Wolves within the Fold

Wolves within the Fold

RELIGIOUS LEADERSHIP AND ABUSES OF POWER

EDITED BY ANSON SHUPE

Rutgers University Press
New Brunswick, New Jersey, and London

Library of Congress Cataloging-in-Publication Data

Wolves within the fold : religious leadership and abuses of power /
   edited by Anson Shupe.
      p. cm.
   Includes bibliographical references and index.
   ISBN 0–8135–2489–X (cloth : alk. paper).—ISBN 0–8135–2490–3
(pbk. : alk. paper)
   1. Clergy—Professional ethics.   2. Sexual misconduct by clergy.
  I. Shupe, Anson, D.
BL630.W65   1998   97–22312
291.6'1—dc21   CIP

British Cataloging-in-Publication information available

This collection copyright © 1998 by Rutgers, The State University

This volume is dedicated to my son and daughter,
Andrew and Abigail,
both artists but on different paths

CONTENTS

Part III *Models for the Study of Clergy Malfeasance*

Wolves within the Fold

The Dynamics of Clergy Malfeasance

ANSON SHUPE

*T*he power of religion as a symbolic, salvation-promising enterprise resides in its authority to create and shape reality for believers and command their obedience. Religion inspires hope, charity, and sacrifice in times of crises, such as natural disasters. Witness outlying churches' responses to the devastation of Hurricane Andrew several years ago. Religion provides succor and assurance during inevitable times of misery and loss, as we saw in the many religious services and the virtual "memorial fence" of mementos and prayerful messages left by grieving families and well-wishers around the ruins of the bombed federal building in Oklahoma City. But in crusades, witch hunts, inquisitions, and pogroms, history shows us a dark side to this power. On this dark side, too, lies the abuse of a religion's followers by its leaders. This phenomenon I have termed *clergy malfeasance*.

I define clergy malfeasance as the exploitation and abuse of a religious group's believers by trusted elites and leaders of that religion. In legal terms such malfeasance represents a violation of fiduciary responsibility. Of course, such violations occur across a broad range of occupations and institutions—for example, in doctors' and counselors' offices, in law firms, and on university campuses (Rutter 1989). According to pastoral psychotherapist James Newton Poling (1991, 12): "Institutions and ideologies determine who has privilege to be dominant and who must defer. Some persons are given great power to make choices for themselves and other people and are protected from the consequences of their choices. . . . These inequities create the occasion for abusive behaviors and unjust power arrangements."

Now, we are coming to recognize, such inequities occur all too frequently in our churches as well. Whatever else their congregants believe them to be, sociologically churches are hierarchies of unequal power. They render some who trust the presumed benevolent motives of more powerful persons and authorities more vulnerable to exploitation and abuse than others. The "trusted" nature of these religious hierarchies thus makes them particularly interesting contexts in which to examine victimization and fiduciary trust violations.

Locating Clergy Malfeasance within Deviance

Our modern recognition of clergy malfeasance, whatever its type, stems at least indirectly from a confluence of factors, principally civil liberties and victimization movements of late twentieth-century North America. I have regarded this sensitivity to exploitation and abuse of laypersons by clerics as a "spillover effect" from the feminist and antiviolence movements of the 1970s and 1980s (Shupe 1995, 13–14). Similarly, Andrew Karmen (1990, 38) describes the U.S. penchant for aggressively expanding our awareness of victim exploitation:

> There is no end in sight to the process of discovering and rediscovering victims. All kinds of victims are beginning to receive the attention, concern, care, and assistance they deserve. They are being rediscovered by investigative journalists who put together feature stories, entrepreneurs who put out new lines of personal safety products, social scientists who explore their plight at conferences, legislators who introduce new laws to benefit them, and self-help groups that organize support networks to overcome the isolation that has divided them.

Over the past decade clergy malfeasance has been discussed largely within a narrow sexual paradigm—the sexual exploitation of youth by pedophiles or of vulnerable females by male clerics. (Even within this paradigm, investigations of female abuse of children and males have been few.)

For example, various studies have compared sexual abuse by clergy to more familiar social problems. Pamela Cooper-White (1991) has likened it to spouse abuse, because the church is so often described as a nurturant, benevolent family. Along the same lines, several observers (Blanchard 1991; Lebacqz and Barton 1991; Milgrim and Schoener 1987) have compared clergy sexual malfeasance to incest. As Blanchard (1991, 239–240) observes:

"Both fathers and clergymen are often seen as having influential and power-ful disciplinary functions. The power of a clergyman is enhanced by the trap-pings of his religious position and the mysterious rituals he enacts. . . . Because of a desire to please, children will tolerate abuses by their fathers much as congregants will submit to sexual exploitation in an effort to avoid displeasing the pastor." Others maintain that such abuse also resembles sexual harassment of women by men in the workplace or of female students by male faculty on university campuses (Dziech and Weiner 1990).

However, such malfeasance has been researched mostly within a family-based sexual abuse paradigm, which limits sociological understanding of it. To be sure, almost half the chapters in this book deal with sexual abuse, and with that problem particularly within the Roman Catholic Church. But by grouping the sexual instances of clergy malfeasance under a broader con-ceptual umbrella, we can enhance our understanding of the more generic is-sues of power and exploitation involved.

To allow for consideration of forms of clergy malfeasance in addition to sexual abuse, it is most useful to locate this entire category of deviance within the concept of *elite deviance*, defined by David R. Simon and D. Stanley Eitzen (1990) as constituting illegal and unethical acts committed by persons in the highest corporate and political strata of society. These actions may be motivated by desires either for personal gain or to enhance the power, profits, and interests of their organizations. In most cases the elite malfeasants run relatively little risk of apprehension or serious punishment. Many such abuses pose actual or potential danger to the safety, health, and well-being of many individuals, at the same time that these elite deviants are typically regarded as pillars of respectability and law-abiding propriety.

Simon and Eitzen dealt with strictly secular malfeasance cases, such as manufacturers distributing known faulty or dangerous products, political corruption, corporate price-fixing, and so forth. That the 1990 edition of their classic *Elite Deviance* does not mention exploitive actions by clergy is not surprising, for media coverage of clergy malfeasance began only in the late 1980s and early 1990s. However, locating clergy malfeasance within the elite deviance model moves it away from the narrower model of sexual deviance and helps us better appreciate continuities across all types of clergy malfea-sance.

One logical reason for considering clergy malfeasance as a subset of elite deviance lies in the corporate status of most churches and denomina-tions. As legal entities, they own land and buildings, have boards and offic-ers, hold meetings, and are recognized by the Internal Revenue Service. Like other corporations, they convey products (such as a sense of community for members, an understanding of the supernatural, even eternal salvation), take in money, market products in a competitive pluralistic system, and provide specific services to "consumers," such as counseling and charitable relief.

Several qualifications are in order, however. Some acts of secular elite deviance are performed to enrich the deviant either directly (as with embezzlement) or indirectly, in the course of furthering the organization's goals (as with corporate price-fixing, illegal contributions to politicians, or the Watergate burglary). In the case of religious elite deviance, however, no one would seriously contend that either pedophilic Catholic priests or treasurers skimming funds from church coffers are contributing to the long-term well-being of their religious institutions. Clergy malfeasance is almost always inspired by lust, greed, or personal problems, rarely by concern for the institution.

Also unlike secular elite deviance, an affective, spiritual bond (even if one-sided) exists between many clergy/religious elites and their victims. Emotional relations between the exploiters and the exploited seldom occur in the economic, rational context of white-collar crimes (Coleman 1987).

But while economic and political elite deviance often affects many persons beyond the immediate corporations' customers and polities, clergy malfeasance usually affects only parishioners and members of groups who put their trust in specific religious leaders. Specific scandals sully only the general reputation of organized religion per se or of specific "industries" within it, such as televangelism.

Yet trust and its betrayal represent the common dimensions of religious deviance and secular elite deviance/white-collar crime: both violate the fiduciary relationship between the client/parishioner/believer and the expert professional to whom the former has turned for services and assistance and thereby revealed vulnerability. We do not usually think of the relationship between guru and disciple or priest and supplicant in such terms, but applying this logic reveals the "fit" of clergy malfeasance and elite deviance. As Shapiro (1987, 626) writes in the context of white-collar crime, trust is "a social relationship in which principals—for whatever reason or state of mind—invest resources, authority, or responsibility in another to act on their behalf for some uncertain future return." In the secular world the return may be high interest and dividends; in the sacred realm it may be healing, good karma, or salvation.

Three Forms of Clergy Malfeasance

The chapters in this volume deal with three forms or types of deviance committed by religious elites: sexual, economic, and authoritative.

The sexual deviance category includes seduction, rape, pedophilia and ephebophilia (erotic attraction to prepubescent and adolescent children, respectively), and homosexuality. Most persons who attend to the electronic and print media are aware that philandering clerics and pedophile priests have received a good deal of attention during the past decade. Some such sexual deviants, such as the pedophile Catholic fathers James Porter and David A. Holley, have preyed upon literally hundreds of young victims. Others, such as the PTL Club's Jim Bakker, have received widespread coverage that bordered on a media circus.

While neither seduction nor homosexuality are illegal in the societies considered here, if they occur within religious organizations whose official policies hold elites to standards of heterosexual marital fidelity or strict celibacy, then they will be judged deviant (if only unethical). Thus in 1994 Irish bishop Eamon Casey was forced to resign after it became known that he had fathered a child in a long-term secret relationship with a woman, as the *Fort Wayne (Ind.) Journal-Gazette* reported on November 20 in "Church Scandals Rock Irish." Later that year the Catholic Church in Ireland suffered further scandal when a sixty-eight-year-old curate suffered a massive heart attack in a gay sauna club and had last rites administered by two other priests who happened to be in the club at the same time, as Thomas Molloy reported in the *Journal-Gazette* on December 8 under the headline, "Scandals Involving Priests Erode Authority of Church in Ireland." Similar scandals that year brought about the resignations of a seventy-five-year-old cardinal in Austria, reported August 16 in the *Chicago Tribune* in "Austrian Cardinal in Sex Case Steps Down," and of the forty-four-year-old head of the Roman Catholic diocese of Basel, Switzerland, detailed in the *Chicago Tribune* on June 3 in "Swiss Catholic Bishop Resigns, Admits Affair Led to Pregnancy." In none of these cases did any of the men necessarily commit any illegal acts, just acts deviant in the eyes of the church hierarchies of which they were elites.

Clergy sexual malfeasance is not a recent invention. Historians of medieval Europe (e.g., Ladurie 1978) have observed how fraught with the potential for sexual abuse were inequitable power relationships between Roman Catholic clerics and laity, between senior clerics and novitiates in orders, and between priests and nuns. Boswell (1981, 182) writes of the unequal power so common in homosexual clerical relations in medieval Christendom that "Saint Peter Damian . . . complained bitterly about the widespread practice of gay priests confessing to each other in order to avoid detection and obtained milder penances, and he alleged that spiritual advisors commonly had sexual relations with those entrusted to their care, a circumstance which would presumably render confessions for the advisee considerably less awkward." Daichman (1990, 106) cites similar instances of heterosexual exploitation of medieval nuns and sisters by priests who "could practically tempt and absolve a sinner in the same breath."

The second category of malfeasance, economic, includes pyramid schemes pitched by fellow religionists or by those claiming spiritual integrity at members of specific religious groups, located and appealed to because of their religious affiliations. For example, "a remarkable number of persons who are or claim to be members of the LDS Church [Church of Jesus Christ of Latter-Day Saints] make their way to Utah, or seek out Mormons elsewhere, to finance illegal quick-buck money-making schemes. Moreover, these grifters frequently try to win endorsements for their operations from LDS Church officials and then use these to reassure investors that the ventures have the approval of the LDS hierarchy and are thus 'blessed' in some special way" (Shupe 1991, 44–75). Chapter 3 of this volume offers a broad array of cases of economic fraud by Christian leaders in North America, such as the New Era scandal of the 1990s.

Economic clergy malfeasance also includes dishonest elite employees of religious organizations and con-artist television evangelists who raise money over the airwaves for missions and causes they know to be nonexistent, who divert for their personal use and enrichment funds raised for ministry, or both.

This form of exploitation illustrates why all forms of clergy malfeasance need to be understood within the broader category of elite deviance and, for several reasons, comes closest to white-collar crime. First, unlike sexual abuse, which often involves physical and psychological attack and injury, the economic category of clergy malfeasance involves persuasion and guile (although these tactics can be part of sexual abuse as well). Second, as Erich Goode (1994, 325) observes about white-collar crimes, many victims may not even be aware that thievery has taken place or that their contributions to religious elites have been misused. Third, many more people fall victim to economic than to sexual exploitation, for sexual abuse is by all accounts relatively infrequent among the totality of clergy persons. Similarly, remarks

Goode (1994, 350), "It is almost certain that the unknown amount of white collar crime is far greater than the amount of unreported common crimes."

An accepted sociological principle that applies to street or common crime vis-à-vis white-collar crime holds true as well for sexual versus economic exploitation by religious elites. Just as white-collar/corporate secular crimes receive much less media attention than street crimes yet are responsible for more widespread damage, the media pays more attention to sexual exploitation by clergy than to clergy economic exploitation, which affects a larger number of individuals and institutions.

For example, accounts of Reverend Jim Bakker's affair with PTL secretary Jessica Hahn, including his intended pay-off to her of more than $250,000 in hush money, filled the print media and received extensive television coverage during the late 1980s. Indeed, Jim and Tammy Faye Bakkers' eleven appearances on ABC's *Nightline* won the show its highest ratings ever, playing to over 20 million viewers (Hadden and Shupe 1988, 6). On the other hand, to learn of the numerous financial frauds and scams involving religious leaders, some of which dwarfed the PTL scandal in scale, one had to read the *Wall Street Journal*, certain business sections of such regional dailies as the *Philadelphia Inquirer*, or publications targeted at other select readerships, such as *Christianity Today*.

The category of authoritative malfeasance is the most sensitive and difficult to examine of the three forms of clergy malfeasance, because what to an outsider looks grossly exploitive may to an insider represent a voluntary trade-off of "outside" goods and comforts for "inside" privileges and promises of spiritual reward.

I define the abuse of authority by a religious leader as excessive monitoring and controlling of members' livelihoods, resources, and lifestyles to enrich that leader, either in money or power. This is admittedly the "grayest" form of clergy malfeasance, which includes a continuum of behaviors from clearly identifiable to less easily discernible wrongdoing (Shupe 1995, 42)—at one end, for example, a Protestant minister who tries to rape a woman (see Fortune 1989) and, at the other, leaders in the shepherding/discipling movement in various conservative Christian sects who micromanage every aspect of their followers' lives.

Besides legal and canonical statutes, as a practical matter—to avoid relying on an outside observer's subjective perspective—I have endorsed turning to specific religions' own definitions and standards of "exploitation" and "abuse" to identify leadership malfeasance (Shupe 1995, 14). For example,

Roman Catholic or Mormon norms (as well as secular law) define pedophilia as abuse. So do they define embezzlement and misrepresentation to believers of the uses to which solicited funds will be put. But submitting oneself to a rigid, spartan regimen of celibacy, poverty, periodic fasting, or pride-reducing rituals is not necessarily "abusive" to psychologically healthy adults if such practices make up part of a lifestyle voluntarily embraced. (Otherwise, we would have to define the regimens of ascetic and monastic religionists, historically important in many world religious traditions, as abusive.)

Thus, clergy malfeasance serves as an inclusive concept with subforms of deviant religious behavior, just as Simon and Eitzen intended their term *elite deviance*, to serve. Clergy malfeasance includes both illegal and immoral activities of religious elites that involve use of their high offices to exploit lay persons or in other ways violate their fiduciary responsibilities.

Overview of This Volume

Drawing upon the explorations of scholars from a variety of backgrounds, *Wolves within the Fold* presents the most recent research on clergy malfeasance in several different religious groups. Broad enough to demonstrate both continuities in clergy malfeasance and its occurrence in a variety of faith traditions, the volume acquires depth from the seven chapters specifically dealing with the Roman Catholic Church, whose prominent position as North America's largest Christian denomination has brought it a generous amount of both media and scholarly attention. Yet this volume also includes chapters that address non-Christian religions, providing evidence of how concepts of deviance, criminology, and conflict theory apply across religious lines.

Some of these researchers were explicitly studying clergy malfeasance when I asked them to contribute to the book. Others, in the course of their fieldwork, had encountered examples of malfeasance about which I learned. All take a sociological approach to clergy malfeasance, seeking to analyze it as a systemic, patterned problem that has to be seen as more than simply the product of a few bad apples among the clergy. Religious organizations, as the authors show, condition not only how the abuse occurs and is replicated but also how victims experience their vulnerability.

The chapters in part 1 emphasize a social structural view of clergy malfeasance and explore how organizational factors influence repeated patterns of deviancy by perpetrators. In the area of deviance, psychology explains motivation while sociology explains opportunity structures that allow motive to translate into action. This is particularly true of the analysis in Theresa Krebs's lead-off chapter concerning pedophilia among Roman Catholic clergy. The Catholic hierarchy's cover-up of sexual scandals from the 1960s to the 1980s became analogous to what criminologists term *corporate crime*, that is, deviant behavior as part of operating policy of the institutional elites. Robert Kisala elaborates on this theme in his examination of doctrinal and leadership issues in the apocalyptic AUM Spiritual Truth Church (Aum Shinrikyo) of Japan, now infamous for releasing lethal sarin gas into Tokyo's subway system in 1995. We now know that the group's operating policies came to include murder, kidnaping, and illegal weapons collection, directed in large part by leaders. Kisala examines the movement's foundation for such actions.

I wrote the chapter on economic fraud and Christian leaders simply because I could find no other social scientist moving beyond specific case studies of such events as the PTL scandal to examine the problem of this kind of economic abuse in a broader perspective. Indeed, many of my data have come from journalism. For example, I have found that virtually every issue of *Christianity Today* (this country's premier evangelical magazine) carries at least one news item on one of the three types of malfeasance defined earlier; it has been a good guide to secular sources as well. My goal in the chapter is to develop the concept of clergy malfeasance and move sociologists' focus beyond sexual abuses.

Authors in part 2 examine reaction to clergy malfeasance: how individual laypersons, leadership, clerical perpetrators, congregations, and the larger public respond to revelations of elite deviance in respected religious institutions. When the structural opportunities for abuse are finally confronted, the results range from a loss of individual faith to a major reexamination of institutional policy, even reverberating into other institutions aligned with religion.

Elizabeth Pullen's chapter turns to a scandal of sexual exploitation in a Franciscan high school in Santa Barbara, California. With unique access to a variety of data sources involving actors in the drama, she analyzes a pattern of victimization that was allowed to continue for years and was only uncovered in the 1990s. The Franciscan order's cooperation in researching the extent of the scandal is a topic worth further examination.

Nancy Nason-Clark, through personal interviews, examines how female victims of clergy sexual abuse in a Canadian community experienced the aftermath of their exploitation. She goes beyond the immediate victims to consider their families (such as parents who often unwittingly encouraged their child-victims to associate frequently with predatory Catholic priests) and the second- and third-order waves of guilt, anger, shame, and weakened faith felt by relatives and the community. E. Burke Rochford also deals with congregants' reactions (whether concern or disenchantment) to violence, sex, drug, and authoritative abuse scandals within the Hare Krishna movement. He considers the consequences for this still precarious religious movement, which dates in the United States only from the mid-1960s.

The remaining three chapters in part 2 present diverse (but not necessarily contradictory) views of sexual abuse by priests in the Roman Catholic Church. In an intriguing analysis that pursues the constructionist approach of his major study, *Pedophiles and Priests: Anatomy of a Contemporary Crisis* (1996), Philip Jenkins looks at the waning influence of the Catholic hierarchy over its own members and the larger non-Catholic community along with the power of the North American mass media as two important factors in the public's emerging awareness of clergy sexual malfeasance. (Public consciousness about the "priest pedophile" and clergy malfeasance problems did not spring full-blown without cultural context.) A. W. Richard Sipe, a former Catholic priest and a practicing psychotherapist, as well as author of several books on clergy sexual abuse, writes of the recent Catholic priest sexual scandals in Northern Ireland and of their effects on the Church hierarchy, the ordinary Catholics in the pews, and the Irish government. His findings from his travels to Ireland and interviews provide a needed corrective to the often-stated view by some Roman Catholic leaders, including Pope John Paul II, that clergy sexual abuse is a problem unique to North America's allegedly decadent culture. Sipe's research dovetails with that of Theresa Krebs in part 1, indicating that sexual exploitation by Roman Catholic priests is a problem international in scope.

Finally, Jeanne Miller provides this volume's second first-person account from the victim's perspective. The mother of a teenage victim of one repeat offender ephebophile priest, she was in large part responsible for the decision by the Roman Catholic Archdiocese of Chicago and its Cardinal to institute reforms in recognizing and dealing with clergy sexual abuse. In 1991 Miller helped found VOCAL (Victims of Clergy Abuse Linkup—now The Linkup), a grassroots family/victims' support group that now serves both as a secular clearing house for information on and victims of interdenominational clergy abuse and as a sponsor of conferences that bring victims, families, counselors, experts, and clergy together for understanding and support.

In part 3, the authors examine issues of special concern to social scientists studying clergy malfeasance. James Thomson, Joseph Marolla, and David G. Bromley use interpretative models from sociological subdisciplines of deviance and social psychology to analyze how abusive clergy self-servingly explain their actions. Using mostly sources from print media, they probe for the dynamics of the perpetrators' *secondary deviance*, that is, how these actors deal in lifestyle and self-concept with the knowledge of their acts. Robert Balch and Stephan Langdon consider the practical reasons why investigators of unconventional religious groups—in this case, the Church Universal and Triumphant (CUT)—might *not* uncover evidence of malfeasance. (They review, for example, group pressures not to discuss or report deviant actions, time constraints, and activities of limited visibility.) This is a particularly important issue because activists in what has been termed the "anticult" movement have often accused sociologists of religion of being "soft" on "cults" (and CUT on occasion has been lumped into the cult category). Balch and Langdon give first-person impressions of their experiences in such research.

The Balch-Langdon chapter should be read as a pragmatic essay that does not settle the issues raised but rather points to a need to look at this area more systematically, with the ultimate goal of moving the definition of clergy malfeasance away from any specific group.

The penultimate contribution in this section is one I deliberately commissioned. Criminologist Peter Iadicola critiques my conflict approach to clergy malfeasance (Shupe 1995) by extending it to consider other dimensions and variables, thereby suggesting a broader inclusive theory of the problem. Whereas I treated religious groups as essentially closed systems, Iadicola considers their social and cultural environments as well.

I conclude this volume with a brief look at where I believe the sociological study of clergy malfeasance is and should be going. I attempt to identify fertile areas for future research.

The social science study of clergy malfeasance, stimulated by the revelations of priestly exploitation of Catholic youth in the 1990s and media coverage of the 1980s' televangelistic scandals, is moving from infancy into childhood. Edwin Sutherland coined the term *white-collar crime* in his 1939 presidential address to the American Sociological Association, but criminologists have continued to ignore clergy malfeasance. The concept of elite deviance, a product of the 1980s, until now has not included acts committed by religious leaders. The few spectacular and widely known examples of malfeasance—Jim Jones and David Koresh, televangelists like Jim Bakker, rogue priests like Father James Porter—represent the tip of a still uncharted iceberg. This book is intended to help inaugurate future studies and lower the water line.

References

Blanchard, Gerald T. 1991. "Sexually Abusive Clergymen: A Conceptual Framework for Intervention and Recovery." *Pastoral Psychology* 39 (4): 232–246.

Boswell, John. 1981. *Christianity, Social Tolerance, and Homosexuality.* Chicago: University of Chicago Press.

Coleman, James W. 1987. "Toward an Integrated Theory of White-Collar Crime." *American Journal of Sociology* 93 (2): 406–439.

Cooper-White, Pamela. 1991. "Soul Stealing: Power Relations in Pastoral Sexual Abuse." *Christian Century*, February 20.

Daichman, Graciela. 1990. "Misconduct in the Medieval Nunnery: Fact, Not Fiction." In *That Gentle Strength: Historical Perspectives on Women in Christianity.* Edited by Lynda L. Coon, Katherine J. Haldane, and Elisabeth W. Somme. Charlottesville: University of Virginia Press.

Dziech, Billie Wright, and Linda Weiner. 1990. *The Lecherous Professor: Sexual Harassment on Campus.* Urbana: University of Illinois Press.

Fortune, Mari M. 1989. *Is Nothing Sacred?* San Francisco: HarperCollins.

Goode, Erich. 1994. *Deviant Behavior.* 4th ed. Englewood Cliffs, N.J: Prentice-Hall.

Hadden, Jeffrey K., and Anson Shupe. 1988. *Televangelism: Power and Politics on God's Frontier.* New York: Holt.

Jenkins, Philip. 1996. *Pedophiles and Priests: Anatomy of a Contemporary Crisis.* New York: Oxford University Press.

Karmen, Andrew. 1990. *Crime Victims: An Introduction to Victimology.* 2d ed. Pacific Grove, Calif.: Brooks/Cole.

Ladurie, Emmanuel Le Roy. 1978. *Montaillou: The Promised Land of Error.* Translated by Barbara Bray. New York: Braziller.

Lebacqz, Karen, and Ronald G. Barton. 1991. *Sex in the Parish.* Louisville, Ky: Westminster/John Knox.

Milgrim, Jeanette Hofstee, and George R. Schoener. 1987. "Responding to Clients Who Have Been Sexually Exploited by Counselors, Therapists, and Clergy." In *Sexual Assault and Abuse: A Handbook for Clergy and Religious Professionals.* Edited by Mary D. Pellauer, Barbara Chester, and Jan Boyojian. San Francisco: HarperCollins.

Poling, James Newton. 1991. *The Abuse of Power: A Theological Problem.* Nashville, Tenn: Abingdon.

Rutter, Peter. 1989. *Sex in the Forbidden Zone.* Los Angeles: Tarcher.

Shapiro, Susan. 1987. "The Social Control of Impersonal Trust." *American Journal of Sociology* 93 (3): 623–658.

Shupe, Anson. 1995. *In the Name of All That's Holy: A Theory of Clergy Malfeasance.* Westport, Conn: Praeger.

———. 1991. *The Darker Side of Virtue.* Buffalo, N.Y: Prometheus.

Simon, David. R., and D. Stanley Eitzen. 1990. *Elite Deviance.* Boston: Allyn and Bacon.

PART I

*Structural Opportunities
for Exploitation
and Abuse*

CHAPTER 1

Church Structures That Facilitate Pedophilia among Roman Catholic Clergy

THERESA KREBS

*I*n 1993 the highest governing official in the Roman Catholic Church revealed his position regarding the sexual abuse of children by clergy and religious in the North American Catholic Church. As reported in the *Edmonton Journal* on June 24, under the headline "Permissive Society to Blame for Abusive Priests—Vatican," the chief Vatican spokesman, Joaquin Navarro-Valls, identified pedophilic clergy in the Roman Catholic Church as a uniquely North American phenomenon: "One would have to ask if the real culprit is not a society that is irresponsibly permissive, hyperinflated with sexuality [that is] capable of creating circumstances that induce even people who have received a solid moral formation to commit grave moral acts."[1]

Navarro-Valls extended the blame to the media for sensationalizing cases of pedophilia when the number of priests implicated in North America amounts to about four hundred, little more than 1 percent. In a further move that denied institutional responsibility for priestly pedophilia, Navarro-Valls pointed out that the percentage of priests involved in pedophilic acts may be less than in other sectors of the general population (see, e.g., Bishop's Administrative Committee 1989, 394). The Vatican's statement demonstrates the Church's protective stance toward pedophilic clergy in its ranks. By continuing to look beyond itself for possible causes, the Church avoids examining how its structure may facilitate pedophilia among some of its personnel.

I argue that pedophilia among Catholic clergy is possible because both longstanding and newly erected structures within the institutional Church facilitate it. The Church's international nature, its organizational hierarchy, and its internal polity allow pedophiles to remain anonymous to all but a few within the Church hierarchy and secular society. It maintains this anonymity through a complex network of archdioceses, dioceses, provinces, and parishes that absorb and protect perpetrators across geographically disparate regions. By acknowledging instances of such behavior and not removing priests from the priesthood (or reporting them to secular officials), the Church hierarchy accords pedophilia a place within its organization.[2]

In addition to these longstanding structural facilitators of pedophilia, newly erected structures, such as official policies and study groups in parishes, further diffuse organizational responsibility. First, in view of current knowledge regarding pedophilia, the hierarchy acknowledged in numerous mea culpae that it had not managed the problem adequately in the past. Consequently, it created policy guidelines and public review boards. Officials, however, continued to justify their past actions by claiming ignorance of the gravity of pedophilic acts committed against child victims.

Second, the Canadian Catholic Church encouraged the organization of study groups and workshops within parishes, with the entire church community working toward a solution. The general consensus arising out of these groups was that abuse in general and pedophilia in particular is no more prevalent in the Church than in other secular institutions. Critics, of course, respond that such generalizations ignore the reality that clergy, as ordained personnel, occupy a category apart from trusted secular officials by their vows of celibacy. Empirically, such claims smack of damage control rather than earnest fact finding.

The Overall Picture

To analyze pedophilia in longstanding structures in the institutional Catholic Church, I build on Anson Shupe's structural conflict model of clergy malfeasance in North American religious organizations. Shupe argues that new structures adopted by the Catholic Church, such as official policies, are positive responses toward effecting change. I, however, offer an alternative interpretation of the Church's remedial response: While no longer denying pedophilia among its ranks, the Church nevertheless continues to deflect institutional responsibility for it. I come to this conclusion with international examples interpreted through Jean-Guy Vaillancourt's study of Vatican control over lay Catholic elites.

Shupe defines clergy malfeasance as "the exploitation and abuse of a religious group's believers by the elites of that religion in whom the former trust" (Shupe 1995, 15). Pedophilia is a subgroup of sexual malfeasance, and it takes place in what he calls hierarchical denominations. A crucial point in understanding a structural relationship between pedophilia and its occurrence in a hierarchical religious group (such as the Catholic Church) is that the local authority of individual clergy is an extension of a bureaucratic authority that legitimizes it (Shupe 1993, 19).

Hierarchical religious organizations exhibit five characteristics of power inequalities that conceptually facilitate pedophilia. First, institutional religion is based on systems of power inequalities termed "hierarchies of unequal power" (Shupe 1993, 10; 1994, 4; 1995, 27–28). The unequal power is spread across several dimensions, such as elites' claims to possess disproportionate spiritual wisdom, experience, or charisma of office as well as their organizational knowledge and insights.

Second, persons occupying elite positions retain a significant capacity for moral persuasion, and in some instances the "theological authority to deny access to privileges of membership, including ultimate spiritual statuses such as salvation," through excommunication or shunning and other forms of ostracization.

Third, unlike their secular counterparts, religious organizations such as the Catholic Church represent what Shupe calls "trusted hierarchies." Individuals in positions of authority explicitly encourage and admonish individuals in lower statuses to trust in their honorable intentions and unselfish motives. More specifically, leaders encourage parents or guardians to socialize children into honoring the intentions and motives of priests by advocating respect and obedience without question.

Fourth, because of their special status as trusted hierarchies, churches provide unique "opportunity structures" or "protected places" that allow leaders to engage in deviance. At a power disadvantage, organization members who do not hold positions of authority are more susceptible to exploitation, abuse, and manipulation.

Finally, in a social structural sense, clergy malfeasance (the elite exploitation of lay members) occurs in trusted hierarchies because they systematically provide opportunities for such behaviors and allow them to continue. Shupe argues that deviance/malfeasance, when occasional, is "normal" to religious hierarchies rather than "the result of psychological pathologies or moral lapses" (Shupe 1995, 31).

An essential dimension of Shupe's typology, and crucial for understanding how established Roman Catholic Church structures facilitate pedophilia, is lay members' ability to gain access to officials in a hierarchically structured religious organization when making claims against pedophilic clergy. He characterizes the locus of control of religious polities by their degree of *permeability*. How receptive is the official hierarchy to complainants' allegations against its administration or its personnel? Traditional authority in hierarchical religious polities is least responsive to complaints against personnel and slowest to implement resolution and remedies.

One reason for this unresponsiveness is that hierarchical religious organizations consciously employ strategies of "neutralization" to protect their personnel or the Church community (Shupe 1995, 80). Moreover, engaging in these neutralization strategies perpetuates the good reputation of the organization and diffuses public perception and awareness of malfeasance. The institutional Catholic Church's neutralizing allegations of pedophilia against its personnel gives perpetrators tacit approval from their superiors to continue engaging in such behavior.

Although Shupe (1995, 81) proposes that hierarchical religious groups "are more likely to develop policies addressing clergy malfeasance" than are local autonomous congregational groups, new structures such as official policies and parish study groups often appear to be responses to public pressure or legal proceedings—in fact, the Church sometimes ignores them. Documented evidence shows that even with sensitive, well-formulated policies in place, as well as uniform plans of action for responding to allegations of pedophilia, some members of the Catholic Church hierarchy continue to neutralize complainants by offering monetary settlements on condition of secrecy.

Yet, the dynamics of secrecy within Catholicism reveal how the Church continues to deflect institutional responsibility for the pedophilic crimes of some of its personnel. In his study of Vatican control over Catholic elites, Vaillancourt (1980, 286) indicates that one of the most ironic aspects of secrecy is that officials "often hide themselves behind an ideology of dialogue, communication, and participation. The leadership remains bureaucratic and secretive, while it veils its manipulation behind a screen of words." Interestingly, the majority of members do not leave the Church when knowledge about pedophilic clergy becomes public. In some respects, membership is even strengthened, because the hierarchy actively solicits lay involvement under the guise of implementing organizational reform while retaining the right to make final decisions.

According to Vaillancourt, therefore, clerical appeals for official policies and open discussion further neutralize critics. Engaging public awareness of policy and encouraging parishioner participation in study groups and workshops are evidence of further neutralization strategies on the Church's part. Combining the observations of both Shupe and Vaillancourt, I argue that newly erected structures further facilitate opportunities for pedophilia for some Catholic priests and religious.

Longstanding Structures That Facilitate Pedophilia

Within the Roman Catholic Church, three longstanding structures facilitate pedophilia among some clergy: the international institution itself, its hierarchical organization, and its government or polity.

The International Roman Catholic Church

The North American Roman Catholic Church engaged in an institutional cover-up of clerical pedophilia for decades. Indeed, the magnitude of the scandal facing the Church today demonstrates its international dimensions. At the same time that Church officials denied that clergy or lay religious leaders engaged in sexual activities with children, they privately assured complainants that the "problem" would be investigated and resolved immediately. In actuality, the Church began to transfer perpetrators either to active ministry in other parishes or to church-affiliated treatment centers. The international scope of the Catholic Church allowed the official hierarchy to relocate offending individuals to distant geographical locations (Isely and Isely 1990, 92–93). For Church officials, such moves solved the problem.

For example, the diocese of Northampton, England, transferred British priest Anton Mowat to Atlanta, Georgia, without informing the Archdiocese of Atlanta about Mowat's "known predilection for young boys." When Georgia police investigated allegations against Mowat of child sexual abuse in 1990, he fled the United States for a monastery in Turin, Italy. Although U.S. authorities repeatedly appealed to his home diocese in Northampton for information regarding Mowat's whereabouts, Church officials denied having any knowledge (Burkett and Bruni 1993, 33). Indeed, if Mowat's home diocese knew where he was, by denying that knowledge it tacitly approved his actions. Moreover, the Church in three separate countries (England, the United States, and Italy) played host to Mowat. By refusing to disclose his hiding place to authorities and by transferring him to another country, the international Church facilitated Mowat's inclination to pedophilic activity.

Earlier, during the 1960s, dozens of priests accused of pedophilia were on assignment in the United States from England, Mexico, Ireland, Sri Lanka, and Italy (Burkett and Bruni 1993, 41). These assignments had already concerned John Salazar, a consulting psychologist for the Servants of the Paraclete treatment facility in New Mexico. In February 1967, Salazar met with the archbishop of Santa Fe, Robert Sanchez, to explain the dangers in allowing pedophilic priests and lay religious "brought from all over the world" to return to working with children at their former, or any, parishes (Burkett and Bruni 1993, 168). Archbishop Sanchez, however, was less than proactive on the issue, perhaps because (as it became known) he himself maintained sexual relationships with young women—as many as five during the 1980s and others before then (Shupe 1995, 3). Sanchez eventually resigned the priesthood in disgrace.[3]

An alternative to transferring alleged pedophilic clergy to distant parishes is transferring them to treatment centers in other countries. Father Canice Connor, former executive director of Southdown Treatment Centre for clergy and religious near Toronto, Ontario, is president and chief executive officer of St. Luke's Institute in Suitland, Maryland. (In 1980, priest and psychiatrist Michael Peterson founded St. Luke's to treat the psychiatric problems of clergy, which include the suffering caused by depression, alcoholism, and other addictions.) In 1983, St. Luke's broadened its treatment to include priests who sexually abuse children. Connor told the *Washington Post* that St. Luke's patient lists include Roman Catholic priests from South Africa and Australia (Miller 1993). On July 16, 1994, Mary Jane Boland reported in the *New Zealand Herald* under the headline "Church Unveils Its Shame" that before that year, the New Zealand Catholic Church responded to allegations of priestly pedophilia by sending priests to treatment centers "overseas"—facilities probably in the United States. (Before it closed, House of Affirmation in Missouri described itself on its letterhead as the "International Therapeutic Center for Clergy and Religious.")[4]

Church officials in North America regard these centers as on the cutting edge in treating addictions and disorders of various types. However, in 1991, Santa Fe lawyer Bruce Pasternack accumulated massive evidence illustrating that patients who initially came to the Paraclete Center in Jemez Springs, New Mexico, for help with pedophilia frequently ended up abusing children in parishes around the New Mexico treatment facility. Bishops had referred clergy suffering from alcoholism, bulimia, depression, and pedophilia to the Paracletes from all over the world. Often when a patient finished treatment at the center, the referring parish would not accept the cleric back. Posted permanently or temporarily to a parish in the Archdiocese of Santa Fe, the priest would continue to commit pedophilic acts (CBS-TV 1993, 3).

For example, the bishop of Winnipeg referred Fr. Jason Sigler to the Paracletes. Following his initial treatment, Sigler received a position in the Santa Fe Archdiocese, where he continued to fondle children. When again accused, he reentered the center for further treatment. Not until Pasternack sued Sigler for sexually abusing a boy under the age of thirteen did sixteen other victims come forward with similar allegations (Burkett and Bruni 1993, 126). When the media began to recount how repeat offenders sent to the center from around the globe perpetrated similar crimes with the Church's awareness, the public reacted strongly and appealed to bishops for accountability.

Hierarchical Organization of the Church

The bishop holds the highest authority in an archdiocese or diocese, and is answerable only to the Supreme Pontiff. His hierarchical roles include teacher of doctrine, priest of worship, and minister of government. As the highest governing official in a diocese, a bishop has executive power to apply the universal laws of the Church, to exercise legislative and judicial power, and to enforce civil law in a diocese. The bishop himself is subject to canon law and, as a citizen, to the civil and criminal laws of the country in which he serves. According to Church and civil laws, the bishop's power, therefore, is limited and not arbitrary. Answerable within the Church only to the pope, bishops nevertheless also possess the potential for considerable power in their dioceses (Archdiocesan Commission of Enquiry [ACE] 1990a, 1:69–70).

Former Archbishop Alphonsus Penney's management of pedophilic clergy in Newfoundland is a particularly telling example of the Church hierarchy's ability to manipulate public perception while denying claimants' allegations. Evidence from as early as 1979 suggests that when Penney assumed the bishopric in the archdiocese in St. John's, he knew that priests and Christian Brothers in Newfoundland were committing pedophilic acts with young members of the Church and wards of the Mount Cashel Orphanage. As the representative official of the Archdiocese of St. John's, Newfoundland, and according to Church law, he was responsible for all juridic affairs, including allegations of pedophilic crimes against Church personnel (Paulson 1988, 103). Therefore, by both canon and civil law, Penney ought to have acted on his knowledge and reported the crimes to Church and civil authorities.

A sex scandal of enormous proportions swirled around Penney's mitre while he followed a tragic course of denial, covering his inaction by transferring or counseling perpetrators rather than indicting them under canon and civil criminal law. Moreover, secular authorities investigating suspected and named abusers met with little cooperation from Church and affiliated institutional officials.

As the highest governing official in a diocese, a bishop is responsible for the physical and spiritual well-being of all Church personnel. Alphonsus Penney reportedly advised priests struggling with their sexual predilections to avail themselves of professional counseling services that he retained for their use. One year after he assumed the office of bishop in the Archdiocese of St. John's, Alphonsus Penney established the Ministry to Priests Program (MPP) to address problems of morale associated with restrictions and requirements of the priesthood, another indication that he knew some clergy were engaged in sexual activities proscribed by their vows of celibacy.

The program, however, served another purpose than that intended. Former members testified that its greatest value lay in the opportunity for socializing with peers. Most clergy, however, avoided associating with the group within the MPP known to have a homosexual orientation. The majority of allegations against and convictions of pedophilic priests were of members belonging to that segment of the MPP (ACE 1990a, 1:96–99).

The MPP represents one example of the way the Church hierarchy facilitates pedophilia by following a course of denial and diffusion rather than by reporting offenses to appropriate secular authorities. As pastor to the priests in his archdiocese, Penney did take steps to address the problem of pedophilia among them. He ignored his obligations to civil law, however, by providing a forum that facilitated rather than eliminated their illegal sexual practices.

When parishioners raised concerns and complaints about the sexual behavior of priests and lay religious to Alphonsus Penney on numerous occasions from 1980 onwards, he followed the requirements of neither canon nor civil law. Regarding the former archbishop's handling of claimants' allegations against Church personnel, the *Report of the Archdiocesan Commission of Enquiry* (ACE 1990,1:99) states that "the measures taken to meet this anxiety within the Presbyterium were insufficient, ineffectual, and, in some respects, inappropriate. The measures which were taken, moreover, were not administered consistently, in an effective manner or in accordance with their design" (ACE 1990, 1:99).

As a result of the devastation caused by pedophilic clergy in the Newfoundland Roman Catholic Church, the public accused the Church of an institutional cover-up. These charges resulted in Penney's resignation in July 1990.[5]

An article treating intervention in allegations of pedophilic clergy states that "the pastoral minister's initial actions when confronted with child abuse may be the most crucial stage in the intervention/prevention process. Often, without the minister's help, nothing could or would be done to stop it" (Isely and Isely 1990, 93). According to the authors, the appropriate response is swift authoritarian intervention to prevent further abuses. Yet the nature of the Catholic Church and its male leaders are "antithetical to a public and swift response to a problem like sexual abuse by clergy. The Catholic Church and the culture that has evolved around it teach laity deference and obedience." Moreover, bishops are not suitable adjudicators in the areas of sex and psychology for the simple reason that they often lack experience and training in those areas (Burkett and Bruni 1993, 60).

Jason Berry, author of *Lead Us Not into Temptation,* followed the pedophilic priest scandal in the U.S. Catholic Church from Louisiana to Washington, seat of the U.S. papal nunciature, investigating Father Gilbert Gauthe, from the Diocese of Lafayette in Louisiana, who managed to commit pedophilic crimes for many years, apparently undetected. Berry blames the complicity between Church personnel and the official Church hierarchy for perpetuating the problem. "The crisis in the Catholic Church lies not with the fraction of priests who molest youngsters but in an ecclesiastical power structure that harbors pedophiles, conceals other sexual behavior patterns among its clerics, and uses strategies of duplicity and counterattack against the victims" (Berry 1992, xx).

A case in point: The *Edmonton Journal* reported under the headline "Church Says Boys Asked for Sex" on February 25, 1995, a clerical counterattack undertaken by the Diocese of Antigonish, Nova Scotia: Priests charged with the sexual abuse of boys between the ages of ten and seventeen pleaded in their defense that any damages suffered by the young boys were the results of their own voluntary actions. (A follow-up article on March 20 in the same paper was headlined "Church Backs Away from Blaming Victims for Sexual Abuse.")

Internal Polity

Shupe characterizes the internal polities of religious organizations by the extent of their permeability and of their neutralization. He measures permeability by the extent to which administrators and leaders in the hierarchy, first, are authentically open to receiving complaints against the organization by lay members and, second, act to eliminate a problem from recurring (Shupe 1995, 118–119). Shupe assesses organizational neutralization by the degree to which administrators and leaders in the hierarchy blame victims, dismiss grievances, or intimidate, bribe, or threaten to ensure the silence and secrecy of complainants. Taking any neutralizing action means that the problem can recur.

The internal polity of the Catholic Church employs numerous methods to neutralize attempts to require accountability or restitution from the Church. Unfortunately, the relationship between parishioners and the Church hierarchy does not encourage, or even allow, demands for institutional accountability. The hierarchy camouflages abuse and abusers against public perception. Relying on their perceived authority, Church officials intimidate claimants, downplay the effects of the acts, or ensure silence from victims by stating that what occurred is an isolated incident. The hierarchy treats each set of allegations in confidence, rather than collaborating and compiling records on named abusers in order to explore behavior patterns. Bishops speak to victims privately, victimizing them further by planting doubts in their minds about possibly having encouraged the attention of the sexual deviant, having enjoyed the attention, and so forth. Bishops also neglect to inform law enforcement officials of sexual abuse. By insulating perpetrators from outside authorities, internal polities of the Catholic Church also promote aspects of pedophilia.

An open letter of July 12, 1989, to Canadian Catholics from Archbishop James Hayes of Halifax, Nova Scotia, exemplifies this neutralization strategy. The archbishop eloquently deprecated the impact of abuse on victims by focusing on the harmful effects of media publicity and public condemnation for both victims and perpetrators. He beseeched the Canadian Catholic community to understand the suffering and shame experienced by both groups. Moreover, he camouflaged pedophilia by employing euphemisms such as "willful immorality," "illness," and "tragedy" (Hayes 1989). Such rhetorical appeals to embrace perpetrators in understanding and a spirit of forgiveness often neglect the victims; they also may facilitate pedophilia through their affective appeal. (One woman with whom I spoke informally told me that, in her experience, the Church favors a policy modeled on "Forgive and forget—forgive the perpetrator and forget the victim.")

Almost invariably, the Church's internal polity insists that officials maintain secrecy regarding claimants' allegations of sexual abuse against priests or other religious leaders. Often secrecy can be negotiated. In Gauthe's case, mentioned earlier, the Church paid an average of $450,000 to each of nine families. Those settlements, however, came with conditions: Accepting payment required signing an agreement of no liability on the part of the Church. Furthermore, the Gauthe case remains sealed, which decreases the Church's risk of media and public exposure (Berry 1992, 6–25).

In the Gauthe case, as in others researched, the hierarchy sought to protect itself and its priests from public exposure by neutralizing claims. Neutralizing claims, however, ultimately deferred scandals only for a short time (Burkett and Bruni, 1993: 60–62). Documented accounts demonstrate that the pedophiles continued to accumulate victims.

Newly Erected Structures

The Catholic Church has recently implemented two structures to deal with pedophilia among its clerics—new official policies and parish discussion groups. Policies are top down and elite driven. Parish discussion groups are bottom up and laity driven. Neither can eliminate the opportunities for clergy malfeasance, but the intent is that together they can discourage incidences.

Policy Making

In the past, looking to some Roman Catholic Church officials for an appropriate response to complaints of sexual abuse was futile, partly because the Church had no established policies in place for intervention. Evidence suggests, however, that even new public policies do not guarantee that complainants will be met with honesty and openness. At times the Church has continued to envelop claimants in the secrecy and silence characteristic of its early response to allegations against pedophilic clergy.

According to Shupe, *compared with congregational groups*, "hierarchical groups ultimately are more likely to develop policies addressing clergy malfeasance" (1995, 81). Without the convenience of comparison, however, it is difficult to discern whether the Church's official policies are a response to complainants' continued pressure for action (Shupe 1994, 32) or to financial pressure from lawsuits. Internal U.S. Catholic Church documents, the media reported in the early nineties, describe priestly pedophilia as a major crisis, projecting that lawsuits might cost the Church as much as $1 billion by 1995. The Archdiocese of Santa Fe alone faced lawsuits totaling $50 million in 1994 (Bennetts 1991, 227; Sheehan 1994, 529–530).

Often parents or guardians initiate lawsuits in frustrated reaction to the Church's apparent lack of public accountability and responsibility for its personnel. As Paulson observes, "Past experience has shown that if the denouncer perceives the bishops' main concerns to be those of the protection of the institution Church, or the protection of his diocese, his priest or himself, then the bishop is likely to have more problems" (1988, 104).

Certainly, the U.S. Catholic Church did not develop policies before the public demanded accountability from it. For example, Ray Mouton (a criminal defense attorney) and Fr. Michael Peterson (also a psychiatrist) helped Fr. Thomas Doyle (a canon lawyer), at his own instigation, prepare a report detailing their observations about the pedophilia crisis facing the U.S. Catholic Church (Berry 1992, 238). Doyle, Mouton, and Peterson presented the report to the National Conference of Catholic Bishops (NCCB) at Collegeville, Minnesota, in June 1985. In their estimation, because of the dysfunctional manner in which the Church had handled allegations of pedophilic clergy, it faced a potential flood of lawsuits. Creating the report and presenting it to the Collegeville assembly was their way of heading off an ecclesiastical financial crisis.

Incorporating insights from their respective fields of expertise, the trio composed authoritative guidelines for bishops faced with allegations of pedophilic clergy, framing legal strategy in moral terms. For example, the experts admonished the bishops that "to allow a priest to continue to function, endangering the health of children, following the receipt of private, confidential knowledge that this priest victimized a child is considered to be 'criminal neglect'" (quoted in Berry 1992, 99). Much of the document outlined possible alternatives to past responses. Using a question-and-answer format, the report then guided bishops through the process of handling allegations of sexual misconduct by Church personnel. The report concluded by suggesting that the NCCB create a uniform national policy.

The NCCB, however, did not welcome the guidelines delivered to them for the conference at Collegeville, whose official agenda did not even include the report. The NCCB never formally acknowledged receiving the report, nor did it discuss the possibility of creating a policy based upon the report's recommendations. Meeting organizers did not make copies of the report, nor did they distribute them to bishops urging them to incorporate the guidelines in their response to claimants' allegations. Neither did subsequent meetings of the NCCB acknowledge or discuss the report. The result is that U.S. bishops as a group never considered instituting a uniform policy across the country.[6]

Perhaps Canadian bishops learned from the costly lessons experienced by their U.S. counterparts. In the face of increasing public censure and outcry, the CCCB resolved to establish guidelines for processing allegations of clerical sexual abuse and in October 1989 convened the Ad Hoc Committee on Child Sexual Abuse to study the issue. The committee's mandate placed priority on the long-term prevention of sexual abuse, the care and support of victims and their families, and the rehabilitation and future of offenders.

The committee's 1992 report, *From Pain to Hope: Report from the Ad Hoc Committee on Child Sexual Abuse*, repeatedly urges Church reform. Its final chapter contains fifty recommendations directed at the entire Church of Canada. The report recommends how to delegate authority, establish advisory committees, and set up protocols for handling claimants' allegations. The recommendations also suggest that authority take the form of community service rather than of power and domination. Church structure, however, receives scant reference.

Even with policies in place, some bishops continue to offer money to claimants to ensure their silence. As Mike Blanchfield reported in the *Ottawa Citizen* on January 15, 1994, under the headline "Church Payoff Broke Rules," the bishop of Ontario's Cornwall diocese, Eugene LaRocque, paid $32,000 in 1994 to persuade a man to discontinue civil action against a prominent Cornwall-area priest. The terms of the settlement specify that the claimant is not to pursue any action, civil or criminal, and that he must end any ongoing proceedings. Such efforts appear misdirected, at the least, in the face of a church struggling to absorb scandal by creating policies.

Parish Study Groups

In his study of papal power over lay elites, Vaillancourt hypothesizes that the Vatican and the episcopate "mobiliz[e] the laity in the defense of the interests of Church authorities" by coercion and manipulation (1980, 6). His findings indicate that an outward show of openness, dialogue, and receptivity conceals the bureaucratic reality. "Appeals for lay involvement do not go beyond a mere token consultation that rarely influences the outcome of decisions. Officials maintain a monopoly over the decision-making process, often trying to give the impression that the ideas and desires at the grass-roots are being taken into account when such is rarely the case" (Vaillancourt 1980, 286).

In short, with regard to priestly sexual abuse, officials retain the right to make final decisions while appearing to demonstrate open and receptive concern for victims and their allegations against clergy. The Church effectively can still neutralize criticism and absorb scandal by involving the laity in a facade of change.

In 1992, the CCCB published *Breach of Trust, Breach of Faith: Child Sexual Abuse in the Church and Society,* a document that draws on recommendations in the two-volume ACE report as well as the CCCB's ad hoc committee report on child sexual abuse. Its format consists of five sessions designed for discussion groups, which the CCCB urged grass-roots Catholics to attend in order to study the issue. The document explicitly aims to foster an environment of awareness and openness in which to address these subjects.

The workshops devote the first session to discussing sexual abuse in the Church, the only session devoted entirely to that topic. Its language subtly deflects clerical responsibility. The session title, for example, is "Sexual Abuse of Children in Our Church." The emphasis on "our Church" rhetorically (and cunningly) deflects institutional responsibility for pedophilic clergy. Through the process of sharing experiences during discussion, parishioners reflect upon abuse in their own lives—abuses that they either experienced or inflicted.

The remaining four sections in the discussion materials address the dynamics of child sexual abuse, factors in society and the Church that contribute to abuse (note the partnering of society with Church), personal and community responsibility for abuse, and preventing child sexual abuse. Completing the five discussion sessions, participants come to realize just how prevalent sexual abuse is in all of society—not just in the Roman Catholic Church (Steed 1994). Implicit in this focus is a diffusion of the Church's role in facilitating pedophilia in the past (and possibly the present).

In April 1992, St. Agnes Parish in Edmonton organized sessions using *Breach of Trust, Breach of Faith*. To date, four groups totaling seventy-five people have completed the discussion materials. Says one St. Agnes parishioner and group facilitator, "To do nothing is to support abuse," as Ramon Gonzalez reported in "Discussing Sexual Abuse," in the February 13, 1995, issue of the *Western Catholic Reporter.*

To paraphrase Vaillancourt, by encouraging parishioner participation in resolving the problem of sexually abusive clergy, the Church effectively neutralizes criticism and coopts watchdogs.

Implications

In the 1970s and early 1980s, despite the Vatican's characterization of pedophilia in the Roman Catholic Church as a uniquely North American phenomenon, the international Church was aware that some of its personnel engaged in pedophilic activities. The Church stalled when it should have recognized pedophilia as a pathology devastating to its victims rather than a moral failing of perpetrators. Longstanding structures in the Church systematically facilitated priests' and lay religious' ability to commit pedophilia. The Church's international status, its hierarchal organization, and its internal polity enabled it to deny allegations of pedophilia perpetrated by its personnel, rendering them relatively invisible to public perception. By maintaining the invisibility of perpetrators' actions, the Church, in turn, insulated both perpetrators and itself from public censure and criminal litigation. In essence, by denying claimants' allegations of pedophilia and by keeping these from the public, the Church engaged in an institutional cover-up. Moreover, by facilitating the sexually perverse activities of some of its members, it acted as what criminologists term an "accessory after the fact."

Today the Church is struggling to recover from the stigma associated with that cover-up and from allegations that often resulted in admissions and convictions. Many members of the hierarchy, however, are proficient rhetoricians who continue to deflect institutional responsibility for the sexual activities of some of its personnel. In this way, the Church absorbs the sexual scandal, even though it has reached the public's awareness.

By implementing two new structures—official policies and parish discussion groups—the Catholic institution wishes to give the impression its approach to pedophilic priests has changed. Yet the Church continues to gloss over the gravity of sexual activity and pedophilic crimes among its personnel. Rather than admit its own culpability, the Church points to the prevalence of all forms of abuse in other institutions and society at large and encourages its members to do the same. A skeptic might conclude that, no longer engaged in denial, the Roman Catholic Church now engages in deflection.[7]

Notes

1. Former Benedictine monk A. W. Richard Sipe estimates that approximately 2 percent of North American priests are sexually fixated on young children and that an additional 4 percent find older youths sexually appealing. Church officials challenge these figures, but Fr. Thomas Doyle, canon lawyer and former advisor to North American bishops regarding sexual abuse by clergy, estimates that three thousand American priests "may be so inclined" (which supports Sipe's estimates). Jason Berry calls disputes over percentage estimates further examples of "concealment strategies" by which Church officials attempt to deny or diffuse the problem of pedophilia among their personnel. The logic runs, "If there are no numbers, [then] it cannot be true" (cited in Berry 1992: xx–xxi).

2. Part of the reason the Church continues to harbor perpetrators rather than dismiss them may be the aging and declining clerical population in North America caused, in part, by resignations and fewer ordinations. The complex canonical

process involved in laicizing clergy also may help to explain why the Church excuses pedophilic clergy within its ranks. See, for example, Gilmour 1992, B6; Schoenherr and Young 1990, 463–481; Schoenherr, Young, and Vilarino 1988, 499–523.

3. Perhaps not so ironically, Archbishop Robert Sanchez's March 19, 1993, letter to the Pope requested permission to resign from his position. CBS-TV's *60 Minutes* segment "The Archbishop," aired March 21, 1993, investigated the New Mexico archdiocese where Sanchez faced accusations of "sexual improprieties." The program suggested that as a result of his own sexual proclivities Sanchez was lenient toward other priests who engaged in sexual activity with children. See Sanchez 1993, 722–724.

4. Private correspondence from House of Affirmation, in possession of the author.

5. The Church hierarchy possibly rewards its personnel for suppressing information about pedophilic priests. Documented evidence suggests that some members who suppressed information regarding known or investigated pedophiles, possibly with the hierarchy's knowledge, advanced in rank. See, for example, discussion about Father Armando Annunziato in Burkett and Bruni 1993, 9–10, 37. See also Brother Gerard Gabriel McHugh's handling of the investigation into sexual and physical abuse at Mount Cashel Orphanage in Harris 1990, 112–118.

6. In a particularly profound example of marginalization by those in command, Thomas Doyle—the brilliant canon lawyer rising through the ranks to bishop—resigned from his position at the Vatican embassy in Washington, D.C., and chose to enlist in the chaplains' corps in the U.S. Air Force. Doyle calls the U.S. bishops' response (or lack of response) to allegations of pedophilia "unChristian, arrogant, and just plain stupid" and says "the phrase 'smart bishop' is like 'military intelligence': an oxymoron" (quoted in Burkett and Bruni 1993, 163).

7. I gratefully acknowledge Stephen A. Kent, associate professor in the Department of Sociology, University of Alberta, for his invaluable comments on earlier drafts of this chapter.

References

Archdiocesan Commission of Enquiry into the Sexual Abuse of Children by Members of the Clergy [ACE]. 1990a. *The Report of the Archdiocesan Commission of Enquiry into the Sexual Abuse of Children by Members of the Clergy*. 2 vols. St. John's, Newfoundland: Archdiocese of St. John's.

———. 1990b. *The Report of the Archdiocesan Commission of Enquiry into the Sexual Abuse of Children by Members of the Clergy: Conclusions and Recommendations*. St. John's, Newfoundland: Archdiocese of St. John's.

Bennetts, Leslie. 1991. "Unholy Alliances." *Vanity Fair* (December): 224–229, 268–270, 272–278.

Berry, Jason, 1992. *Lead Us Not into Temptation: Catholic Priests and the Sexual Abuse of Children*. New York: Doubleday.

Bishop's Administrative Committee. 1989. "Statement on Priests and Child Abuse." *Origins: Catholic News Service* 19 (November 16): 394–395.

Burkett, Elinor, and Frank Bruni. 1993. *A Gospel of Shame: Children, Sexual Abuse, and the Catholic Church.* New York: Viking.

Canadian Conference of Catholic Bishops. 1992a. *Breach of Trust, Breach of Faith: Child Sexual Abuse in the Church and Society.* Ottawa: Canadian Conference of Catholic Bishops.

————. 1992b. *From Pain to Hope: Report from the Ad Hoc Committee on Child Sexual Abuse.* Ottawa: Canadian Conference of Catholic Bishops.

CBS-TV, 1993. *60 Minutes.* "The Archbishop." March 21, 1–9.Transcript.

Harris, Michael. 1990. *Unholy Orders: Tragedy at Mount Cashel.* Markham, Ontario: Viking.

Hayes, James M. 1989. "A Letter to Canadian Catholics about the Church and Sexual Abuse Cases." *Origins: Catholic News Service* 19 (August 31): 216–217.

Isely, Paul J., and Peter Isely. 1990. "The Sexual Abuse of Male Children by Church Personnel: Intervention and Prevention." *Pastoral Psychology* 39 (2): 85–99.

Miller, Jeanne. 1993. "Update." *Missing Link* (newsletter of The Linkup, Inc.) 1 (4): 2.

Nason-Clark, Nancy. 1993. "Gender Relations in Contemporary Christian Organizations." In *The Sociology of Religion: A Canadian Focus*, edited by W. E. Hewitt. Toronto: Butterworths.

Paulson, Jerome E., 1988. "The Clinical and Canonical Considerations in Cases of Pedophilia: The Bishop's Role." *Studia Canonica* 22 (1): 77–124.

Press, Aric. 1988. "Priests and Abuse." *Newsweek* (August 16): 42–44.

Sanchez, Robert. 1993. "Archbishop Sanchez Submits Resignation." *Origins: Catholic News Service* 22 (April 1): 722–724.

Schoenherr, Richard, and Lawrence A. Young. 1990. "Quitting the Clergy: Resignations in the Roman Catholic Priesthood." *Journal for the Scientific Study of Religion* 29 (4): 463–481.

Schoenherr, Richard, Lawrence A. Young, and José Perez Vilarino. 1988. "Demographic Transitions in Religious Organizations: A Comparative Study of Priest Decline in Roman Catholic Dioceses." *Journal for the Scientific Study of Religion* 27 (4): 499–523.

Sheehan, Michael. 1994. "Archbishop's Letter Explains Bankruptcy Risk." *Origins: Catholic News Service* 23 (January 13): 529–530.

Shupe, Anson. 1995. *In the Name of All That's Holy: A Theory of Clergy Malfeasance.* Westport, Conn.: Praeger.

————. 1994. "Authenticity Lost: When Victims of Clergy Abuse Confront Betrayed Trust." Paper presented at the annual meeting of the Association for the Sociology of Religion, Los Angeles.

————. 1993. "Opportunity Structures, Trusted Hierarchies, and Religious Deviance: A Conflict Theory Approach." Paper presented at the annual meeting of the Society for the Scientific Study of Religion, Raleigh, North Carolina.

Sipe, A. W. Richard. 1995. *Sex, Priests, and Power: Anatomy of a Crisis.* New York: Brunner/Mazel.

Steed, Judy. 1994. *Our Little Secret: Confronting Child Sexual Abuse in Canada.* Toronto: Random House.

Theis, John. 1992. "Power and Sexual Abuse in the Roman Catholic Church." *Grail* 8 (4): 34–49.

Vaillancourt, Jean-Guy. 1980. *Papal Power: A Study of Vatican Control over Lay Catholic Elites*. Berkeley: University of California Press.

Wilkes, Paul. 1993. "Unholy Acts." *New Yorker* (June 7): 62–79.

CHAPTER 2

The AUM Spiritual Truth Church in Japan

ROBERT KISALA

On October 13, 1995, Inoue Yoshihiro, the twenty-five-year-old former head of Aum Shinrikyo's "Intelligence Ministry" and a former law student, made the following statement at a court hearing requested by his lawyer:

> Japan will not be awakened by violent means. The way of Vajarayana will not bring salvation. . . . We were willing to sacrifice ourselves, as long as the Master's plan of salvation could be achieved and Japan would awaken to the truth. [However,] in applying the Master's will, the reality was in fact contrary to our ideals, and those disciples who took the lead only increased their own anguish. All we have succeeded in doing is inflicting suffering on innocent people and their families. (*Asahi Shinbun,* October 13, 1995)[1]

At a press conference held after the hearing, the lawyer explained that Inoue, worried that Aum followers still on the run from the police might become involved in further crimes, wanted to appeal to them to give themselves up. In that light, this statement provides an important insight into the beliefs motivating the followers of Asahara Shoko, the founder of Aum Shinrikyo, an apocalyptic group that introduced deadly nerve gas into Tokyo subways in 1995.

Like most of the upper echelon of Aum believers, Inoue belonged to the educational elite of Japan. Although he chose to join Aum's commune rather than attend university, he is a graduate of an elite private high school in Kyoto and had been accepted into the law department of a private university before deciding to leave all in order to dedicate himself to a life of ascetic discipline in Aum.[2] Among the questions frequently posed in the aftermath of Aum's public crimes is how Asahara was able to attract so many highly educated followers to his fledgling religious group and even to persuade them to commit murder.

The media and legal system in Japan seem to have fixed on two theories commonly applied to so-called destructive religious groups in the West, namely, social tension and mind control. These theories are attractive for their logic and simplicity. Clashes with society would tend to increase the isolation and militancy of a countercultural group, and psychological manipulation provides a convenient explanation for criminal behavior. Nonetheless, both are inadequate explanations for clarifying what happened in Aum. Questions concerning the mind control thesis have been well explored in the academic literature.[3] Logical inconsistencies regarding the activities of so-called deprogrammers on the one hand, and evidence of high defection rates among believers supposedly exposed to mind control on the other, undermine the arguments for the effectiveness of the psychological manipulation observed in some religious groups. While the social tension theory is more convincing, the facts show a decisive turn toward apocalyptic and militant thought in Aum before any conspicuous clashes with society occurred.

A close look at the early stages of its doctrinal evolution indicates just when apocalyptic ideas became central to Aum's faith system and at the same time provides clues as to why this development occurred. Indications suggest that tensions within the group, as well as Asahara's desire to enhance his own authority, may have lain behind the early elaboration of an apocalyptic vision. An examination of Aum's early doctrine also helps clarify the religious precepts that motivated Asahara's followers, namely the interpretation of Vajrayana Buddhism and the "plan of salvation" that Inoue alludes to in his statement quoted earlier. While Aum used psychological manipulation, I would maintain that it was ultimately the dynamics of religious faith, supported by elements within the religious and cultural heritage of Japan, that provided Asahara's lieutenants with a reason for their crimes.

Religious Beginnings: Yoga and the Promise of Psychic Powers

Aum Shinrikyo evolved out of a yoga school founded by Asahara Shoko in the Shibuya district of Tokyo in February 1984. Asahara was born Matsumoto Chizuo, one of seven children of a struggling tatami maker from a small town in the southern part of Japan. From his birth in 1955 Asahara was completely blind in his left eye and had only limited vision in his right.

At the age of six he was sent to the city of Kumamoto to attend the prefectural school for the blind, along with two of his brothers who were similarly impaired. At the school he gained a reputation as something of a troublemaker and bully, someone who used the advantage of his limited sight among his more severely impaired peers. However, former teachers and schoolmates report that he also had a likeable, almost clownish, side, and that he could be quite generous with those who would attach themselves to him as his *kobun* (client or disciple; see Nakane 1970, 42–44).

Asahara apparently wanted to attend the medical school of Kumamoto University but was disappointed to find out that he did not qualify for admittance because of his limited sight. Having obtained a license as an acupuncturist and masseur, a traditional occupation for the blind in Japan, he found a job in Kumamoto and set his sights on the Tokyo University law school, the epitome of educational eliteness in Japan. Reportedly he took the exam for Tokyo University in 1977 and failed, after which he remained in Tokyo to retake the exam the following summer. In the meantime, however, he married Ishii Tomoko, and their first daughter was born, forcing Asahara to give up his plans for further education. In July 1978 he started his own acupuncture and Chinese herbal medicine business in a distant suburb of Tokyo, expanding it three years later to include the sale of health food. In June 1982, however, he was convicted of manufacturing and selling his own medicine, an ineffective mixture of ginseng, snake skins, and ethanol advertised as a cure for rheumatism and various other ailments. In the wake of his conviction his business went bankrupt, and he apparently turned to religion.

Asahara himself claims that his interest in religion began shortly after his marriage as the result of the powerlessness he felt at his inability to effect fundamental cures in his patients (Asahara 1991a, 23). He maintains that this experience led him to study traditional Chinese forms of divination, culminating in the practice of *sendo*, traditional Chinese ascetic practices and techniques through which Asahara claims to have obtained supernatural powers. He also says that he read extensively the works of Nakamura Hajime, a noted scholar of Buddhism, and Takahashi Shinji, the founder of GLA (God Light Association), a new religious group with spiritualist and New Age characteristics. He claims that his study of Buddhism led him to Agonshu, another recent entry in the religious world in Japan. It was probably through his contact with Agonshu that he gained his knowledge of yoga, for the founder of this group, Kiriyama Seiyu, combines this practice with his own interpretation of early Buddhist doctrines.

Attention came to Asahara's yoga school in Shibuya with his appearance in the occult magazine *Twilight Zone* in October 1985, wherein he claimed to have achieved the ability to levitate. The magazine carried the now famous picture of him about a foot off the ground, sitting cross-legged with a pained look on his face. A book by Asahara published in March of the following year, *Chonoryoku himitsu no kaihatsuho* (A secret method for the development of psychic power), reproduced the picture on the cover.[4] In the book he claims additional powers, such as the ability to prophesy, see and hear at great distances, bend the flame of a candle at will, transmit his emotions to others, change the weather, and heal sicknesses. The book describes at great length the yoga training leading to Kundalini awakening, a release of latent energy that confers these abilities on anyone willing to take up the practice.

His first book gives a telling description of his beliefs and the aims of the group gathering around him. Although in the book he mentions his study of early Buddhism and the Buddhist concept of deliverance, he provides little explanation of such doctrines. Instead, the group seemed to be exclusively concerned with yoga training, with the attainment of psychic powers presented as the purpose of that training. Furthermore, the psychic powers Asahara describes in the book seem more a matter of ostentation than of salvation or liberation, an impression reinforced by the sometimes puerile examples he gives of these powers. (For example, he relates an incident in which a female student waxed indignant at discovering that one of her male colleagues had achieved the ability to identify the color of her panties.) Finally, only one passing reference to an apocalypse appears in this earliest of Asahara's books, a reference to Nostradamus's prediction of a cataclysm in 1999, found in a short section dealing with prophecy as a psychic power.

From Yoga School to Apocalyptic Religion

Sometime early in 1986, using money collected from members of his yoga classes, Asahara traveled to India. The ostensible purpose of this trip was to find a teacher who could lead him to "final deliverance." After failing to find such a teacher, he claims, with only two months of independent practice in the Himalayas he was able to attain his goal (Asahara 1992, 3). This trip signaled a shift in Asahara and his yoga group toward a more specifically religious teaching, institutionalized in the founding of the Aum Shinsen no Kai in April 1986 and the establishment of a commune in Kanagawa Prefecture, near Tokyo in August of the same year. (The group's name was changed to Aum Shinrikyo in July 1987.) Asahara, presenting himself now as the only person in Japan who had achieved final deliverance, began offering seminars on his teaching. In a book published at the end of that year, *Seishi wo koeru* (Transcending life and death), Asahara gives a fuller description of his interpretation of early Buddhism, identifying the basic concept of the law of causality as the foundation of his teaching, Although he again devotes much of the book to yogic bodily training, in a concluding chapter he identifies a form of Buddhist meditation as one means to attain liberation (Asahara 1992, 133).

Initiation, a transcription of a seminar offered in May and published in August 1987, more clearly reflects the changes in Asahara's teaching during this period. (An unpolished translation, *Supreme Initiation* [1988], is available in English.) Written in the colloquial language Asahara presumably used in his seminars, *Initiation* presents a mixture of Buddhist doctrines and yoga practices. In a further refinement of Asahara's teaching, he draws a distinction between enlightenment (*satori*) and liberation (*gedatsu*); one attained enlightenment through meditation and liberation through the physical training of yoga (Asahara 1987, 30). This distinction disabuses the disciples of the illusion that yoga training can lead to easy and quick results, a promise contained in Asahara's earlier books.[5] In *Initiation*, Asahara warns disciples that they may go crazy or commit suicide if they attempt Kundalini awakening too soon; he advises them to seek enlightenment first through Jnana yoga, described as meditation leading to self-awareness. Ever more elaborate practice leading to liberation characterizes the development of Aum's faith, a trend that bears some relationship to Asahara's increasing turn toward apocalyptic ideas.

We also see in *Initiation* an increased emphasis on Asahara's role in the process of others' liberation. This role is not limited to the teaching of what has become a rather elaborate set of practices but includes the physical transference of psychic energy to the disciple. A set of esoteric initiations is presented as steps along the road to liberation. Central to these rites is *shaktipat*, the transference of energy from the guru to the disciple that Asahara offered as a shortcut to achieving Kundalini awakening. Although he mentioned this practice in his previous books—and indeed credits it for the earlier-claimed rapid awakening of Aum disciples—he places much more emphasis on this rite in *Initiation*.

Two final elements of the teaching presented in *Initiation* are important to note. First, in Aum, memories, thoughts, and feelings are referred to as "data," and a goal of meditation is to replace the mistaken data of the subconscious, such as desires and attachments, with the correct data of the true self, provided by Aum. The attempted manipulation of thoughts, feelings, and desires in this way is characteristic of Aum. Second, in *Initiation* Asahara begins to develop the apocalyptic theme so important to Aum's later activities.

Compared to its later manifestations, vagueness and comparative restraint mark the apocalyptic vision presented in *Initiation*. In a chapter titled "Prophecy and Salvation," Asahara predicts that Japan will begin to rearm by 1993 and that a nuclear war will occur sometime between 1999 and 2003. However, the accuracy of this prediction depends on Aum's establishing branches overseas by that date, for if enough people engage in Aum's practice a war can still be avoided. The salvation indicated here does not necessarily depend on mystic or spiritual agencies but rather on the idea that the world can yet be convinced of the truth and follow a path of nonviolence, led by Aum. Even if the predicted war comes, however, the followers of Aum's practice will be protected, for they will be able to leave their physical bodies behind and enter into the astral world, described here as the "clear light" (Asahara 1987, 114).

Early in 1989 Asahara published a book devoted exclusively to the apocalypse. His interpretation of the New Testament book of Revelation, *Metsubo no hi* (given the English title *Doomsday*), begins with the warning that the day of destruction is surely coming, that now is the time to awake. While Asahara devotes much discussion to Armageddon (defined as humanity's final war), the book remains short on specifics, suggesting only that both China and the Soviet Union would be destroyed in 2004 and that "the American president elected in 1995 [sic] and the Soviet party chief at that time will lead the world to Armageddon" (1989b, 215). Importantly, in his interpretation of Rev. 2:27 Asahara introduces the concept of Tantra Vajrayana, a concept key to Aum's future doctrinal development and to Aum's crimes.

In a companion volume published three months later, *Metsubo kara koku e* (From destruction to the void), Asahara pinpoints the timing of Armageddon. On or about August 1, 1999, a war would begin over oil, involving the United States, the then Soviet Union, the Arab countries of the Middle East, and Japan. Asahara predicts that atomic weapons will not be used at the outset of the war, but between October 30 and November 29, 2003, nuclear devices will be employed, their use peaking on November 25. Asahara also predicts the use of "powerful SDI weapons" at this time (1989c, 52).

Asahara's Plan for Salvation

Why did Asahara begin to emphasize an apocalyptic theme now, devoting two books in quick succession to the subject? As we have seen, a vague concern with apocalyptic issues—based on the prophecies of Nostradamus popular among Japanese of Asahara's generation—was present from early in the development of the group. One wonders, however, at the increased emphasis at this time. Shortly after the sarin attack on the Tokyo subway, it was widely reported that Aum became a "doomsday cult" after suffering defeat in the parliamentary election in February 1990 and encountering other forms of opposition from society at about the same time. In the summer of 1989, when Aum applied for recognition as a religious group under the Religious Corporations Law, the application was held up because of opposition from families of some Aum members. Soon after these families organized in October of that year, their lawyer and his family disappeared. The election came several months later, and clashes with the neighbors of Aum facilities in rural areas west of Tokyo and on the southern island of Kyushu began in the summer of 1990. What is important here is that all of these incidents occurred *after* the "doomsday" books were published. Shimazono (1995) suggests that the constraints of Aum's own doctrine might have led Asahara to turn increasingly to this apocalyptic theme, although Shimazono places the definitive turn to the apocalypse much later, identifying it with a series of lectures on the theme in fall 1992. I would argue that the internal problems to which he attributes this development were already present early in 1989.

A major problem for the movement was the vagueness associated with the liberation promised by Aum. I have already indicated how Asahara backed off from his initial promises of quick achievement of this goal and introduced ever more complex steps for its attainment. Aum was growing at a rapid pace by this time. A large new commune facility was opened at the foot of Mt. Fuji in August 1988, and the group had attained a membership of 4,000 (380 in communes) by late 1989. In the introduction to *Metsubo no hi*, Asahara hints that these increasing numbers were becoming more and more a strain on him personally, saying that the performance of more than 8,000 special initiations and shaktipat had drained him physically. For believers, the road to liberation grew increasingly complex, with various stages of accomplishment now established and long periods of "service" sometimes required of the commune members before they were allowed to undertake fully the practice leading to liberation.[6] Although Aum continued to stress the acquisition of extraordinary powers, these were no longer seen as easily attainable; they were accepted more as proofs of the efficacy of Aum's training, which was to lead to liberation, than as ends in themselves.

Perseverance in this ever lengthening training required a more encompassing motivation. This motivation now presented itself: participation in

Asahara's *plan for salvation*, a term introduced in the doomsday volumes (1989b, 224–225). Participation in the plan of salvation seems to have had a multifaceted meaning. At one point Asahara says that it is already certain that one-fourth of the population of the world will die in the coming destruction and that the number of survivors among the remaining three-fourths depends on Aum's salvific activity (1989c, 54). This activity presumably includes a way to attain personal liberation and thus avoid the cataclysm by moving to a higher realm, as suggested in *Initiation*. It also means providing a place to carry out that training, the Lotus Village Plan to which Shimazono refers (1995, 396–398), that is, establishing Aum communes in various locations. However, even at this stage Asahara hints that his plan of salvation includes the ushering in of Armageddon by a race of superior beings—the followers of Aum themselves. This is where Tantra Vajrayana comes in.

Vajrayana, an esoteric form of Indian Buddhism popularized in Tibet, holds the use of mystical symbols, gestures, and chants to be the most effective means of achieving advanced spiritual states and aims toward achieving psychic powers. Asahara adopted Vajrayana as the core of Aum's teaching and interpreted it in a number of ways, including the idea that it condones the deliberate commission of evil acts.[7] In *Metsubo no hi* Asahara uses the concept to explain why Aum will rule in the postapocalyptic world: "Anybody can see that this means rule by force, the establishment of a world where might makes right. That is precisely the world of Tantra Vajrayana. It is the will of Shiva that the practitioners of Tantra, those who have a strong faith in Shiva, rule over all nations. . . . This hints at the direction that Aum will be taking from now on" (1989a, 50).

In a sermon reportedly delivered on September 24, 1989, at one of the Aum facilities in Tokyo, Asahara explains in unmistakable terms what he means by the practice of Vajrayana. He proposes the hypothetical example of a person who, after leading a good life and accumulating merit to enter heaven, suddenly becomes lazy and is in danger of accumulating bad karma. He then explains how it would be to that person's advantage to die before making such a change in direction. Furthermore, an enlightened being would be able to see the dangerous course this person's life was about to take and would himself gain merit by killing the person, thus saving him from danger. This notion is referred to as *poa*, a Tibetan Buddhist term for the transference of consciousness, especially the transference to the Buddha world after death. This term becomes synonymous with murder in Aum's usage. Asahara concludes the story by saying: "Looked at objectively, that is from the viewpoint of human objectivity, this is murder. According to Vajrayana, however, this would be a splendid *poa*. A person with true wisdom, that is [an enlightened person] with the supernatural powers that I talked about earlier, would see this as being of benefit to both the person killed and his murderer" (Mainichi Shinbun Shakaibu 1995, 26).

In fact, from the results of the national police investigation it appears that it was precisely at this time that Aum embarked on a course of murder. In February 1989 Taguchi Shoji, an Aum believer, was allegedly murdered by fellow members after he tried to defect. Furthermore, sometime during early November 1989 Sakamoto Tsutsumi, the lawyer representing families of Aum members, was allegedly murdered by Aum believers in his home along with his family, and their bodies buried in western Japan.

As Shimazono has pointed out, Asahara's apocalyptic vision becomes increasingly vivid and detailed around 1992. For example, an Aum publication, *Riso Shakai* (The ideal society) in August 1992 begins to feature pictures of Patriot missiles and burning oil fields from the Persian Gulf War on its cover; full-color illustrations of planes, tanks, ships, and a nuclear mushroom cloud adorn its pages. The fascination with weaponry extends to speculation concerning the development of plasma bombs, laser weapons, and even "earthquake bombs," supposedly used by the United States to cause the Kobe earthquake in January 1995.[8] The elaboration of this vision apparently reflected a plan to hasten Armageddon through Aum's own efforts; concrete steps included building a chemical factory to make sarin gas, preparing to mass produce weapons, and buying a military helicopter from Russia.

The doctrine of Vajrayana as developed by Asahara, incorporating a self-initiated Armageddon and the postapocalyptic rule of enlightened Aum followers, apparently served as the religious motivation for those involved in Aum's deadly actions. But the dynamics of relationships within the group had their own role to play.

Guru Worship and the "Mind Control" Issue

As Aum's crimes have come to light, the media and legal profession in Japan have, for the most part uncritically, adopted the mind-control thesis popularized by so-called anticult groups in the West (e.g., Robbins 1988). Much print has gone into fretting over whether Aum members still living in their communes will be able to break their mind control bondage and return to society. Aum members under arrest who refuse to confess to their crimes and denounce Aum and their former guru are judged as still under the sway of Asahara's control. The mind-control thesis is tailor-made for the Japanese legal system, where the vast majority of criminal cases are resolved by the defendant "reflecting" on his crimes and entrusting himself to the mercy of the court. When confronted with the evidence, anyone who chooses not to take this course is viewed as irrational or controlled by outside forces.

Certainly many of the techniques identified with mind control existed in Aum. The members living in communes were cut off from outside sources of information and most forms of contact with society. If press reports are to be believed, many of these members thought that the commune members themselves were under attack, victims of the sarin gas that was in fact being produced within the compound. Members were taught that as a result of their yoga training they could work long hours with little sleep, leading to sleep deprivation. Likewise, they were told that the body needed less food as a result of training and were fed the "Aum diet" of the same two meals daily. Underground *samadhi*, which meant meditating for days at a time in a small wooden room underground, constituted intense training. Members were encouraged to spend long hours viewing tapes of Asahara's sermons or listening to the sermons on the Walkmans as they carried on their work. They were taught to repeat certain phrases thousands of times, pledging their loyalty to Asahara and encouraging themselves to persevere in the training—some of the strategies for the "data replacement" mentioned earlier.

All these, indeed, are techniques of psychological manipulation. As is well known, however, they are not unique to destructive religious groups and have been found useful in presumably healthy contexts. Traditional methods of meditation employed in mainline religious groups encourage periods of fasting, sleep deprivation, and isolation as means to enhance the experience. Athletes in Japan use "image training," a form of positive thinking that replaces fears of failure with mental images of success.

Furthermore, such methods probably cannot completely strip people of their ability to make independent decisions, as critics of the mind-control thesis repeatedly claim. Indeed, as Asahara himself has argued, the believers choose to undertake these practices with some knowledge of what their effect will be (Asahara 1991b, 196). While acknowledging the psychological manipulation that took place in Aum, the mind-control thesis by itself does not adequately explain the believers' actions. Once again, the dynamics of faith, especially as expressed in the Japanese religious and cultural tradition, provide a more useful model for understanding Aum's crimes.

Japanese folk religion promotes belief in the identification of deceased human beings with gods or spirits. At least on one level it is commonly assumed that every person becomes a god after death. For example, the dead are referred to as *hotoke* (buddha) in everyday speech, and in the Shinto tradition the spirits of the dead (or *kami*) are still commonly apotheosized. People who have undergone particularly rigorous training and consequently exhibit some extraordinary power, such as the *yamabushi* (mountain ascetics) or some of the main figures in Japanese Buddhism, are often believed to be living gods. In modern times, the founders of certain new Japanese religious movements have been regarded by their followers in this way, and some of the leaders of the more recent of these groups actively take this mantle upon themselves (see, for example, Astley 1995 on Ōkawa Ryūhō and Kōfuku no Kagaku). Asahara's claim to be the only person to have attained "final liberation" and his repeated demands for absolute faith in him as the "guru" can be understood within this context.

The emphasis on the *oyabun-kobun*, or master-disciple, relationship in Japanese society reinforces demands on the loyalty of followers by religious leaders such as Asahara. Although such a relationship is not necessarily absolute in Japan, nor is it unique to that country, as a cultural element of some continuing importance in daily life we should not overlook it in trying to understand the motivation of Asahara's followers. At the very least its status as cultural tradition would allow these followers to accept the constraints of such a relationship more easily—even when it involves acts of murder.

Aum appears to have reinforced this kind of relationship structurally. Followers were moved frequently between the various communes and branches that Aum had established, discouraging members from forming relationships that might have checked Asahara's power within the group. The members followed individual courses of training, even when gathered together in the same training halls. The rite of shaktipat and other forms of "initiation" emphasized Asahara's role in the individual members' training.[9] Shimada Hiromi reports the presence of a question box at the commune in Namino on the southern island of Kyushu through which members could question Asahara directly concerning the faith or practice (Shimada 1995, 107). Press reports tell us that Asahara always had a phone nearby for one-on-one contact with movement leaders, thus avoiding the need for meetings where several leaders might be present (*Asahi Shinbun*, October 20, 1995).

Less subtle means also maintained discipline and loyalty, such as the murder of Taguchi Shoji, a member who attempted to defect from the group in February 1989. One other case of murder has been documented, and suspicions remain regarding other former members whose whereabouts are unknown.[10] Since May 1994 the group also reportedly engaged in the wholesale manufacture of drugs such as LSD and the truth serum thiopental sodium.

Aum's rituals apparently included LSD, and beginning in November 1994 the truth serum was used to flush out suspected spies within Aum's ranks (*Chunichi Shinbun*, November 14, 1995).[11] Although such methods were principally directed at lower-echelon members, complicity in these crimes probably contributed to the leaders' attachment to Asahara, as they were accessories after the fact and accomplices, and led to the escalation of violence practiced by the group.

Asahara's Armageddon

Statements in a notebook left in Hayakawa Kiyohide's office indicate that Aum might have planned to attack Tokyo in November 1995 with two hundred soldiers fortified by tanks purchased from Russia. Hayakawa, at forty-six considerably older than other Aum leaders, was chief of Aum's Construction Ministry and reportedly Asahara's leading aid. Whether the short entries in his notebook represent concrete plans or merely his own musings, beyond question Aum was preparing to launch an attack sometime in the future. Between November 1993 and December 1994 a chemical plant capable of producing seventy tons of sarin gas was constructed at the group's commune in Kamikuishiki, west of Tokyo.[12] An AK74 automatic rifle was smuggled into Japan from Russia in February 1993 by Murai Hideo, the murdered chief of Aum's Science and Technology Ministry, to be used as a model for the assembly of one thousand rifles by Aum followers (*Chunichi Sinbun*, October 16, 1995). In June 1994 Aum purchased a Mil-17 military helicopter from Russia. It appears that Aum used longtime contacts within the Japanese Self-Defense Forces to gain information on weaponry, even stealing weapons research data from a Mitsubishi facility west of Tokyo (Tokyo Shinbun Shkaibu 1995, 158–163).

Neither the Matsumoto attack nor the Tokyo subway attack, however, represented the opening shot in Asahara's "plan of salvation." Both appear to have sprung from much more mundane reasons. The Matsumoto gas poisoning was allegedly aimed at a panel of judges due to hand down a decision in a case involving Aum's attempted purchase of land in the area. It may also have served as a trial run for a new way to disperse the gas, since two previous attempts directed at Ikeda Daisaku, de facto head of the Soka Gakka Buddhist sect, had apparently failed (*Japan Times*, October 21, 1995). The Tokyo attack smacks of desperation, a hurried attempt to disrupt the police investigation of one of Aum's other alleged crimes, the kidnapping and murder of Kariya Kiyoshi, the sixty-eight-year-old brother of an Aum member.

The Kariya kidnapping does nothing if not indicate how bold Aum had become in its criminal activities, an attitude perhaps engendered by the lack of police response to its growing list of infractions. Kariya had apparently dissuaded his sister from donating a high-priced piece of property to Aum and convinced her to leave the group. Asahara is charged with ordering Kariya's abduction in an effort to obtain information on his sister's whereabouts. The kidnapping occurred on a busy Tokyo street at 4:30 on the afternoon of February 28, 1995. Several witnesses helped identify the van used in the abduction, leading to the identification of Matsumoto Takeshi, an Aum member, as the person who rented the vehicle. With suspicion of Aum's involvement in th kidnapping established, the police planned to raid Aum facilities on the morning of March 22.[13] Aum received a tip about the police plans, and on March 18 Asahara directed Endo Seiichi to produce the sarin gas used in the subway attack. Work on the gas was completed early on the morning of March 20, and the gas was immediately distributed to five teams to be released during the morning rush hour on subways that converge at the Kasumigaseki station, beneath the nerve center of the Japanese bureaucracy. The destructive results instantly became headline news worldwide.

It is hard to imagine how Asahara and his followers could have believed that their plan to disrupt the police investigation would succeed. His followers' motivation is clear, however. Based on Aum's teaching of Vajrayana Buddhism, they believed in the efficacy of murder as a means of salvation; many of them had already been involved in murder or other criminal acts at the direction of Asahara, their guru and master. Armageddon was but one more step on the way to salvation.

Understanding Aum

On one level we can view Aum as a social protest group, as reflected in the comments by Inoue quoted at the beginning of this chapter. In joining Aum, young persons were rejecting a society characterized by opacity and malaise. Despite repeated promises to introduce transparency into public affairs, top political and administrative figures continue to make decisions privately, often over sake at the numerous Tokyo restaurants catering to politicians and bureaucrats. This opacity is reflected in the Aum investigation itself. The public must be content with reports leaked by the police to the press, or with prosecutors' statements filed in court, for no other avenues of information exist in Japan. We may never know why police did not investigate earlier Aum crimes—public inquiries into such incidents are rare in

Japan. Malaise is by its nature a less identifiable problem. Young people perhaps feel increasingly dissatisfied with the rewards offered for long years of hard work in school and a drawn-out apprenticeship in the office with fewer opportunities for promotion than their fathers enjoyed. Perhaps this dissatisfaction has contributed to the contemporary interest in mystic and psychic abilities, forms of empowerment that many may see as more readily available than traditional forms of advancement. For some, dissatisfaction might also make apocalyptic ideas more appealing, offering a spectacular end to the status quo.

What is truly tragic, however, is that Aum repeats and intensifies many of the cultural forms it criticizes. It postpones the promised empowerment, makes authority absolute, and keeps believers in the dark regarding their leaders' true plans. Comparisons have been made with the Japanese Red Army of the 1970s, another radical protest group that copied internally the patterns of power that it sought to destroy in society at large. These groups serve to reflect back to a society its least appealing features—it is little wonder that society wants to treat them as aberrations.

Notes

1. All translations in this article are mine.
2. The term used in Aum for those who undertook this life-style is *shukkesha*, literally, "one who has left home." The term is commonly used for Buddhist monks in Japan, even though the vast majority are married and live with their families. Since Aum's communes were one distinguishing feature of the group, I will use "commune member" as a translation of *shukkesha*.
3. For a useful overview of the arguments in this debate see Robbins 1988, 72–79.
4. Only the revised editions of this and one of Asahara's other early books, *Seishi wo koeru*, are available to the author, which accounts for the discrepancy in dates for these works in this article. The books were not substantially changed from the original, with the main revision being the addition of collections of testimonies from Aum believers at the end of each volume.
5. For example, in *Seishi wo koeru*, Asahara claims that "although it took me four years to attain awakening through the practice of *sendō*, it can be achieved in a matter of months through the use of yoga. My disciples are achieving Kundalinī Awakening in short periods of time" (1992, 34).
6. For example, one believer recounts that after joining the commune in 1989 he was required to wait two years before being allowed to meditate (Asahara 1992, 217). Aum believers defined such service, called *bhakti* from the Hindu word for devotional service to the godhead, as devotion to Asahara and Shiva, the Hindu god of destruction and creation worshiped in Aum. In practice, this often amounted to carrying out tasks assigned to members of the commune or to pros-

elytizing. The English word *work* was also commonly used for both of these activities.

7. See Shimazono 1995, 406, for a summary of some of the meanings attributed to this concept.

8. Earthquake bombs supposedly use microwave technology to vaporize all living creatures in an area while causing no harm to buildings and other structures. Speculation concerning such devices seems especially ghoulish in light of reports that Aum disposed of some of its victims' bodies in a microwave device.

9. For example, the Blood Initiation involved drinking Asahara's blood or a manufactured substance allegedly patterned after the DNA found in it, and the so-called Miracle Pond consisted of drinking Asahara's bathwater. Such practices are not unknown in Japanese religious history, as part of the tradition of veneration of mountain ascetics and living Buddhist saints.

10. Ochida Kōtarō was allegedly murdered on Asahara's orders on January 30, 1994, by a fellow member, Yasuda Hideaki. The two had been caught trying to rescue Yasuda's mother, also a member of the group, and escape together (*Japan Times*, November 9, 1995).

11. Concern about possible spies is already visible in late 1988 or early 1989. For example, in *Metsubō no hi* Asahara claims that he has excommunicated some members as spies for other religious groups (1989b, 46). Police have also documented one case of murder involving a suspected spy: the use of the poison gas VX on Hamaguchi Tadahito of Osaka in December 1994.

12. According to court papers filed by the Tokyo Prosecutor's Office, the plant never worked properly, apparently because much of the equipment was homemade by Aum (*Japan Times,* October 21, 1995). The sarin used in the attacks of Matsumoto, Nagano Prefecture, in June 1994 and on the Tokyo subway in March 1995 was allegedly produced in relatively small quantities by Tsuchiya Masami and Endo Seiichi in their personal laboratories at the Kamikuishiki site.

13. Even with the intervening attack on the Tokyo subway, the official reason for the raid on Aum facilities carried out by more than 2,500 police officers on 22 March was suspicion of involvement in the Kariya kidnapping.

References

Arita, Yoshifu. 1995. *Anoko ga oumu ni!* [That kid joined Aum?]. Tokyo: Kobunsha.

Asahara, Shoko. 1992. *Seishi wo koeru* [Transcending life and death]. Tokyo: Aum Press.

———. 1991a. *Chonoryoku himitsu no Kaihatsuho.* [A secret method to the development of psychic powers]. Rev. ed. Tokyo: Aum Press.

———. 1991b. *Hyaku mon hyaku to* [One hundred questions and answers]. Tokyo: Aum Press.

———. 1989a. *Metsubo no hi* [Doomsday]. (Aum Comics). Tokyo: Aum Press.

———. 1989b. *Metsubo no hi* [Doomsday]. Tokyo: Aum Press.

———. 1989c. *Metsubo kara koku e* [From destruction to the void]. Tokyo: Aum Press.

————. 1987. *Inishieshon* [Initiation]. Tokyo: Aum Press.

Astley, Trevor. 1995. "The Transformation of a Recent Japanese New Religion: Okawa Ryuho and Kofuku no Kagaku." *Japanese Journal of Religious Studies* 22:343–380.

Aum Publications (ed.). 1995. *Kiizuru kuni, wazawai chikashi* [Land of the Rising Sun, disaster Is at hand]. Tokyo: Aum Press.

————. 1992. *Riso shakai* [The ideal society]. Tokyo: Aum Press.

Field, Norma, 1991. *In the Realm of a Dying Emperor*. New York: Vintage.

Hardacre, Helen. 1989. *Shinto and the State, 1868–1988*. Princeton, N.J.: Princeton University Press.

Hori, Ichiro. 1968. *Folk Religion in Japan: Continuity and Change*. Chicago: University of Chicago Press.

Mainichi Shinbun Shakaibu. 1995. *Kurai inori: Asahara Shoko to Shitotachi* [The dark prayer: Asahara Shoko and his disciples]. Tokyo: Mainichi Shinbunsha.

Nakane, Chie. 1970. *Japanese Society*. Berkley: University of California Press.

Robbins, Thomas. 1988. *Cults, Converts, and Charisma*. London: Sage.

Shimada, Hiromi. 1995. *"Oumu Shinrikyo: Sonshi to Shukkeshatachi"* [The master and commune members]. In *Shinshukyu Jidai* [The age of new religions]. Tokyo: Okura Shuppan.

Shimazono, Susumu. 1995. "In the Wake of Aum: The Formation and Transformation of a Universe of Belief." *Japanese Journal of Religious Studies* 22 (2):381–415.

Tokyo Shinbun Shakaibu, ed. 1995. *Oumu soshiki hanzai no nazo* [The enigma of Aum's crimes]. Tokyo: Tokyo Shinbun Shuppankyoku.

CHAPTER 3

Economic Fraud and Christian Leaders in the United States

ANSON SHUPE

$\mathcal{L}$ewis Nobles, former president of private 169-year-old Mississippi College affiliated with the Southern Baptist Convention, had earned a reputation as an extraordinary fundraiser during his twenty-five years in office. During the mid-to-late 1980s he increased the college's endowment fund sixfold to $5.3 million while doubling student enrollment. In 1986 the Exxon Education Foundation named him one of the nation's top eighteen college presidents. His troubles began, however, when it was discovered that he had created secret bank accounts for himself as early as 1978. In August 1993, nine months before his planned retirement from a $125,000-a-year job, he was charged with numerous counts of money laundering, mail fraud, embezzlement ($3 million), transporting young women across state lines for (in the state's prosecutorial opinion) immoral purposes, and spending $379,000 on prostitutes. Early the next year, free on a $15,000 personal recognizance bond, he fled the state shortly before a court date.

FBI agents eventually caught up with Nobles at a plush hotel in San Francisco with $25,000 in cash that belonged to the college. In a suicide attempt he swallowed cyanide, required subsequent emergency surgery to repair damage to his esophagus and stomach, and shortly after suffered a stroke. Meanwhile, at least five women waited to testify against him.

On January 17, 1996, Nobles pleaded guilty in a U.S. district court to two counts of mail fraud, two counts of income-tax evasion, and one count of money laundering. The prosecutors dropped fifteen charges against him in exchange for his guilty plea. By that time seventy years of age, Nobles agreed to donate several parcels of land and stock from several brokerage accounts bought with his embezzled funds, worth an estimated $400,000, to Mississippi College. He faced a maximum sentence of forty years in prison (see "Ex-President" 1996 and Maxwell 1995b).

White Collar Crime and Religion

Economic fraud perpetrated by religious leaders on their religious institutions/denominations or on their followers is a variant of what I have elsewhere termed *clergy malfeasance*, that is, the exploitation and abuse (financial, sexual, or authoritative) of a religious group's believers by elites and leaders of that religious tradition in whom the former trust (Shupe 1995). (I use terms such as *elites, leaders,* and *clerics* in the broadest sense to refer both to ordained and unordained officials in religious groups.) As noted in this volume's introduction, such malfeasance is a violation of fiduciary responsibilities common to a number of professions. In this chapter I specifically examine elite economic malfeasance in religious groups and some circumstantial, conceptually relevant aspects of it.

However, clergy malfeasance occurs within a unique type of benevolent institution, similar to medical practice and psychotherapy, in which power is inequitably distributed. A religious organization, from cult to denomination, is a "trusted hierarchy" wherein the lower echelons believe in (and often are encouraged or even instructed to believe in) the good intentions, sincerity, and wisdom of the upper echelons. Although religion, as Saint Paul observed in 1 Cor. 4:20–21, is very much about power, the positive rather than the negative implications of this power arrangement for vulnerable laity are usually what that group hears about.

Much clergy malfeasance resembles "elite deviance" as defined in Simon and Eitzen 1990—it might or might not be illegal but would generally qualify as immoral (e.g., a Methodist minister caught in an adulterous situation with a congregant). Clerical economic fraud, however, closely parallels "white-collar crime" in the secular world (Coleman 1987; Shapiro 1987; Sutherland 1949). This type of fraud involves perpetrators with relatively high status (which provides opportunities to abuse the group's trust and resources) and relies on guile (unlike most "street crimes," such as burglaries, muggings, or car thefts that frequently involve some force or physical violence), or both.

Moreover, some economic clergy malfeasance resembles corporate crime in which an organization has adopted a policy of law violations or immoral deception to advance its own interests (e.g., Blankenship 1995). No one would seriously argue that the embezzlements discussed here were committed to benefit the organization or group from which financial resources have been taken; rather, the obvious purpose of the malfeasance was to enrich the perpetrator at the group or organization's expense. Investment scams and mission misrepresentations, however, more closely resemble corporate crimes in that entire ministries or religiously directed corporate endeavors are founded on deception and untruth.

No one has made an overall dollar estimate of the costs of economic fraud committed by religious officials on either their own groups or the general public. Indeed, only since the early 1990s have journalists begun offering specific damage estimates in law suit settlements from clergy malfeasance, and then only for specific denominations, such as the Roman Catholic church (e.g., Berry 1992). Part of the problem in amassing data for such an estimate lies in the staggering diversity and number of religious groups in our pluralistic society. Part also stems from the ways many religious hierarchies neutralize embarrassing scandals by cover-ups, sentimental appeals to victims to remain silent, and undisclosed financial settlements with both victims and perpetrators that seek reconciliation (and, on occasion, by sealed court records [see Shupe 1995, 79–116]).

However, as Philip Jenkins demonstrates in this volume, the ability of most religious groups to contain reports of scandals has consistently declined throughout this century. Especially in our modern scandal-preoccupied mass media, where both journalists and news consumers have had their confidence in leaders eroded and their moral shock desensitized (exactly as predicted by Edwin H. Sutherland as a function of increasing public awareness of white-collar crime), reports of clerical economic fraud have become increasingly commonplace.

Cases of Economic Fraud

What follows is a "sampler" of confirmed economic frauds of both white-collar and corporate crime types perpetrated by religious officials, divided into two areas of Protestant and Catholic religion in the United States: recent scandals within mainline denominations and within televangelistic parachurches.[1] These cases illustrate the "domain" of religious economic malfeasance that until now has been largely ignored and certainly not conceptually addressed. I make no claim that they represent either an exhaustive or representative sampling, for we have no way of knowing how many local church treasurers, accountants, or pastors "skim" from the collection plate on a small-time basis.

Mainline Denominational Scandals

Here I offer an overview of four types of economic malfeasance by religious elites: embezzlements, investment scams, misrepresented missions, and televangelistic parachurch financial misuse. Continuing study of such exploitation will likely yield more subtypes.

Embezzlements. Embezzlement represents one of the most common forms of white-collar crime both in secular corporations and in denominations.

As reported in the *Chicago Tribune* on May 2, 1995, under "Church Says Treasurer Stole Funds" and by John Fialka in the *Wall Street Journal* on July 27, 1995, in "Unholy Acts: Church Officials' Thefts Dismay Catholics," national Episcopal Church treasurer Ellen Cooke, after eight years at her $125,000-a-year job, resigned in early January 1995 shortly before denominational officials accused her of embezzling $2.2 million. Later that month she pleaded guilty to transferring at least $1.5 million from church coffers to her private account as well as income-tax evasion. She used the money stolen from this 2.4 million–member organization to finance travel, jewelry (for example, a $16,000 necklace from Tiffany's), school tuition for her children, and new homes. Cooke had been able to divert church funds since 1990 because she had virtually sole supervision over auditing procedures ("Ex-Treasurer" 1996).

One year later, the Episcopal Church had managed to recover $1 million through an insurance policy with the promise of more compensation through the sale of property given to the denomination by Cooke and her husband. She blamed her behavior on faulty memory, her psychiatrist blamed it on job stress, and her lawyer explained it as the result of a "bipolar mood disorder" ("Ex-Treasurer" 1996).

Similarly, Deborah S. Davis, former bookkeeper for the 14,600-member Presbyterian Church U.S.A. Presbytery of Southern Kansas, was fired in April 1995, accused of embezzling $279,000. As Davis awaited trial later that year, the district attorney's office in Wichita charged her with felony theft for funneling restricted church funds over a six-month period to her own uses. Spent by the time it was discovered missing, the money was not recoverable, but denominational spokespersons said they hoped to recoup about a third of it from insurance. The executive presbyter commented: "It's been a heavy emotional and financial loss. It has shaken the confidence people had in us as an institution" ("Funds Missing" 1995).

At approximately the same time, William R. Jones, former comptroller of the United Methodist Board of Global Ministries, was arraigned in New York State Supreme Court on December 1 after a Manhattan grand jury indicted him on grand larceny charges. Jones had earlier confessed to moving $400,000 from the board's bank account into his own personal account a few days before stepping down from the comptroller's post to assume new denominational responsibilities in California. The missing funds were discovered shortly after his departure from the UM's New York offices, according to Fialka's *Wall Street Journal* article.

Such scandals, of course, are not confined to Protestants. For example, between 1992 and 1995 the U.S. Roman Catholic Church (the nation's largest denomination) discovered a half dozen major embezzlement scandals involving church officials. The Diocesan Fiscal Managers Conference, an organization of more than a hundred members that supervises finances in the approximately two hundred dioceses and archdioceses in the United States, decided in June 1995 to draw up new rules of accountability, particularly after three former DFMC members admitted to embezzlement. One, Anthony F. Franjaine, had served as president of the group and stole $1.5 million while comptroller for the Diocese of Buffalo, New York, as John Fialka reported in his July 27, 1995, *Wall Street Journal* article.

Investment Scams. Religious institutions—churches, denominations, or church-affiliated colleges—are as much a part of the late-twentieth-century investment scene as their secular counterparts. Ironically, this involvement has created a potential for financial abuse analogous to that of parishioners in relation to clerics: the trust sometimes misplaced in fiduciary agents. The duplicitous nature of entire organizations also moves us toward a parallel to corporate crime.

For instance, the World Fidelity Bank, officers of which had connections to the 46,000-member Open Bible Standard Churches denomination, sold that group fraudulent certificates of deposit over a two-year period. Instead of expertly investing the money, WFB officers squandered most of it on life-style expenses and wildly speculative schemes. WFB laundered other monies through international banks. An FBI undercover agent posing as an accountant for a drug cartel even offered to lend money to the schemers so that they could pay off their most recent investors. As in any classic pyramid scheme, the Des Moines–based Open Bible Standard Churches earned "incredible" returns from an initial investment of $45,000 between 1988 and 1991. Denominational officials went on to invest 9 percent of the group's total assets in this phony investment plan, eventually suffering large losses. A jury found masterminds of the scheme, including a former minister of the denomination, guilty of conspiracy to commit mail/wire fraud and money laundering (Martin 1993).

In August 1989 the North American Securities Administrators Association and the Council of Better Business Bureaus in a jointly issued study, "Preying on the Faithful," reported that more than 150,000 Americans had lost more than $450,000 since the mid-1980s to religious investment scams (Lawton 1989). For example, an oil- and gas-drilling project proposed to take place in Israel based its specifications on prophecy purportedly found in Deuteronomy. Another scheme organized by a former bank trust officer and treasurer of the largest Baptist church in Atlanta "enticed nearly 200 friends and fellow church members to pool $18 million dollars in stock investments that he promised would yield up to 30 percent profit *per month*" (Lawton 1989, 41; italics mine). Bible verses were printed on the bottom of monthly statements, presumably to reassure religious investors. After the scam was detected (the money spread over forty accounts in seven banks), the former trust officer received a sentence of ten years in prison.

Unquestionably, however, the grossest example of a religious financial rip-off has been the recent debacle known as the Foundation for New Era Philanthropy, another classic pyramid scheme. New Era chair John G. Bennett, Jr., promised charitable and educational groups, including about a hundred religious organizations and missions, they would double their investments in just six months; a pool of anonymous donors, he told them, was putting up tens of millions of dollars in matching grants. Rather than encourage investors to place their funds in escrow accounts or with an independent third party, Bennett required investors to deposit their monies directly with New Era. In reality, as Neff relates, "There were no anonymous benefactors. The ministries that had been depositing funds with New Era were actually funding each other's matching grants" (1995, 20).

As Bennett reportedly assumed "the persona of an inspiring and warm-hearted Christian philanthropist" (Giles 1995, 40), he diverted more than $4 million to his personal businesses and paid himself more than $26,000 a week in consulting fees, according to the Securities and Exchange Commission (Frame 1995, 61). In 1993 alone, New Era's true investments earned a paltry $33,788 compared to the $41.3 million taken in from new clients. In 1994 Bennett contributed $240 million to various institutions, including $20 million to such groups as Planned Parenthood and Harvard University, neither of which had ever invested in New Era (Rubin et al., 1995b). As *Philadelphia Inquirer* investigative reporters David Rubin, Rich Heidorn, Jr., and David O'Reilly wrote in "Near End, a Frenzy at New Era" on June 18, 1995, Bennett wrote $98 million worth of checks in a ninety-day period, or something over $1 million per day. Bennett's confidence and the amounts of money he was transferring astonished and impressed religious and educational organizations. He was fast becoming a high-roller in the world of sacred philanthropy.

Religious organizations "conned" by New Era and Bennett included a who's who of evangelical Protestant institutions: Lancaster Bible College ($16.9 million), Wheaton College ($4.6 million), Gordon-Conwell Theological Seminary ($9.8 million), Scripture Union ($1.62 million), Messiah College ($2 million), International Teams ($2.5 million), CB International ($2.3 million), and John Brown University ($2 million). The loss of $300 by West Catholic High School in Philadelphia illustrates the scope of Bennett's financial malfeasance. Students there had sold more than 1,500 boxes of candy to raise the $300 they invested in New Era, as the *Philadelphia Inquirer*'s Martha Woodall reported June 4, 1995, in "New Era Loses Candy Money" (also Giles 1995; Maxwell, 1995a).

However, a controversy arose in the evangelical Protestant community over other ethical dimensions of the scandal. As in most pyramid schemes, not every investor in New Era had lost money. The initial "show" investors received the promised exaggerated returns to enhance the credibility of the scam. For example, on its original $2.3 million investment, CB International missionary organization, based in Wheaton, Illinois, earned a $4.9 million return. But more than150 Christian organizations founded United Response to New Era when a number of evangelical groups realized that fifty-two of them had received more money from New Era before it collapsed than they had contributed, largely at the expense of sixty-one of their fellow evangelical victims (Frame 1995; and see Steve Stecklow, "Trustee's Filing Identifies 46 Creditors That Made Money before New Era's Fall," *Wall Street Journal*, June 19,1995).

Widespread media coverage—including David Rubin, Rich Heidorn, Jr., and David O'Reilly's "New Era Creditors Choose New Trustee" on June 27, 1995, in the *Philadelphia Inquirer* and Steve Stecklow's "Retired Judge Will Sort Out New Era Mess" on June 29, 1995, in the *Wall Street Journal*— revealed a colossal economic and moral boondoggle for many of the groups involved with New Era, and numerous courts and attorneys found themselves busy in late 1995 trying to sort out the affairs of a bogus philanthropic organization that, when it filed for bankruptcy on May 15 of that year, listed $551 million in liabilities and $80 million in assets (see also Giles 1995).

Misrepresented Missions. With regard to their financial gifts, many Christians take seriously Jesus Christ's instructions to his disciples to undertake the great commission, that is, "Go forth therefore and make disciples of all nations, baptizing them in the name of the Father and of the Son and of the Holy Spirit, teaching them to observe all that I have commanded you" (Matt. 28:19–20). This sometimes renders them vulnerable to slick or convincing appeals for bogus foreign missions projects, a parallel to corporate crime in which company policies knowingly promote deceptive or illegal outcomes.

A case in point: Over a seven-year period, sixty-seven-year-old evangelist Gerald Derstine (a former Mennonite pastor) and his Gospel Crusade, Inc., headquartered in Bradenton, Florida, claimed impressive success in converting Arab Muslims in and about Israel. His "successes" included awe-inspiring miracles, mass conversions, and even martyrdoms. He raised $2.8 million in 1994 alone by selling a book, tracts, and videotapes to support what he portrayed as an expanding but persecuted ministry in the Holy Land. However, it was revealed in March 1995 that Derstine "salted" his materials with nonexistent conversions and confessions and staged "show interviews" with purported converts.

Among other misrepresentations, Derstine portrayed a pseudo-Muslim, sheik-turned-Christian convert, Omar Nufal (actually a Jordanian visiting relatives in Israel), as a former would-be committer of infanticide converted to Christ. In reality, however, "Derstine and [a regional ministry leader, Nufal's brother-in-law] came to his home allegedly 'to help poor families,' gave him $200, took his picture, and left" (Miles 1995, 64). One local ministry leader received $9,000 in ministry funds to add a new level to his home on the pretext that it was going to be a home church. Some local ministry leaders received as much as $500,000 over a six-year period to keep up the ruse. But this ministry produced no martyrs, much less conspicuous converts.

An investigative segment on ABC's *Prime Time Live* reported similar claims of obeying the great commission connected to bogus humanitarian aid to orphans in Haiti ("Apple of God's Eye" 1991). The culprits were evangelists Larry Lea and W. V. Grant, Jr., pastors of two ministries with television extensions based in Dallas, Texas. Their Haitian missions were "smoke-and-mirrors" images of benevolent, caring leaders ministering to unfortunate children, created by video crews on spot visits to an orphanage that loaned itself out to such "media events" for kickbacks. One orphanage laundered donations back to the evangelists, who pocketed the bulk of the monies. Such a practice formed, in fact, one of the bases for the Internal Revenue Service's successful prosecution of PTL's Rev. Jim Bakker: He repeatedly raised money during broadcast time for either misrepresented or nonexistent missions that never received the donations (see, e.g., Martz and Carroll 1988, 55). That practice is illegal, according to the Federal Communications Commission, and Bakker went to prison for federal income-tax evasion. So, eventually, did W. V. Grant, Jr.

Televangelistic Parachurches

The electronic church, or televangelism, is largely composed of *parachurches*, evangelistic organizations who from their beginnings in the nineteenth century "were different from existing churches and denominations. They were totally independent and autonomous . . . they crossed sectarian boundaries and drew their support from Christians who belonged to a wide variety of churches (Hadden and Shupe 1988, 43–44)

Since parachurch ministries first took to the airwaves in the early 1920s, scholars have been interested in how their leaders finance their organizations (e.g., Cardwell 1984; Frankl 1987; Hoover 1988). However, the known instances of deception and misuse of funds by televangelists have generally been examined only in the popular journalistic literature (e.g., Martz and Carroll 1988; Randi 1987) and remain unacknowledged in overview studies of elite deviance literature (e.g., Simon and Eitzen 1990). Most seem to operate within the limits of both federal broadcasting laws and ethical behavior.

Two factors largely drew sociologists to analyze televangelism: the political potential for mobilizing conservative Christians into the Republican Party during the Reagan and Bush eras, and the financial scandals of the late 1980s and early 1990s (e.g., Hadden and Shupe 1988; Hadden and Swann 1981). Here is another parallel between church economic malfeasance and corporate crime—in being rooted in the operating strategies of certain ministries. Although early in this century evangelists such as Billy Sunday and Aimee Semple McPherson had been accused of enriching themselves from parachurch coffers (Blumhoffer1993; Dorsett 1991), not until a trio of sensational scandals occurred in the late 1980s did both media investigators and social scientists take a closer look at televangelistic financing.

First, in March 1987 the nationally prominent televangelist from Oklahoma, Oral Roberts, announced that God had told him in a vision that Roberts would be "taken home to heaven" if his viewers and followers did not produce within one month $8 million to support his ailing medical school and university in Tulsa as well as his television ministry. This theologically deviant (but not illegal) appeal succeeded, but it caused observers to contrast Roberts's desperate plea with his affluent life-style. Second, the next year a private investigator with a camera caught Louisiana's Jimmy Swaggart (at the time the most watched televangelist) in flagrante delicto in a cheap motel with a prostitute (and later in a similar situation after his ministry had all but expired). Money was not the direct issue in the Swaggart scandal, but his sexual antics contributed to the unsavory public stereotype of televangelists.

Revealed the same year as Roberts's "divine hostage" controversy, the third major scandal combined sex and blatant financial malfeasance. The Reverend Jim Bakker, founder, owner, and chief evangelist of the PTL Club program and PTL network, was paying a former PTL secretary to remain silent about having had sex with him. Then it emerged that he and his flamboyant wife, Tammy Faye, had since the early 1980s appropriated for their personal use at least $10 million of PTL viewers' donations originally requested for several nonexistent ministries. Ensuing investigations conducted independently by an interim caretaking committee led by Rev. Jerry Falwell (himself a prominent televangelist), the Federal Communications Commission, and the Internal Revenue Service also discovered that in developing his Heritage Village Christian theme park, his hotel, and a condominium resort Jim Bakker had fraudulently sold $158 million worth of "lifetime" time-share resort partnerships to 116,000 followers.

Barnhart (1988, 11) describes a bureaucratic labyrinth in PTL that made money hard to trace. At one time PTL had forty-seven bank accounts and seventeen vice presidents; financial control was divided into four separate compartments, and only Bakker and his closest aides possessed an overview of PTL's finances. As journalists Martz and Carroll conclude, the Bakkers "weren't accused merely of dipping into the offering plate but of plundering their ministry of millions of dollars in salaries and bonuses and countless thousands more squandered on high living"(1988, 4–5).

That high living included the purchase of seven extravagantly furnished homes in six years, air-conditioned doghouses and tree houses, lavish trips to Europe and the Caribbean (among other places) for the Bakkers and extensive PTL entourages, Mercedes and Rolls-Royces, even gold-plated bathroom fixtures in the Bakkers' suite at the Heritage Grand Hotel (Shupe 1995, 70–73). In the end, Jim Bakker went to prison for almost five years; his wife, Tammy Faye, married his condominium developer, who by the mid-1990s had fallen into his own legal troubles, and for a brief time was an eccentric day-time television talk-show hostess; and PTL, with its theme park, hotel, and other assets, collapsed.

Unlike such prominent national scandals, local and regional economic frauds involving clerics are difficult to chart (without enormous resources) across media accounts, court records, and communities. However, regional scandals appear to abound (a judgment based on my own sampling in various areas over the past half decade).

For example, the Dallas-based *Success n' Life* televangelism ministry of the Reverend Robert Tilton fell apart not long after ABC's *Prime Time Live* aired "The Apple of God's Eye" in 1991, an exposé of his corrupt and cynical direct-mail fund-raising tactics. Until then, Tilton's show had been carried by all 235 U.S. television markets. At his peak, Tilton purchased five thousand hours of airtime monthly, with an estimated 199,000 households watching. His television parachurch took in $7 million in viewer donations each month, sometimes as much as a half million dollars *per day*. These funds, as the ABC report revealed, were conspicuously channeled to support Tilton's expensive homes (at least five), cars, boats, trips, and an investment portfolio worth at least $40 million (Shupe 1995, 73).

Lacking the national profile of the Bakkers or Jerry Falwell, Tilton was nevertheless a rising star in televangelism, with an eccentric and theatric preaching style. But the ABC investigation showed that he had a penchant for dunning widows for pledges to his ministry that their late husbands had supposedly made, sometimes in letters dated after their deaths. And despite his on-air promise to answer individual prayer requests included with mailed donations, Tilton received all the money at a Tulsa, Oklahoma, bank, while "the prayer requests, letters, and even photographs were deposited unceremoniously into a dumpster behind the bank; Tilton never even saw them" (Shupe 1995, 74–75).

By 1995 the ABC segment and a minimum of eleven lawsuits by angry ex-supporters had reduced Tilton's ministry to three hundred people at Sunday services in his five-thousand-seat Word of Faith Outreach Center in Dallas. Nevertheless, he attempted a comeback on cable television with a modest total of four markets for the *Pastor Tilton Show* ("News Briefs" 1996).

Meanwhile, Dallas's W. V. Grant, Jr., was arraigned in federal court on April 15, 1996, for income tax evasion. After a devastating ABC *Prime Time Live* exposé of his bogus missions and "stage magician" healings, Grant sold his Eagles Nest church site in southwest Dallas, along with other properties, for $1.9 million to another Pentecostal ministry. According to Tom Wyatt in "Dallas Televangelist Set to Be Arraigned" on April 14, 1996, in the *Dallas Morning News*, a spokeswoman for the evangelist buyer said: "They were a very good investment. [The new reverend] had no dealings to buy Rev. Grant out. We wish him well."

So What Do We Make of Crooked Clerics? The study of clergy malfeasance has the good fortune to have as resources the conceptual tools of analysis developed by criminologists and sociologists of deviance. Still being refined in interpretation and definition, the dynamics of embezzlement, secular pyramid schemes, corporate crime, and other forms of elite financial deviance are nevertheless no arcane mystery. What remains for further research in the understanding of elite deviance is to promulgate concepts that help relate religious frauds to the special trusted-group contexts in which they occur. (I attempted to find such linkages in Shupe 1991, examining victimization of Mormons in Utah by con artists.)

We also need more detailed case studies of the structural insulation of elites in our more episcopalian- and presbyterian-style denominations, where policy creation and implementation and access to financial resources are more likely to be invisible to rank-and-file laity. Perhaps a new generation of studies will examine the activities of the Lewis Nobles, the Ellen Cooks, the Deborah Davises, the Anthony E. Franjaines, and the William R. Joneses with the same investigative rigor that journalist Jason Berry (1992) brought to his thorough analysis of pedophilia in the U.S. Catholic Church.

One possibility: a further consideration of the roles that *accessories after the fact* play in denominational financial malfeasance. These persons do not directly perpetrate fraud but, by remaining silent or sympathetic, facilitate its occurrence and invisibility. One could hypothesize, for example, that religious embezzlers tend to operate as lone wolves (perhaps out of greed or fear of discovery). None of the examples cited in this chapter involved any conspiracy of culprits.

Alternately, perpetrators of investment scams are involved in more complex and sustained operations that require a division of labor close to the top, hence reliance on accessories. Logically, only a rare economically malfeasant cleric could operate without silent accomplices. Is there a relation between the number of accessories and the scale of the fraud? Who else in New Era, for example, had access to John B. Bennett, Jr.'s account books and was in a position to realize that the philanthropy investment scheme was bogus?

We know that Jim Bakker possessed a board of "directors" and yes-men aides who were all richly compensated and morally coopted during the

PTL scams (Shupe 1995, 70). And Robert Tilton's accountability ended with his two accessories after the fact. First was his wife of twenty-five years who supplied the hands-on money management of his lucrative television ministry (and who unceremoniously divorced him when his direct-mail faith-healing racket fell apart and the donations began to evaporate). Second was Tilton's Tulsa, Oklahoma, attorney, kept on a $1.7 million per year retainer. He helped Tilton stall investigations by the Texas state attorney general's office and loudly rebuked the government for "harassing" a so-called man of God. (As Howard Swindle and Allen Pusey reported in the *Dallas Morning News* September 30, 1993, in "Tilton to Discontinue His Television Ministry," after the 1991 ABC television report, the attorney angrily told a news reporter: "It's just the latest example in a long, long history of persecution that dates back to Rome and even to Christ's crucifixion" [see also Shupe 1995, 75–76]).

The methodological difficulties in cultivating such data are obvious, for they require a researcher's direct access to conversations and decisions or to persons who participated in them and paper trails within bureaucracies. But the same impediments exist for those who study secular forms of white-collar and corporate crimes.

At a cultural level, we need further analysis of the context of religious pluralism in North America, of the "voluntary" (i.e., not state-supported) nature of religion—upon which nineteenth-century observer Alexis de Tocqueville famously commented in *Democracy in America*—and of how such a religious "marketplace" is minimally regulated for "consumer" protection. Clerical economic fraud may be an unpleasant, even embarrassing, subject for some, but so were white-collar and corporate forms of crime when first proposed for consideration. Just as studying corporate crime does not necessarily make one anticapitalist, pursuing clerical economic fraud does not signify that one is against religion. Here lies the challenge for both sociologists of religion and criminologists: to cross-fertilize approaches and open up a new institution for critical analysis.

Notes

1. Controversial nonmainline religious movements and churches have been conspicuous targets of accusations of financial abuse for much of U.S. history. Joseph Smith in the nineteenth century and Father Divine in the earlier part of the twentieth century, for example, were denounced in the popular press for allegedly living exploitively off the pooled labors and resources of their followers (Shupe 1992; Weisbrot, 1983). However, this area of clergy malfeasance, and the process of separating out nativism and prejudice from documented, objective fact, is beyond

the scope of this brief chapter. Excellent case studies consider clergy malfeasance in modern groups such as the Hare Krishnas (Shinn 1987), the Love Family (Balch 1995, 1988), Synanon (Mitchell, Mitchell, and Ofshe 1980), the People's Temple (Hall 1989), and Rajneeshpuram (Gordon 1987); for reliable comparative studies, see Bird and Westley 1988, Robbins 1988, and Bromley and Shupe 1981.

References

"The Apple of God's Eye." 1991. *Prime Time Live.* ABC-TV (November 21).

Balch, Robert W. 1995. "Charisma and Corruption in the Love Family: Toward a Theory of Corruption in Charismatic Cults." In *Sex, Lies, and Sanctity: Religion and Deviance in Contemporary North America*, edited by Mary Jo Neitz and Marion S. Goldman. Greenwich, Conn.: JAI Press.

———. 1988. "Money and Power in Utopia: An Economic History of the Love Family." In *Money and Power in the New Religions*, edited by James T. Richardson. Lewiston, N.Y.: Mellen.

Berry, Jason. 1992. *Lead Us Not into Temptation: Catholic Priests and the Sexual Abuse of Children*. New York: Doubleday.

Bird, Frederick, and Frances Westley. 1988. "The Economic Strategies of New Religious Movements." In *Money and Power in the New Religions*, edited by James T. Richardson. Lewiston, N.Y.: Mellen.

Blankenship, Michael B.(ed.). 1995. *Understanding Corporate Criminality.* New York: Garland.

Bloom, Linda. 1995. "Former Missions Comptroller Arraigned on Larceny Charges." United Methodist News Service release (December 4).

———. 1995. "Ex-Treasurer of Missions Accused of Embezzling." *United Methodist Reporter* (December 1):1.

Blumhofer, Edith L. 1993. *Aimee Semple McPherson: Everybody's Sister*. Grand Rapids, Mich.: Eerdmans.

Bromley, David G., and Anson D. Shupe, Jr. 1981. *Strange Gods: The Great American Cult Scare*. Boston: Beacon.

Cardwell, Jerry D. 1984. *Mass Media Christianity: Televangelism and the Great Commission*. New York: University Press of America.

Coleman, James W. 1987. "Toward an Integrated Theory of White-Collar Crime." *American Journal of Sociology* 93 (2):406–439.

Dorsett, Lyle W., 1991. *Billy Sunday and the Redemption of Urban America*. Grand Rapids, Mich.: Eerdmans.

"Ex-President Guilty of Felonies." 1996. *Christianity Today* (March 4):69.

"Ex-Treasurer Admits Embezzling." 1996. *Christianity Today* (March 4):69.

"Faith Watch." 1995. *United Methodist Reporter* (December 15):1.

Frame, Randy. 1995. "The Post–New Era Era." *Christianity Today* (July 17):60–61.

Frankl, Razelle. 1987. *Televangelism: The Marketing of Popular Religion*. Carbondale: Southern Illinois University Press.

Giles, Thomas S. 1995. "'Double-Your-Money' Scam Burns Christian Groups." *Christianity Today* (June 19): 40–41.

Gordon, James E. 1987. *The Golden Guru: The Strange Journey of Bhagwan Shree Rajneesh.* Lexington, Mass.: Greene.

Hadden, Jeffrey K., and Anson Shupe. 1988. *Televangelism: Power and Politics on God's Frontier.* New York: Holt.

Hadden, Jeffrey K., and Charles E. Swann. 1981. *Prime Time Preachers: The Rising Power of Televangelism.* Reading, Mass.: Addison-Wesley.

Hall, John R. 1989. *Gone from the Promised Land: Jonestown in American Cultural History.* New Brunswick, N.J.: Transaction.

Hoover, Stewart M. 1988. *Mass Media Religion: The Social Sources of the Electronic Church.* Beverly Hills, Calif.: Sage.

Kennedy, John W. 1993. "End of the Line for Tilton?" *Christianity Today* (September 13):78–82.

Lawton, Kim. 1989. "Swindles Prey on Trust of Believers." *Christianity Today* (September 22): 41, 43.

Lester, Mariann. 1978. "Profits, Politics, Power: The Heart of the Controversy." In *Science, Sin, Scholarship,* edited by Irving Louis Horowitz. Cambridge: MIT Press.

Martin, Tom. 1993. "Conviction in Investment Scheme." *Christianity Today* (October 4):57.

Martz, Larry, and Ginny Carroll. 1988. *Ministry of Greed.* New York: Weidenfeld and Nicolson.

Maxwell, Joe. 1995a. "Ministries Pursue Disputed Funds." *Christianity Today* (August 14):56.

———.1995b. "President's Alleged Misdeeds Cost Christian School Millions." *Christianity Today* (April 3):98.

Miles, Jonathan. 1995. "Leaders Falsified Ministry Reports." *Christianity Today* (September 11): 64–66.

Mitchell, Dave, Cathy Mitchell, and Richard Ofshe. 1980. *The Light on Synanon.* New York: Seaview.

Morton, Tom. 1993. "Conviction in Investment Scheme." *Christianity Today* (October 4):57.

Neff, David. 1995. "How Shall We Then Give?" *Christianity Today* (July 17):20–21.

"News briefs." 1996. *Christianity Today* (April 3): 89.

———. 1995. *Christianity Today* (April 3):89.

Omerod, Neil, and Thea Omerod. 1995. *When Ministers Sin: Sexual Abuse in the Churches.* Alexandria, Aus.: Millennium.

Randi, James. 1987. *The Faith Healers.* Buffalo: Prometheus.

Robbins, Thomas, 1988. "Profits for Prophets: Legitimate and Illegitimate Economic Practices in New Religious Movements." In *Money and Power in the New Religions,* edited by James T. Richardson. Lewiston, N.Y.: Mellen.

Shapiro, Susan, 1987. "The Social Control of Impersonal Trust." *American Journal of Sociology* 93 (3):623–658.

Shinn, Larry D. 1987. *The Dark Lord: Cult Images and the Hare Krishnas in America.* Philadelphia: Westminister.

Shupe, Anson. 1995. *In the Name of All That's Holy: A Theory of Clergy Malfeasance.* Westport, Conn.: Praeger.

————. 1992. *Wealth and Power in American Zion*. Lewiston, N.Y.: Mellen.

————. 1991. *The Darker Side of Virtue: Corruption, Scandal. and the Mormon Empire*. Buffalo: Prometheus.

Simon, David R.. and D. Stanley Eitzen. 1990. *Elite Deviance*. 3rd. ed. Boston: Allyn and Bacon.

Sutherland, Edwin H. 1949. *White Collar Crime*. New York: Dryden.

Weisbrot, Robert. 1983. *Father Divine*. Boston: Beacon.

PART II

Responses to Clergy Malfeasance

CHAPTER 4

An Advocacy Group for Victims of Clerical Sexual Abuse

⊶ ⧈⊹⧈ ⊶

ELIZABETH PULLEN

*J*im Gilmore settles into an oversized armchair, surveys the crowd of twenty talking animatedly in small, tightly bunched groups, and loudly clears his throat.[1]

A-hmm. . . . Looks like almost everyone is here. If folks could just get settled at this point . . . it's now 7:15 P.M. and we have a lot of business to get to tonight. Who's still missing? Nancy and Pete? June? Well, she told me she would probably be here late. I ran into Dolores yesterday downtown, and she said she might be joining us tonight.

Well, let's just get started. As our first order of business, Marilyn would like to say a few words to us. This is her last meeting as our therapist-facilitator and she wants to offer some guidelines we can use to run our meetings in the future.

David has a statement he'd like to read about our meeting last month with the IRT [Independent Response Team] . . . we'll all get a chance to talk about what we thought about that meeting.

David also wants to share a letter he wrote to Bishop Kinney of the National Conference of Catholic Bishops regarding the use of residential treatment centers for sexual offenders.

And Warren would like to tell us about his correspondence with Richard Sipe, who wrote *Sex, Priests, and Power.* I understand that he might be visiting California and might come to one of our meetings? Well, you can tell us about that later, Warren.

We have received a few more letters from survivors to share, and

Rosemary brought us copies of some articles she reproduced from *Sojourners* magazine about healing from sexual abuse and violence. If we have time before we break, we've borrowed a video called *Four Men Speak Out on Surviving Child Sexual Abuse* we can show. It's only thirty minutes long, but if it gets too late we can watch it next time.

Here comes Dolores. Come in, we're just getting started.

So begins the eighteenth meeting of the St. Anthony's Seminary Support Group for Sexual Abuse Survivors (hereafter, the Support Group).[2] Formed in the wake of disclosures of clerical sexual abuse of children and young men at St. Anthony's Seminary and in the Santa Barbara Boys' Choir, the group is an independent community organization founded by Robert Van Handel, a Franciscan friar, former teacher, and rector of the seminary.

Many recent studies have examined the incidence of sexual abuse of children in Roman Catholic congregations. Several of the most notable, investigations by journalists, have attempted to expose both clerical child abuse and the institutional secrecy regarding its presence (Berry 1992; Burkett and Bruni 1993). Other works approach the topic from a psychological or policy perspective and seek to counsel either clergy or survivors on proper boundaries, guidelines of care, and resources for treatment (Bera 1995; Fortune 1995; Houts 1995; Lebacqz and Barton 1991; Loftus 1994; Ormerod and Ormerod 1995; Rossetti 1990; Rutter 1989).

While studies focusing upon the causes of clerical sexual abuse and the effects of the abuse upon the child victim and adult survivor have great importance, we also need research that examines the impact of disclosures of sexual abuse on congregations and how communities respond to disclosures. Academic studies have just begun to focus on the short- and long-term effects of clerical misconduct on religious institutions themselves and the damage that can occur within a religious organization that does not openly and fully address internal conflicts (Cradock and Gardner 1990; Hopkins and Laaser 1995; Maris and McDonough 1995; Rossetti 1990,1994a, b; Shupe 1993, 1995).

Although the larger community does not experience the victims' physical abuse, religious congregations can collectively share psychological, emotional, and spiritual trauma when faced with the reality that their most vulnerable members have been sexually violated by individuals the community invested with authority. Support Group members, for example, talk of the "spiritual abuse" they have suffered; they believe that their trust and faith in the credibility and integrity of their religious leaders has been shattered. This sense of betrayal often balloons if people view institutional authorities as seeking to minimize the impact of the sexual perpetrators on the larger church by controlling the situation, isolating the survivors from the congregation and all church members from the facts. Members of a religious community, along with the primary abuse victims, can experience a wide variety of responses over time, from denial, rage, apathy, guilt, and withdrawal from church activities to, as in the case of the Support Group, activism.

This chapter is part of a case study that looks at the formation, development, and activity of a community support group for victims and families of victims of clerical sexual abuse. Field research included more than two years of study of the St. Anthony's Seminary Support Group—participant observation of meetings of the Support Group and its steering committee, formal interviews with group members, and weekly informal discussions about the activities of the Support Group.

While drawing upon media coverage and independent reports, this chapter is an account of the evolution of the Support Group and the sexual abuse crisis as the group members remember and interpret it.[3] The names and locations of the eleven alleged perpetrators in the board of inquiry report have never been publicly disclosed by the Franciscan order, and I name here only offenders identified in the board of inquiry report, criminal or civil proceedings, and media reports.

Saint Anthony's Seminary and the Greater Community

In July 1996, alumni of St. Anthony's Seminary returned to the beautiful seminary grounds for their annual high school reunion. There, in stone buildings with red-tiled roofs adjacent to the scenic Old Mission Santa Barbara and set amidst avocado trees, birds of paradise, and green playing fields, former seminarians and faculty gathered to celebrate the centennial of the founding of St. Anthony's.

As a minor seminary operated by the Province of St. Barbara of the Order of Friars Minor of the Roman Catholic Church in Santa Barbara, California, the school educated hundreds of young men between 1896 and 1987, its years of operation. With its excellent academic reputation, a flourishing program in drama and music, as well as a full slate of athletic teams, Santa Barbara drew high school students from several western states and Mexico, some to determine whether they had a vocation as a Franciscan friar, all to receive a seminary education. An average of 5 to 10 percent of the graduates pursued their vocational interest further and became members of the Franciscan order (Stearns et al., 1993).

As a boarding school, the seminary served as a "total institution," an enclosed environment that provided for, but also controlled, all the students' physical, intellectual, and spiritual needs (Goffman 1961). Until the mid-1960s, the school limited students' interaction with people in the Santa Barbara community, including family members and friends, to vacations, occasional weekend visits, and visiting Sundays. These last occasions, held monthly, provided a regular opportunity for families to have extended visits to the seminary. Guests could attend mass with the seminarians and their Franciscan teachers in the Christ the King Chapel, and picnics on the seminary grounds often occupied the afternoons.

In the liturgical renewal following Vatican II, Sunday worship services at the seminary became known throughout the Santa Barbara area for their innovation and experimentation (Conklin 1971). By 1968, eucharistic services incorporated outdoor settings, electric guitars and drums, fluorescent vestments, pop art banners, and sculptures decorated with mod designs and slogans. At the same time, the Franciscans had decided to open Sunday liturgies not only to the families of the seminarians but to all in the neighboring community. Services began to attract hundreds of local Catholics, and photographs from this period show attendees sitting on the floor, standing in the aisles, and massed around the altar. "Life is where the action is!" the liturgical banners proclaimed one Pentecost, and they invited the approximately seven hundred "Jesus People" at St. Anthony's Seminary to "Feel free (free, free, free, free) to be!"

This expansion of Sunday worship services marks the creation of St. Anthony's Seminary Greater Community. While the style of worship services has changed and attendance has fluctuated since the 1960s, community members still refer to this period in the late 1960s and early 1970s as a primary reference point in their identity as a self-created, nonparish congregation. Members enjoy both the autonomy and participation that is possible for communities outside the traditional parish structure, as well as the association with a large, dynamic religious order. Friars teaching at the seminary or just passing through Santa Barbara often worshiped with the greater community, among them academic scholars, social activists, and gifted artists (Stahel 1995). Close relationships formed between community members and the Franciscan friars; many in the community sent their children to the seminary for their education, served on the high school's accreditation board, tutored students, worked as lay members of the seminary faculty and staff, and supported the school's extracurricular activities. Additionally, many Franciscan friars on St. Anthony's Seminary faculty participated as chaplains for chapters of the Christian Family Movement (CFM) in the early seventies. The most active and social community members opened their homes to both friars and seminarians for Sunday dinners or longer stays around the holidays. Over two decades, longtime community members saw some seminarians arrive as high school freshmen, graduate to the major (college) seminary, profess their vows, become ordained, and return to St. Anthony's Seminary as members of the faculty.

Even after the seminary closed in 1987, the greater community of St. Anthony's Seminary continued to exist, and members contributed their labor to transform the old seminary infirmary into the Franciscan novitiate. In 1990, the year of my first visit to the greater community, the congregation appeared to me to be a tightly knit group of approximately 150–200 progressive Catholics who emphasized participatory liturgy and social support between and among the laity and the Franciscans. The greater community lacked many features of a typical U.S. Catholic parish—there was no parish council, no bingo night, no confirmation or Confraternity of Christian Doctrine classes, no charismatic prayer meetings or Legion of Mary. While not a growing congregation, the greater community appeared to me then to be both extremely contented and self-contained.

The Emergence of the Sexual Abuse Crisis

In March 1989, two former students at St. Anthony's Seminary filed charges of sexual abuse against Fr. Philip Mark Wolfe, a Franciscan priest and teacher at the seminary from September 1981 to June 1984. The molestations occurred between 1983 and 1987, but because of the statute of limitations the charges of only one of the victims could be prosecuted. In September 1989, Phil Wolfe pleaded "no contest" to one count of oral copulation with a person under eighteen and was sentenced to six months in jail followed by six months in a treatment center (Stahel 1994; Stearns et al. 1993).

Although Wolfe was arraigned and sentenced in Santa Barbara, members of the greater community whom I interviewed say they were not aware of the charges, his arrest, or his conviction at the time they occurred. Then, in December 1989, Teresa Clark, a community member, learned from the victims' mother of the sexual abuse of her sons. Soon after, a small group of community members met with the victims' family, the Wrights, to speak with them about what had occurred.

Several actions came out of this meeting. First, seven community members sent off a letter in January 1990 to the Franciscan provincial minister, Joseph P. Chinnici, with copies to the Wrights, Bishop Patrick Zieman (of the Santa Barbara Deanery), and Archbishop Roger Mahoney, offering the Franciscan friars their prayers and sympathy and affirming the church's ability to resolve this crisis. The community members emphasized that as the Franciscans struggled with a resolution to this tragedy, it was important for all parties to be honest and open with each other as they sought to achieve justice and reconciliation.

Second, several members met with Franciscan friar and priest Robert Van Handel, the former rector and current administrator of the now closed seminary and "pastor" to the greater community, to discuss what had occurred. Support Group members recall that, although many parishioners were upset at the abuse perpetrated by Wolfe, he had been considered an isolated case, a loner. They found the sexual abuse he perpetrated tragic but an anomaly. Wolfe's crimes had been identified; he had been punished by the courts and had left the Franciscan Order. After his incarceration, he left California to serve out his probation in New Mexico.[4]

In the summer of 1991, Robert Van Handel left St. Anthony's Seminary and the boys' choir he had founded and directed to move to the San Francisco Bay Area. The greater community threw several parties for him, including one at the home of Kate and Jim Gilmore, as celebrations of his contributions to St. Anthony's Seminary, where he taught from May 1975 until its closure in June 1987.

In May 1992, the Wrights informed the Franciscan provincial minister that one of their sons had told them in December 1991 that, while a member of the Santa Barbara Boys' Choir, he had been sexually molested by Robert Van Handel. The next month, Van Handel was placed on administrative leave and sent for evaluation and treatment to St. Luke's Institute, a treatment center for priests in Maryland. The Santa Barbara Boys' Choir was notified, and in October 1992 the Franciscans and the boys' choir sent a letter to more than a hundred sets of parents of children who had sung in the choir since its creation in 1975, informing them of allegations of sexual abuse against boys' choir founder Van Handel, as Nick Welch reported in "Franciscans Respond to Abuse Complaints" in the *Santa Barbara Independent* on November 5.

On October 28, the Franciscan provincial minister, the boys' choir director, and two therapists, one a Franciscan friar, met to answer questions from the parents of past and current members of the boys' choir. At this meeting, which many greater community members also attended, two additional families, the Gilmores and Bradleys, reported that their sons had revealed that they had also been sexually molested by Van Handel while students at the seminary. It was evident that the sexual abuse was no longer an isolated experience of one family and that victims of sexual abuse included former seminarians as well as members of the boys' choir (Stearns et al. 1993).

In November 1992, Franciscan provincial minister Joseph Chinnici stated that a plan for an investigation was being designed, to be presented the next month. At the same time, approximately two dozen members of the greater community met several times to formulate a set of commission requirements they wanted the Franciscans to incorporate in the investigation (Stearns et al. 1993). In just a few weeks, community members researched the topic of clerical sexual abuse, drawing heavily from the examples of the Hughes and Winter Commissions who had investigated sexual abuse at the Mount Cashel Orphanage in Newfoundland, Canada, as well as the Cardinal's Commission on Clerical Sexual Misconduct with Minors Report to Joseph Cardinal Bernardin of the Archdiocese of Chicago. The group members familiarized themselves with the problems that had occurred in those investigations and drew up a four-page outline of recommended commission purposes, functions, composition, selection, and scope. Among their requirements they stipulated the appointment of a member of the St. Anthony's Greater Community as a liaison to the commission and periodic progress reports to the greater community. This emphasis on regular reports from the investigative body to the congregation would remain a primary concern in all future interactions with the commission as well as the church hierarchy.

At meetings on November 30 and December 4, 1992, the provincial minister, the Franciscan Definitorium, and members of the greater community reached agreement on the investigation into sexual abuse at St. Anthony's Seminary. A formal board of inquiry established by the Franciscan Province of St. Barbara in January 1993 undertook to contact all seminary students from 1964–1987, to investigate any allegations of sexual and physical abuse, and to issue a report on its findings. Consisting of three therapists, a lawyer, a parent of a victim of clerical sexual abuse, and a Franciscan friar from another province, the board solicited detailed testimony from past seminarians and members of the boys' choir.

As one of its first orders of business, the board mailed letters to approximately 350 former seminarians in early February, inviting each to contact the board "if you believe you were the recipient of either physical or non-physical contact by a member of St. Anthony's staff or faculty, which hurt you or left you feeling confused, frightened, guilty or bad about yourself" (Stearns et al. 1993). At one of the monthly meetings held with the greater community in spring 1993, representatives of the board of inquiry revealed that in initial responses to the letter, former seminary students had provided the names of additional Franciscan friars whom they alleged had engaged in sexual misconduct. A second mailing went out to the families of approximately six hundred more former students in an attempt to contact not just those who had graduated from the seminary but also those who withdrew before graduating. Ultimately, approximately three hundred students responded positively and negatively about the inquiry, with about seventy-five indicating they would follow up their initial reply with a further response to the board (Stearns et al. 1993). Additionally, the board created a victim's resource packet that included "a list of recommended therapists, methods of evaluating therapists, a recommended reading list, directives for requesting therapy and obtaining compensation from the province for the therapy" (Johnston 1993a, b; Stearns et al. 1993).

On November 29, 1993, the board of inquiry held a press conference and released its report to the public (Johnston 1993a, b); Andrew Rice's report of the findings ran in the *Santa Barbara Independent* on December 2 under the headline, "Franciscans Admit 34 Boys Were Molested at St. Anthony's." The board's report stated that over the twenty-three years covered by its investigation, thirty-four students said they had been victims of sexual abuse, involving a range of behaviors that included unwanted back rubs, fondling, nude photography, mutual masturbation, oral sex, and sodomy. The board identified eleven friars, among them Wolfe and Van Handel, who had perpetrated sexual abuse on minors at St. Anthony's Seminary. The report stated that "[d]uring the relevant time period, there was in any given year, at least one friar on the faculty that the Board identified to a reasonable certainty as having offended at some point during his tenure at St. Anthony's. One-fourth (11) of the forty-four friars who served on the faculty at St. Anthony's during this time period were identified to a reasonable certainty as having offended at some point during their tenure at St. Anthony's" (Stearns et al. 1993)

The report included not only statistics and details about the extent of the abuse but five composite scenarios of experiences of victimization drawn from the detailed testimony it had collected. The report also included the procedure and guidelines the board of inquiry used to conduct its investigation, a copy of the inquiry letter sent out to seminarians, lists of approved therapists, self-help books and support organizations from the victim's resource packet, as well as recommendations to the Franciscan order regarding changes in policy. Among the suggestions: Create an Independent Response Team (IRT) to handle future abuse complaints and oversee treatment of sexually abusive friars. The report managed to be both professional and pastoral, honestly acknowledging the nature and extent of the abuse while at the same time showing sensitivity to the needs of the victims for privacy and compassion.

The Sunday after the report's release, a Franciscan spokesperson visited the greater community at St. Anthony's Seminary to present church members with copies of the report. Stacks of the report were placed outside the front doors of the sanctuary and were distributed after the service. That marked the last official appearance of a representative of the Franciscan leadership to the congregation at St. Anthony's Seminary. And there would be no pastoral visits at all to the greater community at St. Anthony's Seminary by the hierarchy of the Archdiocese of Los Angeles, who regularly visited the Old Mission Santa Barbara, a historic group of buildings across the driveway from the seminary and the location for many religious and civic celebrations.

St. Anthony's Seminary Support Group for Sexual Abuse Survivors

The St. Anthony's Seminary Support Group for Sexual Abuse Survivors first met in December 1993 in the wake of the release of the board of inquiry report. My participation in the Support Group began soon after; I attended and observed the third meeting of the group in February 1994, when the membership, focus, and structure of the group and of its meetings were still in flux. Although all of these aspects of the group would be subject to some fluctuation over the time I participated in the group, its primary orientation was determined by June 1994 when the Support Group formulated its mission statement.

While the projects and interests of individual Support Group members reflect a variety of perspectives on both the Catholic Church and sexuality, the work of the Support Group has focused on several areas: outreach to victims, support to fellow church members, interaction with the Franciscans and the IRT, and the reform of attitudes within the Catholic Church and society regarding child sexual abuse.

Support to Clerical Sexual Abuse Victims
The support provided to victims has taken several forms. Through informal networking between survivors and Support Group members through

letters and phone calls, members have kept abreast of particular victims in terms of their family life, career, health, and therapy. They inform victims about the group's activities by circulating the minutes from each meeting, which detail actions taken and contacts made. A primary purpose of this correspondence is to keep track of how satisfied victims are with their treatment by the Franciscans through the IRT. Through informal contacts, for example, one Support Group member learned from a victim's family of his addiction problem and his need for inpatient treatment at a substance abuse center. Typically, treatment for substance abuse lies outside the standard provision of therapy provided by the Franciscans. However, because both the family and Support Group members considered the addiction itself a result of the sexual abuse the victim experienced while a student at the seminary, the Support Group requested that this victim be given additional assistance toward rehabilitation. A limited stay at an inpatient substance abuse center was later approved.

Information regarding the status of victims can also come through indirect channels. In 1994, a therapist treating several of St. Anthony's sexual abuse survivors informed the Support Group of financial problems besetting several of the victims. Although these individuals were in the process of making claims against the Franciscan order and anticipated receiving settlements, the intensive process of therapy for childhood sexual abuse had made it difficult for them to maintain regular job schedules, and sometimes they had problems finding a job or meeting their basic expenses. The Support Group decided to hold a collection at St. Anthony's Seminary, which raised over $6,000, put into a short-term emergency loan fund for victims.

The Support Group also tries to help victims connect with one another. In the summer of 1996 Support Group members worked with victims to organize and host the second St. Anthony's Seminary survivors' gathering. While the content and scheduling of the sessions was left to the survivors to determine, the Support Group secured facilities for meetings and housing for the survivors and their families.

Support to the St. Anthony's Seminary Greater Community

Although most of the Support Group's energy goes to providing support to the victims of sexual abuse at St. Anthony's Seminary, members also see themselves as serving the greater community, the "secondary" victim of the sexual abuse crisis.

In its first year, the group petitioned the Independent Response Team to help finance therapeutic services for the greater community on the grounds that the community itself had been victimized by the sexually abusive friars. After four months of negotiating on the nature, extent, and structure of the therapy, a local therapist was hired to facilitate group meetings. For twelve months, the therapist helped community members work through the complex layers of feelings about the sexual abuse as well as the responses of the Franciscans and lay members of the community to the disclosures. This took three focuses: education, group therapy, and a mission statement.

Education about child sexual abuse relied on handouts from the workbook *Breach of Trust, Breach of Faith*, published by the Canadian Conference of Catholic Bishops (CCCB). Meetings included an educational segment that offered information on sexual abuse and a longer period in which members discussed in small groups aspects of child sexual abuse, profiles of perpetrators, and the cultural, societal, and religious influences on the occurrence of sexual abuse. Both the therapist and group members judged the CCCB materials, located and obtained by Support Group members, extremely helpful in providing information and guidelines for group discussion.

Inseparable from the intellectual discussion and education about sexual abuse was the process of group therapy itself. Through cathartic exercises and talking about emotions, group members expressed their disappointment, embarrassment, anger, despair, bewilderment, frustration, and grief arising from the disclosure of the sexual abuse perpetrated by the previous religious leader of the greater community and several other friars.

During these twelve months of group therapy, a victim came forward whose abuse by Robert Van Handel fell within the statute of limitations. In March 1994, the police removed Van Handel from his residence in Northern California, arresting him for sexual abuse; he was sentenced in August 1994 to eight years in prison, events reported in the *Santa Barbara News-Press* on March 23 by Morgan Green in "Ex-St. Anthony's Priest Held on Molest Charges," on March 24 by Green and Rhonda Parks in "Ex-Seminary Head Pleads Not Guilty in Sex Case, and in the *Santa Barbara Independent* on March 24 by Andrew Rice in "Ex-Saint Anthony's Priest Arrested on Abuse Charges." Attendance at his arraignment and sentencing by many members of the greater community proved to be a catalyst for much emotional exploration at subsequent Support Group meetings. While Support Group members had differing levels of participation in these exercises of group therapy, membership in the group was at its highest during this period when meetings were structured and professionally facilitated.

Finally, the Support Group therapist-facilitator helped the group toward composing its mission statement, which took most of an all-day workshop to articulate, revise, and approve. The result: "In the spirit of a loving Christ, our purpose is: to create a safe open forum; to educate and communicate about sexual abuse by the clergy; and to act as a healing force committed to the support of victims, families, and community through outreach and positive action."

Although in the two years since its adoption some group members have noticed limitations in the group's mission statement, particularly regarding its lack of specific goals, the members have made no attempt to alter it. The statement appears on minutes of the group meetings, and members refer to and reread it when a dispute arises over the direction of a meeting or group discussion. Although usually unobtrusive, the development and regular repetition of the Support Group's mission statement has proved an invaluable tool for the group as it seeks to maintain its focus; with many possible directions open to the group, the possibility of the group splintering always exists. Members have used the mission statement to help determine whether the level of group activities directed toward the victims, their families, and the Franciscans reflects the group's original priorities.

The Support Group meetings also serve as an ongoing source of friendship and support for group members through social interaction, sharing of feelings and concerns, affirmation of support, and reiteration of commitment to the group. Monthly meetings are the primary sites of these continued displays of support, although much discussion occurs at Sunday services, at the steering committee meetings, and during social activities.

I estimate that approximately 20–25 percent of the entire greater community has participated in at least one Support Group or informational meeting, and a range of attitudes still exists regarding its activities. Although most greater community members appreciate the Support Group's activism, others stay away from its meetings; three to four and a half hours of intensive and sometimes heated discussion about the consequences and effects of the sexual abuse of children in the church and society can prove emotionally exhausting.

Activity with the Franciscans and IRT

The Support Group directs much of its energy and activity toward following up the efforts of the Franciscans and the IRT to address the sexual abuse that occurred at St. Anthony's Seminary. At times this involves direct inquiry into whether the IRT is following the recommendations of the board of Inquiry report. In April 1995, for example, several members of the Support Group went page by page through the report and public statements by the Franciscans, generating a four-page list of new policies and policy changes the Support Group believed had not been fully implemented. This led to a meeting in June 1995 with the entire IRT in Santa Barbara. Although the meeting did not address all of the issues in question, Support Group members expressed hope at the time that the personal contact between the Support Group and the IRT would facilitate and encourage more collaboration between the groups.

Other activities relate to issues that have surfaced since the board of inquiry report came out, among them questions about monetary limitations on therapy the victims can obtain; a request for more responsive, speedier treatment of the victims' claims; inquiry into the HIV status of accused perpetrators; and questions about disclosing the identity and location of perpetrators and about sharing information about the existence and activity of the IRT with locations outside California, where there might be additional victims of the eleven abusers.

Even as the group continues to pursue ongoing dialogue with both the IRT and the Franciscan order in its role as victim advocate, many members recognize that its efforts have had only a limited effect upon the policy decisions of the institutional church. Although pressure exerted by the group has occasionally led to extensions or changes in treatment of individual survivors, the group's major demands about disclosing and disseminating information as to the identity, location, and HIV status of the perpetrators have met with consistent refusals on the grounds of confidentiality.

The Support Group has also asked the IRT to publicize its efforts in locations where the Franciscan perpetrators had lived and worked before coming to Santa Barbara. Although the IRT told the Support Group in June 1995 that work continued in this direction, including the appointment of regional ombudsmen and the distribution of a brochure on the IRT, members have questioned whether these efforts have been timely, visible, or accessible. The consensus of Support Group members is that the work of the IRT, due to limits in its authority and funding, has focused on monitoring treatment of the perpetrators and processing the claims of victims who emerged during the board of inquiry investigation into St. Anthony's Seminary. What is being neglected, these advocates say, is further outreach toward sexual abuse survivors among the laity throughout the entire Franciscan Province, which extends from Spokane, Washington, to Mescalero, New Mexico.

Other Activities

The Support Group has directed a number of other activities toward addressing the larger problem of sexual abuse in the Church and society. Some effort had gone into developing educational programs on child abuse in the Archdiocese of Los Angeles. After the Support Group tried unsuccessfully in 1993 and 1994 to establish forums on child sexual abuse at the diocesan level, through the annual Los Angeles Archdiocesan Religious Education Congress, the group began to focus its efforts on the local level. A meeting between members and newly installed Auxiliary Bishop Thomas Curry led in 1996 to a half-day workshop for local clergy on issues of child sexual abuse in the church. The Support Group has sought to have education on sexual abuse conducted in every parish and parochial school but have recently reduced its efforts in this area, awaiting more interest and support on the diocesan level toward developing these programs.

Additional efforts of the group have focused on advocating changes in child sexual abuse legislation. The group members have contributed money and actively supported bills that would extend the statute of limitations for child sexual abuse and of a bill that would make clergy mandatory reporters of colleagues' abuses. So far, due in part to the current political climate in California regarding crime and to strong state advocacy groups, these efforts have met with success, and as of this writing the bills have passed through all stages of committee review and received the approval of the legislature. California is now in the forefront, creating a criminal justice climate conducive to making clerical perpetrators accountable for their actions.

The Aftermath

The St. Anthony's Support Group for Sexual Abuse Survivors has responded to the disclosure of sexual abuse in the church with action, engaging the issue on both personal and institutional levels. On behalf of the wider parish community, the group has helped some victims pay their overdue utility bills, lobbied the state legislature to include clergy as mandatory reporters of child sexual abuse, sought to create regional educational programs on child sexual abuse, conducted a year-long program of community therapy, and recently initiated a series of informal meetings with several Franciscan friars to discuss mutual concerns about the effects of the sexual abuse at the seminary. Although these activities have had varying levels of success, group participation and commitment continues high eight years after the first instance of sexual abuse at the seminary came to light.

At this early stage of analysis, it appears that a significant strength and weakness of the Support Group is the fluidity that comes from existing outside the bureaucratic structure of the Roman Catholic Church.[5] Yet although the group has the ability to change directions and respond to problems as they emerge and develop, it has no institutionalized position of authority from which to pursue structural change. The Roman Catholic Church assigns no institutional role to laity interested in participating in policy making at the diocesan level or in the leadership of the Franciscan order. Members of the Support Group are free to pursue their self-directed course of action toward addressing the problem of sexual abuse in the church, but the church hierarchy can also choose to ignore or deny their requests for information or policy changes, with little chance of appeal.

For example, in late 1995, a victim in contact with several Support Group members asked to come and speak to the entire Support Group. One meeting was completely devoted to listening to his story of molestation at the seminary and asking him questions regarding the response of the Franciscans at the time of his abuse, how his initial request for treatment had been handled by the IRT, and the quality of his subsequent dealings with them. There was considerable questioning because the victim's alleged abuser was still involved in parish ministry. The Support Group devoted several meetings to discussing possible courses of action, drafting letters, and making phone calls. To a letter sent to the Franciscans requesting the removal of the friar from active parish ministry, the response was that the friar in question denies the alleged abuse and that he will remain in his pastoral position. Stymied in their efforts to effect a change through the institutional process, the Support Group has put the matter on hold for now but has considered several more dramatic courses of public action that they might pursue should they receive information of subsequent abuse by this friar or if the group's relationship with the IRT deteriorates. As the direct, procedural approach was judged unsuccessful, many in the Support Group see as their only alternative working outside the institution through a more public discussion of the problem. A majority of members rejected this course of action, but it remains a possible strategy as the Support Group pursues its goal of eliminating and preventing the sexual abuse of children within the Catholic Church.

This instance, I believe, illustrates both the responsiveness of the Support Group to issues they identify as social problems as well as the group's lack of sustained institutionalized influence on church policy and procedure. In the current environment of the U.S. Catholic Church, as long as the Support Group focuses its efforts upon structural changes, it remains dependent on the institution to acknowledge its existence and legitimacy. It is too soon to determine the overall impact of groups like St. Anthony's Support Group for Sexual Abuse Survivors, but this group remains an excellent example of the many external advocacy groups seeking a role for lay participation in reforming institutional policy in the U.S. Catholic Church.

Notes

1. I use pseudonyms for all Support Group members at their request, in order to preserve the privacy of survivors of childhood sexual abuse and those with children who are survivors of clerical sexual abuse.
2. Strong opinions exist within the sexual abuse recovery movement that the terms *victim* and *survivor* reflect distinctly different stages of empowerment and healing. During the tenure of the Support Group both terms have been used, and for the purposes of this paper I use the two synonymously.
3. Given the emotionally charged events that unfolded and the evolving understanding concerning the scope and nature of the sexual abuse that occurred, interpretations of the "crisis" at St. Anthony's Seminary differ among members, just as do levels of involvement and allegiance to the Franciscan order and to the greater community. One constant appears to be the almost universal respect for the dedication and thoroughness with which the board of inquiry conducted its investigation. Its report of findings has been accepted by many community members as accurately capturing the dimensions of the abuse at the seminary.
4. As the *Los Angeles Times* reported on November 11, 1994, in "Former Priest in Seminary Molestation Case Commits Suicide," less than a month after completing his probation, Philip Wolfe hung himself in his apartment in Albuquerque. He faced a lawsuit brought by the two survivors. See Rossetti 1994b for one perspective on suicides among priests accused or convicted of sexual misconduct.
5. The importance of this extrainstitutional role of Catholic advocacy groups has been formalized and described in Anson Shupe's model of institutional response to clergy malfeasance, which seeks to correlate the organizational structure of the religious institution with the responses of the church hierarchy and church membership (Shupe 1995).

References

Bera, Walter H. 1995. "Betrayal: Clergy Sexual Abuse and Male Survivors." In *Breach of Trust: Sexual Exploitation by Health Care Professionals and Clergy*, edited by John C. Gonsiorek. Thousand Oaks, Calif.: Sage.

Berry, Jason. 1992. *Lead Us Not into Temptation: Catholic Priests and the Sexual Abuse of Children.* New York: Doubleday.

Burkett, Elinor, and Frank Bruni. 1993. *A Gospel of Shame: Children, Sexual Abuse, and the Catholic Church.* New York: Viking.

Conklin, Hal. 1971. "A New Focus Interview at St. Anthony's." *New Focus* 3:6 (November–December):4–6.

Cradock, Carroll, and Jill R. Gardner. 1990. "Psychological Intervention for Parishes Following Accusations of Child Sexual Abuse." In *Slayer of the Soul: Child Sexual Abuse and the Catholic Church*, edited by Stephen J. Rossetti. Mystic, Conn.: Twenty-Third Publications.

Fortune, Marie M. 1995. "Is Nothing Sacred? When Sex Invades the Pastoral Relationship." In *Breach of Trust: Sexual Exploitation by Health Care Professionals and Clergy*, edited by John C. Gonsiorek. Thousand Oaks, Calif.: Sage.

Goffman, Erving. 1961. *Asylums: Essays on the Social Situation of Mental Patients and Other Inmates*. New York: Doubleday.

Hopkins, Nancy Myer, and Mark Laaser, eds. 1995. *Restoring the Soul of a Church: Healing Congregations Wounded by Clergy Sexual Misconduct*. Washington, D.C.: Alban Institute.

Houts, Donald C. 1995. "Training for Prevention of Sexual Misconduct by Clergy." In *Breach of Trust: Sexual Exploitation by Health Care Professionals and Clergy*, edited by John C. Gonsiorek. Thousand Oaks, Calif.: Sage.

Johnston, Rosemary. 1993a. "Parents of Molested Sons Tell of Alienation from Church." *National Catholic Reporter* (December 17).

———. 1993b. "Pedophilia Board Focused on Victims First." *National Catholic Reporter* (December 17).

Lebacqz, Karen, and Ronald G. Barton. 1991. *Sex in the Parish*. Louisville, Ky.: Westminster/John Knox.

Loftus, John Allan. 1994. *Understanding Sexual Misconduct by Clergy: A Handbook for Ministers*. Washington, D.C.: Pastoral.

Maris, Margo E., and Kevin M. McDonough. 1995. "How Churches Respond to the Victims and Offenders of Clergy Sexual Misconduct." In *Breach of Trust: Sexual Exploitation by Health Care Professionals and Clergy*, edited by John C. Gonsiorek. Thousand Oaks, Calif.: Sage.

Ormerod, Neil, and Thea Ormerod. 1995. *When Ministers Sin: Sexual Abuse in the Churches*. Alexandria, Australia: Millennium.

Rossetti, Stephen J. 1994a. "Parishes as Victims of Child Sexual Abuse." In *Restoring Trust: A Pastoral Response to Sexual Abuse*. Vol. 1. Bishops' Ad Hoc Committee on Sexual Abuse, National Conference of Catholic Bishops. Washington, D.C. November.

———. 1994b. "Priest Suicides and the Crisis of Faith." *America* 171 (October 29): 8–12.

———, ed. 1990. *Slayer of the Soul: Child Sexual Abuse and the Catholic Church*. Mystic, Conn.: Twenty-Third Publications.

Rutter, Peter. 1989. *Sex in the Forbidden Zone: When Men in Power—Therapists, Doctors, Clergy, Teachers, and Others—Betray Women's Trust*. Los Angeles: Tarcher.

Shupe, Anson. 1995. *In the Name of All That's Holy: A Theory of Clergy Malfeasance*. Westport, Conn.: Praeger.

———. 1993. "Opportunity Structures, Trusted Hierarchies, and Religious Deviance: A Conflict Theory Approach." Paper presented at the annual meeting of the Society for the Scientific Study of Religion, Raleigh, N.C.

Stahel, Thomas H. 1994. "One Pastoral Response to Abuse: Interview with Joseph P. Chinnici, O.F.M." *America* 170, 2 (January 15–22):4–8.

Stearns, F. B., K. Baggerley-Mar, E. Merlin, D. Bonner, and R. Higgins. 1993. *Report to Father Joseph P. Chinnici, O.F.M. Provincial Minister, Province of St. Barbara*. Independent Board of Inquiry Regarding St. Anthony's Seminary, Santa Barbara, California (November).

CHAPTER 5

The Impact of Abuses of Clergy Trust on Female Congregants' Faith and Practice

NANCY NASON-CLARK

*F*ather James Joseph Hickey was an extraordinary clergyman. Enthusiastic in his work with youths, tireless, and adored by most of his parishioners, Father Jim became the most celebrated priest in the Canadian province of Newfoundland. When official visitors arrived on Newfoundland's shores—whether pontiff or prince—Church leaders called upon James Hickey to share the platform and the microphone. He was especially highly regarded for organizing mammoth teenage rallies or "altar boy jamborees" for Catholic youths around the province, and he held an elected position as the first president of the Newfoundland and Labrador Association of Youth Serving Agencies.

In short, the Newfoundland community will long remember James Joseph Hickey as a champion of the young who "never missed a chance to praise, promote, or defend the group he felt most comfortable with"—Roman Catholic teenagers (Harris 1990). In fact, the community—sacred and secular alike—will struggle to overcome its collective memory of Father Hickey. For Father Jim was a priest who used his charismatic appeal to seduce and manipulate altar boys for his own sexual pleasure.

Understanding the Events

On January 11, 1988, James Joseph Hickey was charged with multiple sex crimes. The following September 8, he pleaded guilty to twenty counts of either sexual assault or gross indecency against adolescent and preadolescent boys in parishes where he had served. The Hickey scandal became a media sensation. But as tragic as the Hickey case proved for the Roman Catholic community on the island, it represented only the tip of the iceberg. In the following year, a series of cases of sexual abuse of young boys by Catholic parish priests unfolded in the Archdiocese of St. John's, Newfoundland. In response to intense public reaction, Archbishop Alphonsus Penney initiated a commission of enquiry headed by Gordon A. Winter. The Winter Commission reviewed events involving seven Newfoundland priests. When the Winter Report came out in June 1990, five of these men had pleaded guilty to a total of twenty-eight sex-related charges.

During the same period, allegations surfaced regarding both physical and sexual abuse of young boys that had occurred during the 1970s at Mount Cashel Orphanage, a Roman Catholic institution staffed by a lay order of Catholic brothers in the provincial capital. Mount Cashel became a household name across Canada, as millions of television viewers learned of the crimes of brothers charged with caring for dislocated children. Moreover, the justice system contributed to the scandal by ensuring that the perpetrators escaped the consequences of the law. The orphanage abuse became the subject of a government-ordered commission of enquiry, the Hughes Commission. The Church closed the facility, and the building was later demolished. Meanwhile, shock, pain, and anger were directed toward the abusive priests and brothers, the bishop of St. John's, and the Church in general.

When the reports of allegations and charges first surfaced, the media focused mostly on victims' recollections of abuse and on the long-term implications of an abusive past. Information about the priestly misconduct spread rapidly, as did the sordid details of the clergy's liaisons with male minors in their care. The media's fascination with the events as they unfolded kept the story in the public ear and eye. Few Canadians—and probably not a single Roman Catholic in Newfoundland—escaped learning about the allegations and subsequent charges. For months in Atlantic Canada, one could not pick up a newspaper, turn on the radio, or watch television without being bombarded with the latest on the sexual abuse story. In a sense, it was Newfoundland's version of the O. J. Simpson trial. What began as sympathy for the victims and shock at the sexual misconduct turned into outrage at Church and government bureaucracies that failed to protect vulnerable children and disregarded their pain and suffering. Journalist Michael Harris called it a "conspiracy of indifference" on the part of secular and sacred officials (Harris 1990). Among many interesting questions left unanswered in this saga of sex, politics, justice, and religion: Why did the disclosures suddenly meet with a sympathetic hearing? Why did the Newfoundland story of sexual abuse by priests receive so much media attention and garner such public anger?

The Timing of the Disclosures: Publicizing the Scandal

Few scholars have shown much interest in understanding why events in Newfoundland ignited public outrage. I have argued elsewhere that answers to the "why now" question lie in part in: (1) greater public knowledge of the prevalence and consequences of child sexual assault, including the deleterious impact of a "breach of trust"; (2) the impact of the women's movement; (3) the changing relationship between the state and the church; (4) the geographical, economic, and political realities of Newfoundland; (5) the role of the media; and (6) the innovative measures introduced by the judicial system to respond to cases of child sexual abuse (Nason-Clark 1991).

Child sexual abuse has come out of the closet in the last two decades (Bross et al. 1988). Although reported incidences of child sexual assault are on the increase, the problem is not new (Finkelhor 1984). The reaction of society to a child's allegation of sexual misconduct at the hands of an adult, however, has changed—whether the reactors are parents, grandparents, teachers, social workers, or the justice system (Nason-Clark 1989). Thanks to the women's movement's effort to reconceptualize sexual abuse from a crime of passion to a crime of power abuse (Walker 1990; Martin 1981), society is now less likely to blame child sexual abuse on the perpetrator's misdirected sexual urges. Factors contributing to society's increased willingness to condemn abuse include greater concern for the rights of children (Bross et al. 1988), volumes of research indicating the deleterious long-term affects of childhood sexual and physical abuse (Finkelhor 1984; Straus 1992), and more knowledge about, and intolerance for, family violence (Rosenberg and Gary 1988; Straus, Gelles, and Steinmetz 1980). With the growth of child sexual abuse research and debate, we have learned the great significance of the violation of trust involved. The breach of trust magnifies the long-term consequences, decreases the child's willingness to disclose the abuse, and increases the likelihood that the child's report will be dismissed upon disclosure. The present openness to survivors' stories of sexual abuse has developed only recently. By the late 1980s secrecy and silence became harder to maintain beyond the closed doors of the orphanage, the judge's chambers, or the presbytery.

The first piece of the puzzle, then, that explains why events surrounding the sexual assault of children at the hands of Roman Catholic priests and brothers have lately come to light relates to the recent increase in knowledge about child abuse in our society. This knowledge base, while still incomplete, reduces the possibility of dismissing children's claims without question or refusing to act upon them.

A second piece lies in the impact of the women's movement. Although the struggle for women's full and equal participation with men in all dimensions of modern society goes on, several accomplishments have increased social receptivity to disclosures of child sexual abuse. First, one of the central foundations of modern feminism was the proclamation that the personal is political (Friedan 1963; Steinem 1986). Feminism challenged women to see that their personal struggles had political overtones and political solutions (Landsberg 1983). Second, feminism highlighted the power imbalance between victim and perpetrator in crimes involving sex as well as the role of fear on the part of the victim—fear for one's life, fear of reporting, fear of retaliation, and even fear of terminating an abusive relationship (Martin 1981). And third, feminism gave many church women and men new ammunition in the struggle for equitable relations between male and female members of congregations, clergy and laity, the religious powerful and the powerless (Ebaugh 1993; Ruether 1985; Wallace 1992).

A further piece of the puzzle of why events in Newfoundland surfaced in the late 1980s concerns the altered religious environment and, in particular, the changing relationship between the Church and state. Newfoundlanders held Roman Catholic priests in high esteem; these were men purportedly without spot or blemish. Like priests everywhere, they had taken a vow of poverty and obedience, not to mention celibacy. At the Archdiocesan Commission of Enquiry into the Sexual Abuse of Children by Members of the Clergy, known as the Winter Commission, parents reported how delighted they had felt when their adolescent sons spent time with a priest: they considered this a worry-free environment, in contrast to "local youth hang-outs." This adoration for the parish priest also explains a teenager's reluctance to disclose the abuse to his parents. Moreover, the offending priests offered financial and emotional inducements to their young victims, virtually ensuring their sexual cooperation and enhanced secrecy about it. In passing sentence on Father Hickey, the provincial court judge Reginald Reid said:

> The twenty sexual offences committed by Jim Hickey are unsurpassed in seriousness in this province, at least. The enormity of what happened can be best understood by realizing the twenty sexual offences were coupled with a serious breach of trust and faith placed

in their moral and spiritual leader by persons who all but idolized him as parish priest. . . . The priest offered the boys a continuous and calculated regime of inducements such as holding his home out as a virtual hang out for children to escape parental discipline, providing a liberally accessible supply of alcohol, and loaning his car to minors not old enough to drive. (ACE 1990)

At the same time, the religious scene is changing, with declines in the numbers of active parish priests and ordinands (Hoge 1987; Wallace 1992). Shrinking clerical numbers translates into a strong vested interest on the part of the Church in avoiding public disclosures that would reduce them still further—an incentive to keep silent and simply move offending priests to another jurisdiction. At the same time, Vatican II paved the way for ordinary Catholics to play a greater part in parish life (Hoge 1987). With attendance at mass declining across the country and Canadian Catholics reporting behavior and attitudes that opposed official Catholic teaching, the power and mystique of the Catholic hierarchy had begun to fade (Bibby 1987, 1993). In the aftermath of the charges against priests, Newfoundland's more confrontive and vocal Catholic laity led to a crisis of confidence in the spiritual leaders that culminated in both the Winter Commission enquiry and the eventual resignation of the archbishop of Newfoundland.

A fourth piece of the puzzle relates to the economic and political reality of Newfoundland, an isolated, mostly rural province on the east coast of Canada. The secrecy about abuse at the Mount Cashel Orphanage exemplifies the relationship between the Church and the state, which functioned to maximize the benefits of secrecy while minimizing the costs. In terms of its child welfare and criminal justice systems, the state earned economic and political dividends from keeping the orphanage viable. First, Mount Cashel offered the province much-needed housing for children deemed "wards of the state"; the government contributed money but made no attempt to interfere with programs or operations. Second, as celebrations for the facility's centennial got under way, no politician wanted to damage a relationship with the Catholic electorate by questioning the orphanage's care, nor did any want to jeopardize their networking opportunities at the many highly publicized fund-raisers and celebrations at Mount Cashel; better to keep the sordid activities of the Christian Brothers at one of St. John's most esteemed institutions under cover.

However, shortly after the charges against parish priests (as well as the events involving the Christian Brothers) became public knowledge, the isolation and cultural distinctiveness of Newfoundland society ensured a captive audience and a rather unanimous response. Cultural homogeneity thus contributed to both the speed and intensity of the public outcry.

As surely as the social, economic, and political environment protected the priests and brothers and denied justice to the victims, the media deserves credit for raising and continuing to highlight the stories of abuse. On Easter Sunday 1989, an article in the *St. John's Sunday Express* alleged sexual and physical abuse at Mount Cashel. Prompted by the publicity given priests in Newfoundland who had sexually abused altar boys and encouraged by the possibility of seeing justice done, Shane Earle, a twenty-three-year-old former resident of the orphanage, had contacted the editor of the paper, hoping to expose the scandal that had left dozens of young men like himself haunted by memories of violation and betrayal. According to Michael Harris (1990), at least eighty-seven people in positions of authority knew of the abuses taking place at Mount Cashel, but none were willing to expose a potential scandal. That a victim would choose to reveal his personal horror in a newspaper feature article, that an editor would agree to publish it, and that the public would rally as a result testifies to the enormous power of the media to increase visibility and accountability for crimes involving sex.

One final reason to account for why these events surfaced in the late 1980s in Newfoundland relates to innovative techniques and measures for processing cases of child sexual assault, among them Bill C-15, a piece of Canadian-passed legislation that encourages the adoption of modern technology in courtrooms. The use of screens and video-taped testimony means that child victims do not necessarily have to face their accused in court; the rules regarding collaborative evidence have also changed. Other changes have affected how some jurisdictions detect, investigate, process, and adjudicate cases involving the sexual abuse of minors. Coordinated interagency investigative teams reduced the number of times victims were interviewed and increased the possibility of approaching the alleged offender quickly, reducing the risk of a collaborated alibi. These efforts sped due process in the criminal justice system while treating victims and their families, so that child welfare workers grew more optimistic about the advantages of involving judges in cases of abuse. While innovative technologies per se did not affect the adult men coming forward to testify to the abuse they had experienced as adolescents or preadolescents, the discussions surrounding Bill C-15 produced an environment of optimism regarding the criminal justice processing of child sexual abuse.

Taken together, these factors created an environment less hostile to victims of abuse and more open to the criminal justice processing of offenders. Moreover, the Church as an institution was undergoing change, affecting both lay attendance and clerical "callings." Public awareness of the prevalence and seriousness of childhood physical and sexual abuse was growing, and the media seized an opportunity to "break a story." That Newfoundland Catholics were relatively strong both numerically and as supporters of "separate" schools for their children gave that story even greater impact.

Telling the Story from Catholic Women's Perspective

Rome mandates Catholic women to have large families and to educate and train their children to follow the teaching of the Roman Catholic Church in both belief and practice. Mothers, then, have a special role as guardians of the faith tradition, in terms of both regular involvement with the parish community and keeping the Catholic way alive at home. In traditional Newfoundland coastal communities, the mothers tended the home fires as the fathers fished the seas. Not surprisingly, the Church was important for social as well as religious rituals and activities. With the demise of cod fishing in Newfoundland and the disintegration of many small fishing villages, despair about the present and the future crept into homes. But Catholics on the island retained a strong sense of community, rooted in the life of their parish churches and priests.

When news of the scandal broke, did Catholic women rally around their Church? How did they respond to the growing number of charges and convictions among priests in whom they had confided? Did they find themselves caught in a crossfire between allegiance to the Catholic Church and their concern for the safety and protection of children? And finally, what were the implications of sexual scandal for the beliefs and practices of Roman Catholic women? Did they undergo a "crisis of faith"?

To explore such questions related to the impact of scandal by religious elites on their female followers, a sample of twenty-four Roman Catholic women were contacted and interviewed in parishes around the Diocese of St. John's. The taped, semistructured interviews, most often conducted at the woman's home around the kitchen table, lasted between one and two hours. An initial analysis of the interview data appeared in Stapleton 1992 and Stapleton and Nason-Clark 1992.

Early Reactions to the Story

All twenty-four women who participated in our initial Newfoundland study could remember exactly where they were and what they were doing when the supper-time news broke the story of James Hickey's sexual abuse of altar boys. As one homemaker in her sixties recalled: "I think that women everywhere were caught up with a dish in their hand from the oven or on their way to the sink. . . . A friend of mine told me she actually dropped a dish and broke it on the floor."

The six o'clock evening news, supplemented by later press reports, served as the first source of information. Once the news had been released, phone lines around eastern Newfoundland communities became clogged, as family, friends, and co-workers scrambled to spread the news to others.

Most Newfoundland Catholics reacted to the story with disbelief, the response reported by exactly half of the women in our study. A secretary in her thirties explained that Hickey "worked hard for the parish and community and we just totally believed in him. And, of course, we were brought up to believe that priests could do no wrong. And, I mean, we just couldn't understand. We thought that maybe somebody was framing him or telling lies until the truth really come [sic] out that it was true."

Though only five women initially felt angry, by the time our research was conducted three years after the story broke, nineteen of the twenty-four reported anger as one of the emotions they felt in the aftermath of the sexual scandal. One woman in her forties spoke of the irony of confessing one's sins to a priest himself guilty of sexually abusing boys in the parish: "And this is what really shocked me, to think that I actually really liked this person and he could do these things that were beyond me. I mean to think that we were going to confession to them. I just can't believe that I actually went to confession to this man and confessed things that were so childish and so insignificant and were not sins, I mean were not sins at all. And these men were committing the biggest, in my opinion, the biggest sins on earth. . . . I find it difficult to find words."

As one might expect, the primary targets of their anger were the offending priests, but most of the women eventually also felt angry at the bishop, other Catholic priests, the Church hierarchy, and those who disbelieved the early reports; some of the women were angry at Catholics who happened to live in parishes where priests had been charged. This sense of outrage with local Catholic believers was rooted in disappointment that parishioners continued to support a system that allowed priest misconduct to occur and failed to act decisively when it did. What is particularly interesting about this viewpoint is that several women later commented in the interview that they personally accepted responsibility for "failing to see" the abusive behavior or "failing to hear" the warning bells. One mother in her fifties summed it up this way: "I had worked so hard for the parish and for my community. I'm still very involved with it. And to know that the money that I had raised had gone to buy liquor and porno movies to lure young boys, it was just . . . I couldn't cope with it. I really couldn't."

Although the women at first responded with disbelief and shock, these feelings gave way over time to anger, hurt, guilt, and a sense of betrayal. Two-thirds talked about feeling betrayed, hurt, guilty, and embarrassed; some reported a "beaten-down spirit." The guilt that women experienced literally consumed them and explains why so many Catholic women in Newfoundland chose to alter their personal relationship with the parish church in the aftermath of sexual scandal. As a teacher in her forties reflected: "Why were we so stupid? Why did we allow these people to have so much control over our lives? You know, looking back now, it was always little things that we should have connected but we didn't. . . . We're to blame for some of this too, for taking all this, excuse me, shit that we took from them for years and years."

The Impact of the Story

Parish life changed in the aftermath of sexual scandal in Newfoundland. Devout Catholics—both men and women—boycotted the Church with their feet and their pocketbooks. What was less clear, however, was why the story had struck them with such an impact. During the interviews, most women spoke of strained relations with the incumbent priest, the bishop, and the rigid hierarchical structure of Roman Catholicism as they internalized the scandal. Their growing hostility came in response to the Church's failure to act quickly to bring priests and brothers to justice; accept responsibility for the abusive priests; ask forgiveness of the victims, their families, and Catholics throughout the region; help victim's pay for professional counseling; and begin a process of personal, collective, and structural renewal. The words of this woman in her thirties make clear the displeasure and dismay of Newfoundlanders to the Roman Catholic elite's response to the crisis: "I have seen this Church in positions where they could have made responses that made sense, that rooted themselves both in the theology and faith of the Church and rooted themselves in the faith of the people who were hurting. And what I saw each and every time they were given an opportunity, was that they still had not learned and always tended to stand with the people who were more powerful or to stand in the place that was going to protect the institution, rather than care for the people of faith."

In fact, the poor response of the Roman Catholic elite to the sexual abuse crisis made the process of dealing with the scandal even harder for Catholic believers. Those leaders had failed to react swiftly and decisively to the allegations. Moreover, the hierarchy never made it clear that it understood the pain and long-term consequences of what had happened to the altar boys and their families, the children who called Mount Cashel home, and the wider community, both religious and secular. Sweeping the events under the carpet, a strategy that in the past had succeeded in keeping the sordid sex lives of priests and brothers from public scrutiny, now augmented the downward spiral of confidence in both the Church and those who had vowed to serve it.

According to our interviewees, this breach of clerical trust had markedly affected women's participation in the life of the Church. They were less likely to attend mass or confession and volunteered less for Church office or duties. Interaction with all areas of the life and ministry of the institutional Church declined. Yet the women reported little or no impact on their personal faith journeys. Their anger and frustration was directed toward priests and the Church hierarchy, but their faith in God remained.

From our interviews we learned that these women of faith passed through a series of stages as they came to grips with the misuse of clerical power and privilege. They blamed themselves for blind allegiance, but most of all they blamed clerical leaders for failing to respond to the people.

Later Reflection on the Scandal

To address the longer-term impact of sexual scandal on believers' faith and practice, we contacted the same group of Newfoundland women four years later, in 1995. Nineteen of the original twenty-four granted us a telephone interview of from thirty to sixty minutes.[1]

In the almost ten years since the scandal, some women have chosen to come back to their parish church, some have stuck it out "through thick and thin," and others have chosen to stay away.

Almost all of the women we interviewed claimed that the Church in Newfoundland has not recovered from the scandal. Moreover, all save one reported dissatisfaction with the Roman Catholic Church's response to the scandal. While the women are adamant that their personal faith has suffered little (and perhaps even grown stronger) as a result of the clerical sexual abuse, they say they never again will trust priests as they once did; Catholic priests in Newfoundland have been collectively "struck from the pedestal" (Stapleton and Nason-Clark 1992).

A Story of Coming Back

Mildred Small (a fictitious name), born and baptized into a Roman Catholic family, attended a Church school in Newfoundland during her childhood. Her family offered grace at their meals, said family rosary, discussed religion at home, and invited the parish priest to join them for dinner during times of family celebration. In 1991 when we interviewed her, Mildred Small was in her thirties, worked outside the home as a clerk in an office setting, and had two children. She reported that when the news first came out about James Hickey she didn't believe it. "As a matter of fact," she admitted, "I remember I cried for three days." Like many other women, she contacted another priest to ask whether the radio reports about their beloved priest, Father Jim, were true. Small told us of the petition circulated in her community to support James Hickey, and how painful it was for people like herself to gradually realize the truth of the allegations and subsequent charges. "We thought that maybe somebody was framing him, or telling lies, until the truth really came out," she said. "I used to thank God all the time 'cause my son was an altar boy."

Shock, dismay, and sadness set in as the weeks and months passed. Though the accused Hickey made contact with her, she remained cool and aloof toward his attempts to garner community support; for Small, like many other women, disbelief turned into bitterness.

Her son (though he himself was not abused) ceased to be an altar boy; neither of them wanted that contact with the Church any longer. Mildred Small stopped attending mass altogether, no longer volunteered for parish committees, quit baking for Church sales and pouring tea for parish garden parties, resigned from parish council, and no longer served as a reader. Her response to sexual scandal in the Catholic Church was to cut her ties altogether, which created guilt and sadness for her. "I want to go back desperately," she told us in 1991. "It nags me on Sunday. It nags inside of me. And I want to go . . . [but] I don't know how to deal with it."

Small found most painful the failure of the Church—her church—to come to the people, admit the pain and the problem, and work with faithful Catholic followers toward renewal.

By 1995, Mildred Small had begun to attend mass again. "I've pretty well returned to church since we last spoke," she said quietly. "I felt the message was still there. The message was not the problem. The problem was the messenger and not the message itself. That's how we dealt with it." But her relationship with the Church has changed forever. She is no longer willing to serve on Church committees or to take on major responsibilities within the parish, though from time to time she bakes some cookies for sale. "I think people in the parish are more cautious. I think they give things more thought. It's not automatic anymore just because the priest said so."

Mildred Small's story is not unique. Her response typifies that of many Roman Catholic women in Newfoundland. She has come back to the Church, but her allegiance to the parish and her faith in its leaders have not been restored. Returning to the religious practices of her past filled a personal void. She missed the Church and the message that it preached. But, like many of the women we interviewed, she does not encourage her children to return to mass or to participate in the activities offered for their age groups. And they have not.

A Story of Staying Put

Georgina Jones (a fictitious name) has always been a faithful Catholic, attending Church schools as a child as well as mass and confession and teaching her own six children to do likewise. When we first talked with her in 1991, she was in her midforties, a woman whom her church could count on to volunteer when a job needed doing. The first allegations of James Hickey's sexual abusiveness had no great impact on Georgina Jones, who did not know Hickey personally; though many of her friends struggled with his arrest, the issued remained at arm's length to her. However, with the arrest of her own parish priest some time later, she found herself in shock. "My first reaction was, it was a mistake, that they had arrested him falsely." As more allegations surfaced and the stories of boys she had known became public, her reaction intensified. "There was nights I didn't sleep because of it, you know. I'd toss and I'd turn and everything went on in my mind."

As time went on, Jones found herself wondering about all priests, "Well, as more and more charges came out I didn't know what to do. I just didn't know who was going to be brought out next . . . like you're looking at a priest who'll come into your parish and say mass and you're looking at him and thinking is he another one of them going to be accused."

Though she found it very difficult, Georgina Jones never turned her back on the parish or her commitment to the Church. "I can stay involved and not . . . let it happen again, and try and to watch for things like this, be more aware." Like several other women, Georgina Jones felt personal responsibility for the priest's sexual misconduct. She blamed herself for not watching his behavior more diligently or picking up his cues over time, particularly after the first priest was arrested. Unlike her, Jones's husband has not entered the parish church since the arrest of their priest. In fact, Jones indicated that he will not even discuss with her the sexual abuse, the Church's failure to respond, or his own anger.

According to Georgina Jones, time has not erased the impact of sexual scandal on Newfoundland's Catholic Church. "It hasn't gone away. It has not cleared up. We were affected deeply in our parish because our priest was arrested. It goes up and down hill, but it still comes out." She told of one family who had called the priest to say the last rites over their father, who died just before daybreak. Three hours later, that priest was arrested.

The scandal altered Jones's willingness to volunteer in the parish and changed forever her view of priests and the Church hierarchy, yet when asked if her faith in God had declined since the scandal, she replied, "No change. No matter what happens, even if all the priests were arrested, because my faith is in God not the priest. Perhaps that's where we went wrong in the past. We had too much faith in the priest back then." While Georgina Jones has continued to support her parish throughout the scandal and to the present day, the priests' sexual abuse did not leave her unscathed.

Like Georgina Jones, 40 percent of the women we interviewed reported that their attendance at mass remained constant over the last ten years. Yet, like her as well, each woman reported that, while her personal faith in God was untouched by the abusive episodes, she was less likely to give unconditionally of her time and devotion as she had in the past. Although other factors may have contributed to the women's changed pattern of volunteerism, by their own accounts these Newfoundlanders claimed that the scandal had taken its toll on them personally.

Has Roman Catholic Church attendance dropped in the aftermath of scandal? One in every two Catholic women we interviewed in 1991 indicated that they attended mass less frequently after the scandal broke than before, while 10 percent indicated increased attendance. By 1995, 35 percent of the women whose attendance had dropped had come back to church, though their participation had not returned to its prescandal level. So most of those whose attendance had suffered in the years immediately following the crisis were coming back, but on different terms—less frequently and with less willingness to serve the parish as volunteers. Had healing taken place? Were they responding to an invitation by the clerical elite to replace pain with hope?

In June 1992, the Canadian Conference of Catholic Bishops published the report of their Ad Hoc Committee on Child Sexual Abuse (consisting of three bishops, two members of religious orders, and two lay Catholics). *From Pain to Hope* lists fifty recommendations to "our Catholic brothers and sisters of Canada" (CCCB 1992, 45). Although some have criticized the report's tone and content (Redmond 1993; Stapleton 1992), whether it spoke to "ordinary Catholics" remained a question, and particularly whether it spoke to Catholics in parishes whose incumbent priests had been charged. Of the nineteen women we reinterviewed in 1995, only one had seen the booklet, while two others seemed to recall that such a report was being prepared. Because several said during the interview that they were interested in reading *From Pain To Hope* (once we had alerted them to its existence), we wrote each of them several months after the telephone interview to find out whether they had tried to locate and read it. We heard from three women who attempted to obtain a copy of the report, only one of whom was successful. She wrote us of her difficulty locating the report—apparently even the episcopal office did not have a copy. She finally borrowed a copy from a woman academic at Memorial University.

It is ironic that a report that proposed to heal the pain and offer hope to ordinary Catholics in the aftermath of sexual scandal was so difficult to access, and virtually unheard of, even in the parishes where priests had been charged. If these "ordinary Catholics" were not the target population of the Canadian Conference of Catholic Bishop's commissioned findings, who was?

The Widened Network of Victims

The sexual scandal involving Roman Catholic priests and brothers that came to light in the late 1980s in Newfoundland offers an interesting example of the longer-term impact of abuse by clerical leaders. Intensive media coverage of the allegations and charges alerted nearly everyone in Canada's most easterly province of the sexual misconduct that had occurred on their island. Among a myriad of reasons that might be postulated for why these events surfaced in the late 1980s, we focused on greater public awareness of the nature and prevalence of child sexual abuse; changes affecting the church as an institution; the enhanced role of the media and investigative journalism; and economic, geographical, political, and legal factors.

Almost all of the Catholic women we interviewed in 1991 and 1995 who lived in or near parishes where priests had been charged claimed that the Church in Newfoundland has not recovered from the ten-year-old scandal. Some of the women have chosen to come back to their parish church, while others never entirely left. Yet most told of pain and shame as they first disbelieved the allegations, then became angry and bitter at the offending priests and the institution that protected them, and subsequently internalized the frustration by accepting some of the blame themselves.

Skeptical about clerical power as they had never been before, these Catholic women have removed the blinders from their own eyes and the pedestal from under their priest's feet. In this sense, they qualify as what Shupe (1995, 132) has termed "secondary victims" of clergy malfeasance, those indirectly hurt as trusting members of congregations.

Notes

Portions of this chapter have been presented at professional conferences and meetings. See Nason-Clark 1991, 1989; Stapleton and Nason-Clark 1992.

1. Anne Stapleton, a master's student in the Department of Sociology at the University of New Brunswick (UNB), conducted the 1991 interviews as part of the completion of her thesis; Nancy Nason-Clark was the thesis supervisor. The first phase of the study was supported by monies from the Nels Anderson Fund. Stapleton, herself a Roman Catholic mother of three, grew up in Newfoundland, factors that no doubt influenced the positive response to her request for interviews; not one woman approached refused to participate in the study. Portions of those data were reanalyzed for this chapter. The 1995 follow-up was supported by a research grant to Nason-Clark from the UNB Research Fund. Stapleton conducted the telephone interviews. We were unable to locate three women; one woman had died; and one woman caring for a sick, elderly parent was not available for an interview.

References

Archdiocesan Commission of Enquiry into the Sexual Abuse of Children by Members of the Clergy [ACE]. 1990. *The Report of the Archdiocesan Commission of Enquiry into the Sexual Abuse of Children by Members of the Clergy.* Vols. 1, 2, and Summary and Recommendations. St. John's, Newfoundland: Archdiocese of St. John's.

Bibby, Reginald. 1993. *Unknown Gods: The Ongoing Story of Religion in Canada.* Toronto: Stoddart.

———. 1987. *Fragmented Gods: The Poverty and Potential of Religion in Canada.* Toronto: Irwin.

Bross, D., R. Krugman, M. Lenherr, D. Rosenberg, and B. Schmitt. 1988. *The New Child Protection Handbook.* New York: Garland.

Canadian Conference of Catholic Bishops [CCCB]. 1992. *From Pain to Hope: Report of the Ad Hoc Committee on Child Sexual Abuse.* Ottawa: Canadian Conference of Catholic Bishops.

Ebaugh, Helen Rose. 1993. *Women in the Vanishing Cloister: Organizational Decline in Catholic Religious Orders in the United States.* New Brunswick, N.J.: Rutgers University Press.

Finkelhor, D. 1984. *Child Sexual Abuse: New Theory and Research.* New York: Free Press.

———. 1983. "Removing the Child—Prosecuting the Offender in Cases of Child

Sexual Abuse: Evidence from the National Reporting System for Child Abuse and Neglect." *Child Abuse and Neglect* 7:195–205.

Friedan, Betty. 1963. *The Feminine Mystique.* New York: Penguin.

Harris, Michael. 1990. *Unholy Orders: Tragedy at Mount Cashel.* Markham, Ontario: Viking Penguin.

Hoge, Dean, 1987. *Future of Catholic Leadership: Responses to the Priest Shortage.* Kansas City, Mo.: Sheed and Ward.

Landsberg, Michele. 1983. *Women and Children First.* Toronto: Penguin.

Martin, Del. 1981. *Battered Wives.* San Francisco: Volcano.

Nason-Clark, Nancy. 1991. "Broken Trust: The Case of Roman Catholic Priests in Newfoundland Charged with the Sexual Abuse of Children." Paper presented at the annual meetings of the Society for the Scientific Study of Religion, Pittsburgh, November 8–10.

———. 1989. "The Frequency and Severity of Child Sexual Assault: Implications for Religious Bodies." Paper presented at the annual meetings of the Society for the Scientific Study of Religion, Salt Lake City, October 26–29.

Nemeth, Mary. 1994. "Sex and the Vatican." *MacLean's.* December 19, 32–33.

Redmond, Sheila A. 1993. "It Can't Be True and If It Is, It's Not Our Fault: An Examination of Roman Catholic Institutional Response to Priestly Paedophilia in the Ottawa Valley." *Canadian Society of Church History Papers*, 229–245.

Rogers, Carl M., and Terry Tremaine. 1984. "Clinical Intervention with Boy Victims of Sexual Abuse." In *Victims of Sexual Aggression*, edited by I. R. Stuart and J. G. Greer. Toronto: Van Nostrand Reinhold.

Rosenberg, Donna, and Nancy Gary. 1988. "Sexual Abuse of Children." In *The New Child Protection Team Handbook*, edited by D. Bross, R. Krugman, M. Lenherr, D. Rosenberg, and B. Schmitt. New York: Garland.

Ruether, Rosemary Radford. 1985. *Women-Church: Theology and Practice.* New York: Harper and Row.

St. John's (Newfoundland) Sunday Express, 1988–1991.

Shupe, Anson. 1995. *In The Name of All That's Holy: A Theory of Clergy Malfeasance.* Westport, Conn.: Praeger.

Stapleton, Anne. 1992. "The Power and the Pedestal: Roman Catholic Women in Newfoundland Reassess Their Beliefs and Attitudes in the Aftermath of Scandal." Master's thesis, University of New Brunswick.

———, and Nancy Nason-Clark. 1992. "The Power and the Pedestal: Roman Catholic Women in Newfoundland Reassess Their Beliefs and Attitudes in the Aftermath of Scandal." Paper presented at the annual meeting of the Society for the Scientific Study of Religion, Washington, D.C.

Steinem, Gloria. 1986. *Outrageous Acts and Everyday Rebellions.* Winnipeg: Signet.

Straus, Murray A. 1992. "Sociological Research and Social Policy: The Case of Family Violence." *Sociological Forum* 7 (2):211–237.

———, R. J. Gelles, and S. K. Steinmetz. 1980. *Behind Closed Doors: Violence in the American Family.* New York: Doubleday/Anchor.

Walker, Gillian A. 1990. *Family Violence and the Women's Movement: The Conceptual Politics of Struggle.* Toronto: University of Toronto Press.

Wallace, Ruth. 1992. *They Call Her Pastor: A New Role for Catholic Women.* Albany: State University of New York

CHAPTER 6

Reactions of Hare Krishna Devotees to Scandals of Leaders' Misconduct

E. BURKE ROCHFORD JR.

The post 1977 guru project of the Krishna consciousness movement alleges to be the "continuation" of a five-thousand-year-old "pure guru lineage." Up to 1977, this lineage (called guru parampara) was always completely free from all defect, illusion, cheating, sensory defect; and what to speak of as immorality. Yet, the alleged post 1977 guru succession (created by ISKCON's Governing Body Commission or GBC) contains every horrific device known to man, including theft, drugs, homosexuality, pedophilia, sex with disciples, . . . repressive cover-ups, murder of dissenters, "gurus" breaking up marriages. (Prabhupada Anti-Defamation Association 1993)

Some mainline religions as well as new religious movements have faced wrong-doing and illegal activities by clergy and other leaders (Jacobs 1989; Shupe 1995). In cases of sexual abuse and misconduct, the behaviors often exact great personal cost of those directly affected (Berry 1992). Yet the implications of these and other acts of wrong-doing extend far beyond the parties involved. To the extent that the untoward behavior of clergy becomes public knowledge, the religious organization as a whole may be held up to scrutiny; questions may arise about possible cover-up activities by church authorities, as L. Matchan and S. Kurkjian reported in their *Boston Globe* article on October 21, 1992, "Porter Personnel Files Show That Church Knew." Such collective "soul searching" may also result in factionalism, defection, and schism as the legitimacy of a religious organization becomes the target of doubt from within.

In this chapter I consider the interrelationship between leader misconduct, declining religious authority, and the development of the International
Society for Krishna Consciousness (ISKCON), popularly known as the Hare
Krishna movement.[1] What one ISKCON insider has called "the crisis of authority that shook ISKCON to its foundation in the years after [ISKCON's
founding guru] Srila Prabhupada's demise" provides the focus for my discussion of how leader malfeasance, and related struggles over religious authority, influenced the development of ISKCON in the 1980s (R. S. dasa
1994,10).[2]

Religious Authority and Organizational Change

My work builds conceptually on Mark Chaves's model of conflict and
change within religious organizations.[3] Secularization, according to Chaves,
involves "the declining scope of religious authority" as a result of "concrete
struggles among social actors" over its legitimate limits (1993b, 7). Authority in general is vested in leaders and others capable of withholding access
to things that individuals desire. When that ability to withhold "is legitimated
by reference to the supernatural, authority is religious." Defined as declining religious authority, secularization thus refers to the shrinking influence
of social structures whose legitimation rests on the world of the supernatural (Chaves 1994, 756).

Chaves's investigation of Protestant denominations found that internal
secularization was an outcome of conflict between competing organizational
structures—religious authority structures, on the one hand, and agency structures, on the other.[4] Organizations moved toward secularization when dominant structures of religious authority lost influence and power to competing
agency structures. These conflicts and struggles over authority were often
accompanied by denominational factionalism, and even schism.

Although mainline religious organizations typically have both religious
and agency structures, some denominations, and perhaps most sectarian
movements, lack this differentiation. The lack of a distinct agency structure
makes such religious organizations qualitatively distinct from their dual-
structured counterparts. Given the dominance of a religious authority structure,
these groups remain preoccupied with regulating access to "religious goods"
or spiritual principles and rights. Congregations thus become the "*object of
control,*" subject to the decisions and will of religious authorities (Chaves
1993b, 9).

Conflicts between two competing structures of *religious* authority within ISKCON, and related grass-roots mobilization, are the central issue here. The first of these, the guru institution as it came to be defined by the movement's leaders in the aftermath of Prabhupada's death, rested on the traditional, if not the charismatic, authority of the newly appointed gurus.

The competing religious authority was the movement's international governing board—the Governing Body Commission (GBC). The GBC initially collaborated with the appointed gurus to legitimize the new guru system. Within two years, however, the GBC sought to limit the collective authority of the gurus after several deviated from the movement's moral principles or became involved in illegal activities. Failing to constrain the gurus' authority, the GBC too lost legitimacy in the eyes of rank-and-file members. In a situation defined by leader conflict and declining religious authority, a grass-roots movement sought to reform ISKCON's structures of power and authority.

Succession, Scandal, and the Decline of Religious Authority

In the fall of 1977, the charismatic founder of ISKCON died in Vrndavana, India. Srila Prabhupada's death represented a major turning point for ISKCON's development. Over the next decade, ISKCON faced continuing and often bitter internal conflict (Gelberg 1988, 1991; Rochford 1985, 221–255, 1989). Because Prabhupada had left the movement without a clear and legitimate heir or power structure, two structures of religious authority competed for control—the Governing Body Commission and the guru successors to Prabhupada (R. S. dasa 1994, 11; Rochford 1985, 221–222).

Like some other charismatic leaders, Prabhupada established a governing board of directors to oversee the administrative affairs of his movement. As detailed in Prabhupada's final will, "[t]he Governing Body Commission (GBC) will be the ultimate managing authority for the entire International Society for Krishna Consciousness" upon his death (R. S. dasa 1994, 12).

Meanwhile, during the months before his death Prabhupada appointed eleven of his closest disciples to serve as gurus (Rochford 1985, 283–286). When he died, the appointed gurus assumed responsibility for initiating new disciples into Krishna Consciousness, thus assuring the continuation of the traditional disciple succession. Soon after their appointment the gurus began to assert their independence from the GBC. Having proclaimed themselves *acaryas*, the gurus viewed themselves as immune from the decisions and will of the GBC. They effectively became heads of their own institutions, albeit working within the context of ISKCON.[5]

In keeping with their acarya status, each of the new gurus took charge of a designated geographical territory over which he exercised complete political, economic, and spiritual authority. New recruits found themselves with little choice but to take initiation from the regional ISKCON guru. Initiated disciples were expected to recognize their gurus as advanced and infallible spiritual masters. This structure of religious authority that would define ISKCON for nearly a decade became known as the "zonal acarya system."

The eleven gurus shared the responsibility for governing ISKCON with fourteen other GBC members. These twenty-five men comprised the major decision-making body within ISKCON. The alliance between acaryas and nonguru leaders on the GBC proved a tenuous one that would give rise to an ongoing conflict, only exacerbated when the gurus established their own GBC subcommittee to address all matters relating to the guru institution, such as initiations, decisions to appoint new gurus, and problems associated with individual gurus (R. S. dasa 1994, 10). The question of which of the two structures of religious authority held ultimate power to govern the movement became a source of continuing debate and struggle.

Soon, however, the gurus gained the upper hand politically, as a result of the religious authority they laid claim to as acaryas. "Indeed," writes R. S. dasa (1994, 11), "the gurus, with their status as sacred persons, a status constantly emphasized by formal deference and ceremonial honors, and their growing numbers of personally devoted followers, quickly eclipsed the GBC."

But even with religious authority in the organization established, questions remained about the gurus' spiritual credentials. Most Prabhupada disciples believed many, if not all, of their guru godbrothers unqualified spiritually (R. S. dasa 1994, 13; Rochford 1985, 237). A series of controversies and scandals that arose around several of the gurus only strengthened this belief.

Initially, these controversies served to more firmly establish the institutional—if not the popular—status of the gurus. In a major confrontation at ISKCON's 1979 international meetings in India, the GBC ruled that the new gurus should have the same relationship with their disciples as Prabhupada had with his. Thereafter, each guru had a *vyasasana* (an elevated ceremonial seat reserved exclusively for him) in each temple in his zone and received worship each morning from his disciples (*guru puja*). The gurus argued that these and other measures were necessary to develop and deepen the faith of their disciples (Rochford 1985, 229).

In 1980, the GBC imposed sanctions on three of ISKCON's newly appointed gurus, two for illegal behavior. In a case that received national media attention, authorities in northern California charged ISKCON guru Hansaduta with possessing a large cache of weapons and ammunition (Rochford 1985, 230–231). Although some members of the GBC sought to have Hansaduta excommunicated from ISKCON, in the end he received a one-year suspension from his guru duties, that is, he could not initiate new disciples. The second guru, Jayatirtha, found to be taking "LSD," also received a one-year suspension from the GBC.[6]

In the third such controversy, Tamal Krishna, then residing in Bombay, began preaching in the spring of 1980 that he was the true successor to Prabhupada and directed the Prabhupada disciples in his zone to embrace him as their spiritual leader. Following the precedent of the previous two cases, the GBC stripped Krishna of his guru duties for a year.

Shortly after being suspended from their duties, two of the gurus sought to have their suspensions overturned. One of Prabhupada's godbrothers in India, Sridar Maharaja, sided with them over the GBC, affirming the supremacy of the guru. Shortly thereafter, the GBC convened and withdrew the sanctions, allowing both gurus to return to their zones and resume their duties as gurus. In backing off from its original decisions, the GBC acknowledged the religious authority of the gurus as the dominant structure of power in ISKCON.

The last guru controversy of 1980, in retrospect, represented the first of the challenges to the status and position of ISKCON's gurus. Ramesvara, a guru in Los Angeles, sought to redefine the role of newly appointed gurus like himself. Because some had proven fallible and less than spiritually pure, he argued for limiting their role to initiating disciples on behalf of Prabhupada (Rochford 1985, 234). In a gesture consistent with this philosophy, Ramesvara removed his vyasasanas from the temples in his zone and discontinued morning guru puja worship of him by his disciples. The GBC, under intense pressure from the other eleven gurus, rejected Ramesvara's proposals. To have accepted them would have dramatically reshaped the guru institution and undermined the religious authority of the gurus (Rochford 1985, 235).

In 1981 the GBC again sought to limit the authority of the gurus. Facing mounting criticism from a substantial and growing number of Prabhupada disciples in and outside of the movement, the GBC ruled that henceforth the gurus must accept the collective GBC as the ultimate and final authority in ISKCON (Rochford 1985, 235–236). Individual gurus could no longer claim independence from the GBC, because the gurus collectively held their positions only under GBC authority. This decision ultimately had little practical impact, for it left the zonal acarya structure of authority intact.

In the years that followed, other scandals emerged around individual gurus. In 1982, Jayatirtha, who was based in England, left ISKCON with as many as a hundred of his disciples, after he unsuccessfully tried to have Prabhupada's godbrother, Sridar Maharaja, brought formally into ISKCON as an initiating guru (Rochford 1985, 250–252). In 1983, after years of controversy, the guru Hansaduta was expelled from ISKCON by the GBC (Rochford 1985, 259–260). Between 1985 and 1986 three more gurus— Ramesvara, Bhagavan, and Bhavananda—charged with sexual misconduct and corruption, were forced to resign their positions and leave the movement (Gelberg 1991, 154; Rochford 1995b, 218).

In a well-publicized legal case, Kirtanananda, the guru leader of ISKCON's West Virginia farm community known as New Vrindaban, was convicted of a number of charges stemming from the murder of a dissident devotee. In 1987, ISKCON excommunicated Kirtanananda, leaving only five of the original eleven gurus in ISKCON. Until 1994, New Vrindaban remained estranged from ISKCON.[7]

The Reform Movement and the Reshaping of Religious Authority

The various guru scandals convinced most Prabhupada disciples, and many new disciples whose own gurus had left ISKCON in disgrace, that the guru system needed fundamental alterations. As one early disciple of Prabhupada's commented in my survey. "During the 'guru' phase of ISKCON it was impossible to remain a devotee. Many devotees were told if we didn't like what was going on that we should leave. Many devotees did just that! The political atmosphere at that time made it almost impossible to practice Krishna Consciousness in a peaceful manner."

A formally organized reform movement emerged in North America beginning in 1984. The reformers at first met with "dogged resistance from most GBC members and gurus" (Gelberg 1991, 154), but the political tide had begun to turn against the gurus and the zonal acarya system. As scandal weakened their collective religious authority, a grass-roots mobilization confronted the gurus and their GBC supporters.

The reform movement as an organized group had its origins in ISKCON's second level of leadership, the movement's temple presidents and regional secretaries. Organized dissent emerged at an annual North American Temple Presidents meeting in New Jersey in September 1984. Thirty-five leaders had come together to conduct official ISKCON business and to discuss preaching strategies for North America. Spontaneously, however, the participants turned their attention to questions concerning "the role and position of guru, the behavior and standards of the gurus, and the impact of the guru institution on ISKCON" (North American Temple Presidents, Regional Secretaries, and Sannyasis 1984, 1).

A survey conducted during the meetings revealed that the leaders present felt "deeply unhappy with many aspects of the guru institution" and saw an immediate need for change (North American Temple Presidents, Regional Secretaries, and Sannyasis 1984, 2). More than 90 percent of the leaders present agreed with the following statements: (1) There were "fundamental and compelling problems with the guru institution"; (2) ISKCON's gurus were not "exemplifying the spiritual standard expected of a *Vaisnava acarya*"; (3) "[t]he GBC should regulate the personal use of funds by gurus"; (4) the "standard of spiritual purity in ISKCON" had been "seriously compromised by the way the GBC has neglected, and at times covered up, discrepancies in the personal behavior of gurus and its own [non-guru] members"; and, (5) the evolution of the institution of acarya in ISKCON has "seriously diminished Srila Prabhupada's position in ISKCON (i.e., removed him from the center)." More than 80 percent agreed to the need for an "immediate and significant expansion of the number of initiating gurus," found "serious problems with the current system of zonal gurus," and believed that "the gurus should not continue to be worshiped at the current level" by their disciples.

The group scheduled a follow-up meeting for the following month. In the interim a committee would research exactly how the guru system had been implemented following Prabhupada's death and draft a position paper outlining its conclusions. The resulting paper concluded "that Srila Prabhupada's order, establishing how the *parampara* would continue in ISKCON after the founder-*acarya's* departure, was not clearly understood and hence not properly followed. As a result, the position of initiating guru has become institutionalized in ISKCON in a manner that is contrary to the desire of Srila Prabhupada and incompatible with his plans for ISKCON" (quoted in R. S. dasa 1985a, 1).

As one longtime ISKCON member and Prabhupada disciple explained: "After so many Godbrothers had been ostracized, kicked out, etc., there was gradually a recoil effect and that was when the reform movement began. We all met in New Vrndabana [sic] in September of '85 and tried to rectify things in a Vaisnava manner—although I think a hanging would have been more appropriate in retrospect."

Because of the GBC's complicity in implementing and then supporting the zonal acarya system, this body also came in for intense criticism. A resolution drafted in 1986 following a joint meeting of the North America Temple Presidents and North American Prabhupada Disciples Organization in Towaco, New Jersey, stated:

> The erosion of confidence in the GBC among senior devotees [and] junior devotees . . . has gathered to a point of crisis, and ISKCON is de facto without an ultimate managing authority. If nothing is done very swiftly to revive faith in the leadership of the GBC body, ISKCON may well dissolve forever as a unified preaching movement. This radical loss of faith in the GBC body is caused by the perception that the GBC has not accepted the fact that it made a grievous error in the way the position of the guru was established in ISKCON after Srila Prabhupada's departure. . . . At the same time, the GBC has not had the will to police its own members, especially its established '*acaryas*'; it has acted only when forced to do so by public scandal or severe pressure from non-GBC devotees. (North American Temple Presidents and the North American Prabhupada Disciples 1986, 1)

Various position papers and publications raised still further doubts about the legitimacy of the zonal acarya system (R. S. dasa 1985a, b, c; Goswami 1986). Reformers took the position that Prabhupada must once again become the central source of religious authority around whom all devotees could unite. Any other course risked the further fragmentation of ISKCON.

> The paradigm of the institutional acarya envisioned a zone unified and made coherent by a common devotion and submission to a single person. The guru zones became more unified than ISKCON as a whole, which was becoming increasingly fragmented, turning into a kind of amphictyony of independently empowered leaders. The paradigm of the reform movement, in contrast, envisioned ISKCON temples in which the disciples of many different gurus could all work together for their common cause. The underlying personality was to be the founder-acarya of the institution, Srila Prabhupada. (R. S. dasa 1994, 15)

The political goal of the reformers was to pressure the GBC into transforming the guru system altogether.

> The effort was to persuade the GBC to dismantle the "zonal acarya system" efficiently and decisively. We were able to put forward two

proposals to the GBC, which taken together, would dismantle the system. The first was to make the process of receiving authorization to initiate radically more open. . . . [T]he central intent of this proposal was to eliminate a *de facto* "property requirement" for becoming an initiating guru. Since a guru had to have his exclusive initiating zone, one or more of the established gurus had to lose territory to create a zone for any new gurus. . . . And many of the gurus were reluctant to shrink the area of their authority. (R. S. dasa 1994, 15)

The second proposal involved eliminating the exclusive vyasasana reserved for the use of the acarya within his zone. This seat symbolized his status as "head of the institution," the traditional autocratic guru associated with many forms of Hinduism (R. S. dasa 1994, 11).[8]

Under growing pressure from reformers, beginning in 1985 the GBC implemented a number of policy changes that fundamentally altered the guru institution. By 1987, after removing three gurus for "moral impropriety and corruption," the GBC had acted on virtually all the demands of the reform movement for change in the GBC itself, as well as in the position and authority of the gurus (Gelberg 1988, 181). Among the most significant changes in the guru institution:

1. The GBC approved the appointment of nine new ISKCON gurus in the fall of 1985, added eleven in 1986, and by 1990 had approved more than thirty altogether worldwide; by 1995, the number had grown to more than eighty. As the reformers intended, the addition of new gurus brought with it the demise of the zonal acarya system. Some of the original gurus tried to establish a two-tiered guru system comprised of acaryas and *diksha* (i.e., initiating) gurus, which would have increased the number of initiating gurus but allowed the zonal acaryas to retain control over their geographical territories—and their spiritual and political power. This attempt led to a revised system under which gurus no longer exercised exclusive authority over exclusive geographical zones.

2. In a significant symbolic gesture, the GBC ruled that the term *acarya* could refer only to Prabhupada. This ruling tied the religious authority of the gurus directly to ISKCON; no longer were they autonomous heads of their own institutions. Moreover, this change reestablished Prabhupada as the source of religious authority in ISKCON.

3. The GBC restricted guru worship (guru puja) in ISKCON temples to

honor Srila Prabhupada exclusively. Disciples of the new gurus could continue worshiping their guru, but not within the confines of the temple room.

4. Exclusive vayasasanas for zonal gurus were abandoned, leaving only a *murti* (a life-sized image) of Prabhupada sitting on his vyasasana in each ISKCON temple.

Other changes involved reorganizing the GBC. In 1987, a committee of fifty senior and respected Prabhupada disciples reviewed each member of the GBC to judge his suitability for governing ISKCON. Although the committee did consider expelling a limited number of GBC members, in the end it recommended expanding the group. The fifteen devotees appointed to serve on the GBC had all actively supported the reform movement.

Clearly, the reform movement did help resolve some of the issues that had divided ISKCON for nearly a decade. Yet these problems have not been finally resolved. Findings from the Prabhupada Centennial Survey in North America revealed that half (51 percent, or 141) of ISKCON's full-time members believed that the reform movement had not fully resolved the guru controversies within ISKCON. Far more (64, or 88 percent) of the devotees no longer affiliated formally with ISKCON agreed.[9] As one Prabhupada disciple who was forced out of ISKCON by one of the eleven zonal acaryas explained:

> The so-called dissidents were placated by being assimilated into the corrupt regime. . . . But as soon as they were made into GBC's and gurus the whole thing started again. It's not as bad as it was but I can assure you that the exploitation, black-balling and condescension goes on. . . . The guru-disciple relationship in our movement has become a farce. Srila Prabhupada warned against accepting "many" disciples, but there are men [ISKCON gurus] who have accepted thousands; sannyasis who live in the lap of luxury (if Beverly Hills isn't the lap of luxury, nothing is!) getting fat, being chauffeur-driven by their supposed disciples in Cadillacs, etc., to "speak" here or there while their unsuspecting (or suspecting!) servants work hard day and night to pay for their "guru's" high living standards. . . . This sort of trickery is so far from the way that Srila Prabhupada wanted his senior GBC/guru disciples to live that it is actually funny to many of us living on the outside.

The Ritvik Issue and the Restoration of Religious Authority

The controversies surrounding the gurus not only led to protest and demands for change from within ISKCON. Mobilization also occurred on the margins of ISKCON as ex-ISKCON members joined to condemn the gurus and the GBC.

Following Prabhupada's death a substantial number of devotees defected or were expelled from ISKCON (Rochford 1985, 236, 1989). Many who left did so because of abuses of power they had been subject to or had witnessed. Like many ISKCON members who remained, these devotees found reason to challenge the authority of the appointed gurus and the GBC. But although dissidents in and outside of ISKCON expressed similar grievances, one protest frame resonated more strongly with dissidents outside the ranks (Snow et al. 1986).

In the May and June before Prabhupada's death in November 1977, Prabhupada designated eleven of his disciples to serve as *ritviks*, officiating priests who would initiate new disciples on his behalf. His deteriorating health made it virtually impossible for him to personally initiate the growing list of devotees seeking initiation.

Upon his death, the GBC and the designated ritvik gurus assumed that the latter would automatically become "regular gurus" with the authority to initiate their own disciples. In movement terminology, the previous ritvik gurus would become diksha gurus. As more details of the gurus' appointment became known, especially the widespread dissemination of the May and June appointment conversations, some began to argue that Prabhupada had never intended the ritvik gurus he appointed to become initiating diksha gurus. This line of reasoning seemed all the more logical to dissidents given the many scandals and other controversies that had involved the gurus. Aware that Prabhupada had often expressed the view that none of his leading disciples were yet qualified to serve as his successor, those holding the line on ritviks argued that Prabhupada had intended them after his death to remain ritviks—not to become diksha gurus—until a qualified diksha guru emerged.

As Ravindra Svarupa dasa comments (1990, 127): "[I]t seems very certain that [Prabhupada] did not feel that any of his disciples were immediately, or even very soon, capable of being *diksha*-gurus, or *acaryas*, in the strict sense of these terms. It also seems quite clear that he never appointed any *gurus*, but only named some *r[i]tvik* or ceremonial priests. It can also be ascertained with an equal measure of certainty that *diksha* in the true and deepest sense of . . . the term can only be conferred or transmitted by a self-realized soul."

This interpretation meant that Prabhupada would remain as ISKCON's spiritual master even in death, and that all devotees initiated by his ritvik representatives would become his disciples. Moreover, it was thought that any of Prabhupada's disciples had the potential to serve as officiating priests.

A limited number of initiations—as few as fifty worldwide—have taken place outside ISKCON in accordance with the ritvik-as-initiator philosophy. In 1995, I received an invitation to attend a ritvik initiation at the Prabhupada Sankirtan Society in New York City, a schismatic group organized around that viewpoint. The invitation read in part: "You are cordially invited to attend the initiation of Mother (name) *Given By* His Divine Grace A.C. Bhaktivedanta Swami Prabhupada, Founder-Acarya-*Spiritual Master* on his Disappearance Day" (emphasis added). A quote attributed to Prabhupada appeared just above his picture on the invitation: "I shall always be your personal guide, whether physically present or not."

Supporters of the ritviks-as-initiators remain in the minority inside ISKCON but are more numerous among disaffected devotees outside the movement. The North American Prabhupada Centennial Survey found that less than a quarter (23 percent, or 142) of ISKCON's full-time members and somewhat fewer than half (45 percent, or 66) of the devotees no longer active in ISKCON agreed with the statement, "To my understanding, Prabhupada wanted the 11 *ritviks* he appointed to continue as *ritviks* after his departure." A considerable majority (86 percent, or 156) of the full-time ISKCON members agreed that "[a] devotee not yet initiated must accept a living *guru* if he or she is to make full spiritual advancement." By contrast, just over half (52 percent, or 70) of those no longer active in ISKCON agreed with this statement.

Setting aside theological debates about whether initiation requires a "living guru" (see, e.g., K. dasa 1990), those championing the ritvik-as-initiator position offer one solution to the crisis of religious authority that has confronted ISKCON and the broader movement. Continuing to honor Prabhupada as spiritual master and the source of religious authority within the movement has restored legitimacy to the guru institution, if not to ISKCON as a whole.[10]

Prabhupada and Religious Authority

While the ritvik-as-initiator interpretation of succession provided those outside of ISKCON with a structural basis for maintaining Prabhupada's religious authority, those within ISKCON had to find other ways to maintain their faith in Prabhupada and ISKCON. In the midst of scandal and divisive internal politics, many sought solace and renewal in the purity they associated with Srila Prabhupada and his teachings. As one Prabhupada disciple who joined ISKCON in 1969 commented: "Every aspect of my life has been and is influenced by Srila Prabhupada. . . . I love his ISKCON and am sorry for the all the duplicity, hypocrisy, problems, and fallen leadership, etc., but I cannot and will not let it ever effect my spiritual growth or faith." Although we might expect Prabhupada disciples to turn to their spiritual master in the face of organizational crisis, in fact many other devotees chose to do so as well.

A near equal percentage of Prabhupada disciples (85 percent, or 155) and those of the new gurus (88 percent, or 114) agreed with the statement, "Whatever ISKCON's past or present faults, it still represents Prabhupada and on that basis I will forever be connected to ISKCON." Illustrating this commitment to Prabhupada—and through him to ISKCON—are comments made by two disciples of ISKCON's new gurus. The first is a disciple of a guru expelled from ISKCON in 1986: "Prabhupada is the absolute authority. He gave us our direct connection to Krishna and the *Parampara* through his books and instructions. Without the pure devotee, we would have nothing. He gave (and still gives) us everything as individuals, and as a society."

The second is a disciple of one of the remaining five original gurus following Prabhupada: "I see Prabhupada as my grandfather, hero, saint, scholar-teacher, inspiration and friend. I feel greatly indebted to Srila Prabhupada and will sincerely try to please him for the rest of my life. I really feel that I love Prabhupada and long for the day when I will meet him, speak with him, and personally serve him. This is my constant meditation and life's goal. I see my Spiritual Master as Prabhupada's associate and so for that reason I also feel great attachment and respect for him."

And finally, an eighteen-year-old second-generation woman who intends to take ritvik initiation from Srila Prabhupada in the future explained: "Srila Prabhupada is like a guiding beacon in the fog of *maya* [material illusion]. Sometimes the fog is so thick, I cannot see his light, but when I do catch a glimpse of that light I navigate towards it. Every morning and evening I worship my Prabhupada *murti* [image], offer obeisances, and offer all food that I cook. By daily remembering him I continually re-evaluate my spiritual standing and try to progress more on the path. Srila Prabhupada gives us the highest treasures and I want to develop my love and faith and understanding. Someday soon, I want to render great service to please his Divine Grace."

The Timing of Insurgency

Social protest and movement mobilization historically have emerged in contexts of political instability, especially where elites are in a state of disarray, with relatively weak authority and power. Such a situation presents opportunities for successful collective action. Politically and socially fragmented elites cannot mobilize effectively against the forces of change.

Within the first year after Prabhupada's death, some Prabhupada disciples mobilized politically against the gurus and what they referred to as the "appointment myth" (Rochford 1985, 236–245). This insurgency failed, however, as activists were forced out of the movement by ISKCON's leadership, or they exited voluntarily seeing little or no scope for change (Rochford 1985, 1989). Prospects for organized protest changed when several gurus became involved in illegal, corrupt, and immoral behavior and increased after the GBC was implicated in the widely discredited zonal acarya system.[11] This combination of guru misconduct and GBC complicity defined ISKCON's "crisis of authority" in the early 1980s, providing dissidents with both the political opportunity and leverage necessary to challenge successfully the prevailing structures of power, and thereby to reestablish the centrality of Srila Prabhupada's religious authority in ISKCON and throughout the broader movement.

Notes

1. The Hare Krishna movement originated in India and was brought to the United States in 1965 by A. C. Bhaktivedanta Swami, or Srila Prabhupada, as he is called by ISKCON members. Dedicated to spreading Krishna Consciousness throughout the world, ISKCON has communities and preaching centers on every continent. At its height during the mid-1970s, approximately 5,000 core members lived in its communities. During the 1980s ISKCON became a congregation-based movement, a shift furthered by the involvement of Asian Indian immigrants in various communities. More recently the movement has successfully recruited new members in Eastern Europe and the former Soviet Union. The Krishna devotee seeks self-realization through *bhakti-yoga* (devotion to God), a practice that requires chanting Hare Krishna and a life-style free from meat, intoxicants, illicit sex, and gambling. On the movement's historical roots in India, see Judah 1974 and Brooks 1989; for a more detailed history of ISKCON's development in North America, see Rochford 1985, 1989, 1995a and b, 1997; and Shinn 1987.
2. This study is based on twenty years of research on ISKCON in North America that has combined participant observation, interviewing, and surveys. All numerical and narrative data presented here are from 1994 and 1995 surveys of present and former ISKCON members in the United States (N=390), part of the "Prabhupada Centennial Survey," a nonrandom survey conducted in more than

forty countries with more than 1,800 devotee respondents. For a more detailed discussion of my research methods, see Rochford 1985, 1992.

3. I rely to a great extent in the discussion that follows on Chaves 1993a and Chaves 1993b.

4. Agency structures view the congregation as a source of funds and other resources (e.g., legitimacy, power, expertise) critical for organizational maintenance and the realization of goals. Congregations also represent a primary market for organizational services and products (religious literature, social services) (Chaves 1993b, 9). More precisely, for religious authority structures, congregations are primarily objects of control and secondarily a resource base. For agency structures, congregations represent a resource base only (Chaves 1993a, 155).

5. The Sanskrit word *acarya* can mean "guru" but is more often reserved for a charismatic teacher and leader around whom an institution emerges.

6. As elsewhere (Rochford 1995b), I have chosen to use the actual names of guru leaders because other scholars (Shinn 1987), journalists (Hubner and Gruson 1988), and former ISKCON members (Gelberg 1988, 1991; Muster, 1994) have done so in their writings on the movement.

7. After being expelled from ISKCON, Kirtanananda made a number of changes in his New Vrindaban community, most significantly introducing interfaith practices. Until 1994, the spiritual life of New Vrindaban blended Christian, Native American, and other religious traditions with Krishna Consciousness. The community hosted numerous interfaith conferences until 1993. After winning his appeal for a new trial, Kirtanananda returned to New Vrindaban in the fall of 1993, only to be discovered to be involved in illicit sex. Thereafter he left New Vrindaban and, in 1995, was living nearby with a handful of his disciples while awaiting trial. New Vrindaban in all likelihood will reunite with ISKCON after various legal cases involving the community are finally resolved. Other communities in Ohio and India previously aligned with Kirtanananda have already rejoined ISKCON. New Vrindaban has returned to its former Krishna conscious religious practices and way of life, having abandoned the interfaith experiment.

8. Ravindra Svarupa dasa, one of the leaders of the reform movement and a religion scholar, argues that eliminating the exclusive vyasasana for the zonal acaryas was crucial to eliminating the system itself. "This proposal abolished the exclusive *vyasasana*, the symbol of the zonal *acarya's* sovereignty. . . . I realized . . . that if the symbol of the system [was] eliminated, it would go far to eliminate the system" (1994, 16).

9. These percentages are based on responses to the following Likert scaled item: "The 'reform movement' of the mid-1980s basically resolved the guru controversies within ISKCON." Here, as elsewhere in the chapter, I report data for full-time ISKCON members and ex-ISKCON members only. The response pattern of congregational ISKCON members in each case fell between these two categories of devotees, although their attitudes more closely approximate those of full-time ISKCON members.

10. The *ISKCON Journal* devoted an entire issue in 1990 to respond to the ritvik question after the GBC was provoked into a response by the editors of the *Vedic Village Review*, the official publication of the dissident, but now disbanded, New

Jaipur community in Mississippi. Seventeen interviews, articles, and letters addressed the guru issue in general, and the ritvik question in particular.

11. Ironically, the scandalous guru behavior may have preserved ISKCON as a religious organization. Had the gurus been able to establish their religious authority within the context of the zonal acarya system, there is reason to believe that ISKCON would have splintered into separate institutions led by individual gurus.

References

Berry, Jason. 1992. *Lead Us Not into Temptation: Catholic Priests and the Sexual Abuse of Children*. New York: Doubleday.

Brooks, C. 1989. *The Hare Krishnas in India*. Princeton, N.J.: Princeton University Press.

Chaves, Mark. 1994. "Secularization as Declining Religious Authority." *Social Forces* 72(3): 749–774.

———. 1993a. "Denominations as Dual Structures: An Organizational Analysis." *Sociology of Religion* 54 (2):147–69.

———. 1993b. "Intraorganizational Power and Internal Secularization in Protestant Denominations." *American Journal of Sociology* 99 (1): 1–48.

dasa, Karnamrta. 1990. *Living Still in Sound*. Washington, Miss.: New Jaipur.

dasa, Ravindra Svarupa. 1994. "Cleaning House and Cleaning Hearts: Reform and Renewal in ISKCON." Typescript.

———. 1985a. "Reflections of Brahminical Management." Typescript.

———. 1985b. "Serving Srila Prabhupada's Will." Typescript.

———. 1985c. "'Under My Order . . .': Reflections on the Guru in ISKCON." Typescript.

dasa, Rupavilasa. 1990. "Ritvik or Guru." In *Living Still in Sound*, edited by K. dasa. Washington, Miss.: New Jaipur/

Gamson, William. 1975. *The Strategy of Social Protest*. Homewood, Ill: Dorsey.

Gelberg, Steven. 1991. "The Call of the Lotus-Eyed Lord: The Fate of Krishna Consciousness in the West." In *When Prophets Die: The Postcharismatic Fate of New Religious Movements*, edited by T. Miller. Albany: State University of New York Press.

———. 1988. "The Fading of Utopia: ISKCON in Transition." *Bulletin of the John Rylands University Library of Manchester* 70 (3): 171–183.

Goswami, S. 1986. *Guru Reform Notebook*. Washington D.C.: Gita-nagari Press.

"Guru Is Never Appointed." 1980. Mimeograph.

Hubner John, and Lindsey Gruson. 1988. *Monkey on a Stick: Murder, Madness, and the Hare Krishnas*. New York: Harcourt.

ISKCON Journal. 1990.

Jacobs, Janet. 1989. *Divine Disenchantment: Deconverting from New Religious Movements*. Bloomington: Indiana University Press.

Judah, Stillson. 1974. *Hare Krishna and the Counterculture*. New York: Wiley.

Muster, N. 1994. "Betrayal of the Spirit." Typescript.

Prabhupada Anti-Defamation Association. 1993. "Child Molesters: Gurus? The False Krishna Gurus." California.

North American Temple Presidents and the North American Prabhupada Disciples. 1986. Resolutions of the Joint Meeting of the North American Temple Presidents and the North American Prabhupada Disciples, November 17–18. Towaco, N.J.

North American Temple Presidents, Regional Secretaries, and Sannyasis. 1984. Report to North American GBC from the North American Temple Presidents, Regional Secretaries, and Sannyasis, October 12–13. Towaco, N.J.

Rochford, E. Burke, Jr. 1997. "Family Formation, Culture, and Change in the Hare Krishna Movement." In *Srila Prabhupada*, edited by W. Deadwyler, E. B. Rochford, Jr., and S. Rosen. Los Angeles: Bhaktivedanta Book Trust.

———. 1995a. "Family Structure, Commitment, and Involvement in the Hare Krishna Movement". *Sociology of Religion* 56 (2): 153–175.

———. 1995b. "Hare Krishna in America: Growth, Decline, and Accommodation." In *America's Alternative Religions*, edited by Timothy Miller. Albany: State University of New York Press.

———. 1992. "On the Politics of Member Validation: Taking Findings Back to Hare Krishna." In *Perspectives on Social Problems*, edited by G. Miller and J. Holstein. Greenwich, Conn.: JAI Press.

———. 1989. "Factionalism, Group Defection, and Schism in the Hare Krishna Movement." *Journal for the Scientific Study of Religion* 28 (2): 162–179.

———. 1985. *Hare Krishna in America*. New Brunswick, N.J.: Rutgers University Press.

Shinn, L. 1987. *The Dark Lord: Cult Images and the Hare Krishnas in America*. Philadelphia: Westminister.

Shupe, A. 1995. *In the Name of All That's Holy: A Theory of Clergy Malfeasance*. Westport, Conn: Praeger.

Snow D., E. B. Rochford, Jr., S. Worden, and R. Benford.1986. "Frame Alignment Processes, Micromobilization, and Movement Participation." *American Sociological Review* 51: 464–481.

CHAPTER 7

Creating a Culture of Clergy Deviance

PHILIP JENKINS

*S*ince the early 1980s, child sexual abuse by clergy has become one of the most urgent issues in organized religion in North America, the subject of a series of scandals that have caused unparalleled damage to the prestige and credibility of certain groups, above all the Roman Catholic Church. Popular perceptions of this issue may well contain much that is erroneous: Perhaps Catholic clergy are not uniquely prone to this form of offense, and the link between pedophilia and mandatory celibacy less automatic than it is sometimes portrayed (Jenkins 1995, 1996). However, Catholic authorities have faced a large number of these complaints, which at least until the late 1980s they tended to handle in a fashion that was both secretive and unsympathetic toward the child victims and the families concerned (e.g., Burkett and Bruni 1993; Berry 1992; Rossetti 1990). The assumption appears to have been that the offenses, though regrettable, could easily be covered up and the priest concerned moved to a less tempting environment. In many cases, this optimistic approach was unfounded, and a few priests survived to become serial molesters of epic proportions.

The collapse of this discreet approach resulted from a variety of factors: Changes in the legal profession made it both more tempting and more profitable to sue large corporate institutions like the Catholic Church, while political divisions within the Catholic Church itself enhanced the likelihood that scandals would be highlighted to serve the rhetorical goals of respective factions. However, the most critical factor concerned the role of the mass media. Essentially, before the late 1970s, it was all but unthinkable to report publicly on events that would cast the Catholic Church in a bad light; even stories that today seem relatively trivial were quashed. This was all the more true of extremely damaging actions like child sexual abuse. Some improper sexual behavior by Catholic or other clergy is likely to occur in any society or era, and there will always be a few disturbed individuals who offend on a frequent basis. In any society too, at least some children will complain to elders or parents, some of whom will become sufficiently indignant to insist on sanctions or reparation. However, the complete lack of scandals before the 1970s is striking. Except in vulgar squibs and anti-Catholic tracts, the most assiduous search of media sources in any period between, say, 1900 and 1970 will find virtually no evidence of such scandals, no records of Father X being accused (still less convicted) of child molestation or rape. As a visible social problem, clergy sexual abuse simply did not exist in these years.

In such an environment, church authorities could rely completely on immunity from a "bad press" resulting from clergy scandals, sexual or otherwise, and this security had many implications. It meant, for example, that prosecutors who were already unwilling to take on such a powerful adversary would face no external media pressure to pursue these difficult cases, so the likelihood was that complainants would have no recourse outside the institution and would face overwhelming pressure to settle grievances on the terms offered by ecclesiastical authorities. If the Church transferred a deviant priest, the absence of news reports meant that investigators or victims could never construct a pattern of multiple offenses widely separated by time and place. The lack of reports of priestly abuse meant that professionals had no body of data to study, that no one had any means to discern warning signs, in short, that parents and potential victims had no reason to adopt even the most rudimentary forms of protection. Only this thorough news blackout can explain the astonishing circumstances that so frequently come to light in abuse cases in which teachers or parents happily send young boys to spend the night with a priest, to share a room or tent, without the slightest suspicion that anything improper could occur (e.g., Harris 1991).

By far the most important consequence of the news blackout involved the clerical offenders themselves, who found themselves in an environment in which malfeasance was effectively removed from the possibility of sanction. This inevitably created a sense of invulnerability among real or potential wrongdoers, who knew that the most extreme actions could be undertaken in relative safety. We therefore have a perfect illustration of the principles of classical or Beccarian criminology, in which natural hedonism is controlled only by the fear of detection and the certainty of punishment. A social setting totally lacking either of these controls will be characterized by free and unrestricted indulgence in the pleasurable or profitable behavior. The sense that such actions were not only taking place but also evading sanction may well have encouraged others in a given community to experiment with the illicit behavior, which would explain the frequent charges of virtual pedophile rings operating in certain seminaries and closed institutions.

Before the 1960s, both external and internal constraints might have moderated temptations somewhat: respectively, the severe internal discipline exercised by a highly autocratic ecclesiastical structure, and the moralistic ideology that condemned all improper sexual expression. Even these factors did not deter some of the most egregious clerical offenders like the New England priest James Porter, who was educated under the clerical ancien régime and molested dozens of children in the 1960s. However, matters must have deteriorated in later years with the collapse of internal discipline and the extreme shortage of priests, which led the church to ignore all but the gravest personal failings in a desperate effort to keep clergy in orders. Without the external controls provided by the possibility of detection and scandal, the collapse of internal sanctions effectively declared open season for that tiny minority of clergy willing to exploit their position to gratify their sexual desires.

The Silence

The clergy abuse problem must therefore be understood as at least in large part a consequence of the media's abdication of even a notional attempt to observe or chastise the behavior of a very large social institution. In the flood of reporting that has followed recent scandals, it has been common to suggest that this silence was a craven response to "Catholic power," an image that unwittingly or otherwise partakes of anti-Catholic stereotypes throughout U.S. history. In reality, the Catholic Church was by no means the only institution that enjoyed relative immunity from public scandal, whether in sexual or financial matters. Other churches and religious groups tended to be treated gently by police and editors, as much from a fear of undermining public confidence in the institutions as from fear of their economic power. For example, in the area of child sexual abuse, the Boy Scouts of America enjoyed an almost identical news blackout for most of the century, a media attitude that collapsed at almost exactly the same time as the Catholic Church came under assault (Boyle 1994).

Although media reactions depended on more than a simple fear of Catholic power, reactions to Catholic scandals do provide a valuable illustration of the very different investigative standards prevailing for most of the century. Studying these attitudes raises challenging methodological questions, as the most powerful single piece of evidence is, in fact, the total lack of news coverage of child abuse scandals between, say, the 1920s and 1970s. But how is it possible to argue from this negative datum that offenses were in fact occurring, and were in turn being covered up? I maintain that we can proceed by examining media attitudes to less serious offenses or even news depicting the Catholic Church in a negative light and then considering the treatment of sexual issues. In this chapter I draw heavily on examples from Pennsylvania as one of the most heavily Catholic states, and one likely to be representative of the experience of other northern and midwestern industrial regions.

Catholic attitudes to hostile media coverage are sometimes depicted in terms of a hypersensitivity to criticism characteristic of a closed hierarchical institution. Although there may be some truth in this image, since the mid–nineteenth century Catholic clergy and laity had been the targets of virulent antipapist propaganda in U.S. newspapers and pamphlets, which commonly depicted lay people as ignorant and violent, and priests as sexually exploitative and conspiratorial (with the alleged sexual abuse directed at adult women). Mass political movements aimed at destroying Catholic power included the Know-Nothings of the mid–nineteenth century, the American Protective Association of the 1890s, and the Ku Klux Klan of the 1920s. Each had its scurrilous press and its own lecture circuit that paraded legions of purported "defectors," such as alleged former priests or nuns, who would regale audiences with salacious tales of sexual misdeeds behind the walls of rectories and convents. This whole genre was epitomized by the rumored "secret tunnels" that linked the dwellings of priests and nuns, and the hidden cemeteries in which were buried the offspring of these liaisons (on such nativism, see Franchot 1994; Bennett 1990; Schwartz 1984; Greeley 1977; Kinzer 1964; Higham 1955).

By the 1920s, the abundance of such charges provoked ecclesiastical authorities to undertake antidefamation activities of the sort then being pioneered by Jewish community leaders, and tales of lascivious priests or nuns acquired the same ludicrous character as the notorious legends of Jews sacrificing Christian children on the Passover. As in the Jewish case, Catholic papers kept track of the most active enemy speakers and actively discredited their stories wherever possible. Throughout this crucial decade, Catholic diocesan papers carried frequent reports on appearances by alleged ex-nuns and how their tales were challenged and dismantled. The Philadelphia archdiocesan paper offered a characteristic headline in 1925: "New Jersey Towns Hear Neva Miller, Ex-Nun Lecture. Notorious Fake Religious Was Inmate of Reformatory and Magdalene Home, Official Police Records Show," as the

Catholic Standard and Times reported under the headline "Camden News-paper Supports Claim of Faker as Ex-Nun" on May 23.

Catholic leaders also created liaisons with the press to aggressively and proactively prevent the spread of anticlerical slanders. These efforts were co-ordinated through the National Catholic Welfare Council, "an efficient and aggressive organization that is the envy of many other American religious groups." Those suspicious of Catholic ambitions viewed the hierarchy as an Orwellian juggernaut: "The bureaus of the N.C.W.C. are full of busy young priests, lobbyists, pamphleteers, journalists, and lawyers who coordinate the Catholic population of the country as one great pressure group when any 'Catholic issue' arises. The Press Department sends out about 60,000 words a week in the form of news releases and feature articles to 437 Catholic pa-pers in this country and beyond . . . in American Catholicism the bishops speak for Catholic power" (Blanshard 1949: 29).

Some of the bitterest early battles concerned the journalistic writings of militant antipapist Katherine Mayo. Her widely published stories and travel tales included the full panoply of anti-Catholic horrors: the ignorance and incest permitted by lax Catholic morality in the Philippines; the U.S. soldiers betrayed and killed by a sly pro-German priest; and vituperative attacks on the Virgin Mary and the Immaculate Conception (e.g., Mayo 1925).[1] In the years 1924–1925, at the height of Klan antipopery campaigns, Catholic pres-sure forced the removal of Mayo's writings from several leading publications and demanded apologies from others. The *Philadelphia Public Ledger* de-scribed the article it had published as "baseless, irreverent and offensive," while the *Saturday Evening Post* and *Ladies Home Journal* came under bit-ter attack. In retrospect, it is perhaps less remarkable that such columns were driven from the mainstream press than that the editors still, at this late date, felt they could flout the opinions of such a large and well-organized pres-sure group. The battles had a long and bitter aftermath.

By the 1920s, a series of such conflicts and boycotts had created a modus vivendi between the secular press and the Catholic Church, which in effect removed from the press not merely the gross tales of the militant big-ots, but virtually any hostile reporting concerning the clergy, or even the Catholic population at large. Any such story would be challenged, usually with a suggestion that the media outlet in question was repeating the "secret tunnel" legend. For the next four decades, the best tribute to the success of this stringent unofficial censorship was not only the lack of critical stories, but the virtual absence even of complaints about media timidity.

However, some illustrative exceptions occurred, especially in the anti-

Catholic journalism of George Seldes and Paul Blanshard, who published a series of exposés about the excesses of the hierarchy and its threat to free speech. In 1938, for instance, Seldes wrote that the Catholic Church was "one of the most important forces in American life, and the only one about which secrecy is generally maintained, no newspaper being brave enough to discuss it, although all fear it and believe that the problem should be dragged into the open and made publicly known." For the media, the consequences of non-compliance could be painful, and Seldes (1941, 34–35) claimed that "[t]o criticize the Catholic Church is to invite a boycott, the withdrawal of advertising, loss in circulation and in revenue." As Paul Blanshard (1949, 195–198) wrote in 1949, "As a result of this policy of siege and boycott, very few publishers in the United States are courageous enough or wealthy enough to deal frankly with Catholic social policy or stories of priestly crime."

Not all newspapers and magazines observed the censorship as fully as the hierarchy would have liked, though when scandals did erupt they usually concerned matters that seem quite trivial in retrospect. In 1944, for example, a brief report of a priest found driving drunk with a woman companion attracted costly reprisals against the *San Francisco News*. In response to inquiries, the archdiocesan office responded, probably accurately, that "[n]o one in San Francisco has ever used a story like that"; and the crime referred to was a relatively minor offense by the standards of the 1940s ("Catholic Campaign" 1944). *Time* magazine was regularly targeted for its willingness to offend Catholic sensibilities on issues like the Spanish Civil War, where the Church regarded any sympathy for the leftist republican cause as tantamount to an endorsement of anticlerical persecution (see "Time Magazine Scored for Anti-Catholic Slurs," *Catholic Standard and Times,* September 1, 1944). *Time* attracted further ecclesiastical ire for reporting both the San Francisco arrest and the ensuing media controversy.

Offending the sensibilities of the hierarchy brought on more than mere displeasure. In one 1940s case, a teenage girl died attempting to escape from a home for delinquents in Washington D.C., and subsequent coverage in one city newspaper painted a hostile picture of the nuns operating the institution, charging what would today be termed physical abuse. Catholic organizations mounted an advertising boycott and a campaign among the readership with the result that "in two weeks the paper lost forty percent of its circulation" (Blanshard 1949, 195–198). Boycotts could be devastatingly effective weapons and, in 1947, Philadelphia's Cardinal Dougherty threatened to shut down the city's cinema industry by ordering Catholics to observe a year-long boycott of theaters showing unpalatable films like *Forever Amber* and *The Outlaw,* as a *Catholic Standard and Times* editorial noted in November of that year. Nor were Church authorities modest about their ability to invoke secular sanctions. In 1939, the newspaper of the Philadelphia archdiocese, the *Catholic Standard and Times*, noted on January 6 under "Notable Events in the Church in America during 1938" that "[t]here were in the course of the year sporadic slurs upon the Catholic church in publications in various parts of the country. In at least one instance the offending publication was a secular college paper. The Government found it necessary to ban certain issues of these publications from the mails."

Boycotts were usually organized through powerful groups like the Knights of Columbus, the Legion of Decency (1934), and the National Organization for Decent Literature. Though the last two groups focused their attention on obscenity, they were also called on to attack films or publications that seemed anti-Catholic, a label that could cover anything opposing fundamental Catholic political beliefs (Boyle 1994). In the 1930s, for example, the Legion of Decency attacked films that supported the Spanish republicans. By the late 1940s, the Legion of Decency was censoring some 450 films each year, demanding changes in films that took a less than rosy view of the clergy of any denomination (e.g., Black 1944; Skinner 1993; Blanshard 1949). Formal legal sanctions also applied; until 1952, for example, New York state law prohibited showing "sacrilegious" films, however serious their artistic intent.

Those who violated the rules had to make humiliating apologies. In Philadelphia, for example, the great liberal paper of the 1930s and 1940s was the *Philadelphia Record*, owned by J. David Stern, a maverick press lord who resigned from the conservative publishers' cartel, and who consistently supported organized labor and the New Deal. Throughout the 1930s, the *Record* was the only paper in the city and sometimes in the state that would publish stories seen as too difficult by other proprietors. George Seldes (1941) described Stern as one of a tiny minority of owners in America who really wanted to publish a free newspaper. However, even Stern found the Catholic Church too powerful an enemy. One condemnation of General Franco and the nationalist cause in Spain proved too strong for the local Catholic archdiocese, which threatened a boycott and forced a groveling retraction of the pro-Loyalist stance. In 1940, the *American Magazine* of Milwaukee was coerced into a similar capitulation after publishing a short story that contained a perceived attack on the Catholic priesthood, as the *Catholic Standard and Times* reported under "Magazine Editor Apologizes for Slur on Clergy" on July 12.

Once the Church had brought mainstream newspapers and radio stations into line, the hierarchy could concentrate on a second tier of publications, including satirical and sectarian publications that hoped to exercise more freedom. In 1934, for example, the *Harvard Journal* on April 16 published an attack on "the well drilled corps of priests" who ran the Legion of Decency, "a powerful lever in the hands of the Jesuitical and morally indignant Archbishop," and referred to the "Catholic organization, with its regimental draft of blindly obedient underlings on the one hand, and its Machiavellian pontiff on the other." Though Harvard may have been too daunting an opponent to bring into line, even here the Legion coordinated a strenuous protest, well supported by political allies (Boyle 1994).

In this environment, there was an impressively long catalog of untouchable stories that could not be used or printed. Obviously, the media had to treat any story about criminal priests with extreme tenderness, but clergy could not even be reported unflatteringly; nor could Catholic groups or organizations, even if operating outside the protection of the official Church. In the late 1930s, for example, there were extensive pro-Nazi and anti-Semitic activities by demagogues like Father Charles Coughlin, whose Christian Front followers undertook extensive violence in cities like New York, Boston, and Philadelphia. Though the press occasionally reported these actions, they are virtually never treated for what they were—the work of Irish Catholic gangs often inspired by priests—but were euphemistically attributed to "Nazis" or "Bund supporters." Boston media went still further in 1943, when they refused to cover anti-Jewish rioting by local Irish gangs organized by the Christian Front. "Concealed behind a thorough news blackout," the riots were reported in no paper in the city or state (Gunther 1951, 529).

Fictional treatments of Catholic issues had to tread as gingerly as did news coverage, and the motion picture industry was especially sensitive, as the *New York Times Magazine* pointed out in "Hollywood Walks Warily" on August 23, 1936. Apart from the obvious boycott threat, Hollywood magnates were vulnerable to comments about the overwhelmingly Jewish composition of the industry and feared charges of anti-Christian bias. The situation was all the more perilous in the mid-1930s, when Coughlin's followers emphasized the role of Jewish Hollywood in corrupting America and spreading Communism. In consequence, film treatments of Catholic clergy in the 1930s and 1940s never fall short of the heroic or saintly. The high point of this near hagiography came between 1938 and 1944, also the apex of popular anti-Semitism in U.S. cities: These were the years of film classics like *The Keys of the Kingdom, Going My Way, Boys Town, The Bells of St. Mary's,* and *Angels with Dirty Faces* (Keyser and Keyser 1984). In 1947, John Ford's *The Fugitive* was based on the novel *The Power and the Glory*, and here the priest-hero usually appears accompanied by streams of light and angelic music. Moreover, the movie version omits the priest's alcoholism, a key theme of the book. *I Confess* (1953) featured a priest suspected of murder but only because of his laudable refusal to breach the secrecy of the confessional. Ultrarespectful treatment of Catholic priests also extended to the clergy and faithful of other denominations and religions.

Sexual Scandals

If the media could not report or depict a priest who was drunk, how much more unthinkable that they could suggest sexual impropriety. At least occasional cases of drunk driving or physical brutality might occur in the media, if only long enough to be denounced by the local diocese. Suggesting sexual liaisons fell into an utterly different category, and for evidence we have to look at the scurrilous anti-Catholic tracts that had considerable clandestine circulation through these years. *Converted Catholic Magazine* favored horror stories of Catholic misdeeds, which apparently included sinister alliances with every dictatorship and massacre in modern history. Several authors specialized in this material, often former clergy like Joseph McCabe (1926, 1937, 1946) and Emmett McLoughlin (1954, 1960, 1963). Sexual charges are much in evidence. In *The Truth about the Catholic Church* (1926), ex-monk McCabe recounted many scandals involving drunkenness and sexual license, which commonly took the form of priests living in virtual marriage with their ostensible housekeepers, while McLoughlin published a study titled *Crime and Immorality in the Catholic Church* (1962).

However, there is an oddity here. For all their zeal to expose Catholic atrocities, even these works contain no accounts of the child sexual abuse that one presumes to have been endemic. The scandals McCabe relates all involve stable heterosexual liaisons, and he suggests that he was in effect shielded from most of these tales because of his youth and innocence. McLoughlin similarly focuses little attention on the pederast/pedophile issue, although he grew up in a California Christian Brothers seminary, where one might hypothesize that he at least heard rumors of such activities. Indeed, his *Crime and Immorality* mainly addresses charges that Catholic education, moral practice, and (above all) celibacy encouraged crime, illegitimacy, and mental illness, rather than the sort of child exploitation one would today expect from such a title.

Pederastic behavior may have been rare in those years, but we should not overlook the possibility that the act was simply too shocking, too horrifying to describe in print, and even to mention it placed a work in the category of obscenity. In support of this view, we note the largest "priestly pedophile" investigation in history, which occurred in 1936–1937 when the German Nazi government wished to destroy the prestige of the Catholic Church (Grünberger 1974, 557–558; Micklem 1939, 156–161). As the *Catholic Standard and Times* reported under "Immorality Trials Extended to Austria" on July 8, 1938, and the *Catholic Register* reported under "Nazi Charges of Immorality Are Poorly Founded" on November 7, 1939, the Nazis arrested and tried hundreds of priests and religious on charges of child molestation and homosexuality, the vast majority of which are generally taken to be fraudulent and based on evidence improperly taken from mentally defective children. In Germany itself, the party press covered the charges extensively in the most obscene detail, causing a reaction from the most unexpected quarter. Nazi women's organizations protested the public availability of the graphic detail, and widespread public sympathy for the priests was reported. Even the Nazi courts were soon returning acquittals. In the United States, the child molestation charges were scarcely mentioned in the vast literature cataloging the horrors of the Nazi regime. When they were addressed at all, they were described as "immorality charges" and the "scandal trials." The unsuspecting reader of a Church periodical or secular journal would conclude that the priests were charged, at worst, with violating their celibacy rules with adult women, or perhaps consorting with prostitutes. Pedophilia or pederasty was literally a crime that could not be named; *clerical* pedophilia was an offense that could not even be conceived.

Breaking the Wall

Although media restraint toward clerical misconduct seems to belong to a very different world, it is a recent one. The remarks of a journalist about one suppressed scandal in Massachusetts as late as the mid-1970s applied to almost any community with a strong Catholic presence: "If any priest had any sexual problems or was involved in a compromising incident—even if it involved an arrest—the diocese could prevail upon the local papers not to write about it and upon the district attorney's office not to prosecute. To reveal a priest's shortcomings was akin to blasphemy in the eyes of diocesan officials, and they were ever vigilant against such disclosures" (Wilkes 1993, 68). In 1981 a conservative Catholic reminisced that "[i]t was not long ago that the press would file the story of a bishop arrested for drunken driving" (Kelly 1981, 315).

Not until the late 1970s did a thaw clearly set in, as suggested by an outpouring of fictional works between about 1976 and 1982. This was for example the era of the lurid television miniseries *The Thorn Birds*; of films like *Monsignor* and *Nasty Habits*; of novels like Iris Murdoch's *Henry and Cato*, Patricia Nell Warren's *Fancy Dancer*, and John Gregory Dunne's *True Confessions*. Most of these works depicted clerical sexuality; some explored still more delicate themes of homosexuality, and some even hinted at pedophilia. In addition, true-crime exposés purported to reveal sinister financial and criminal enterprises associated with the Vatican. The most sensational product of this era was Andrew Greeley's 1981 novel, *The Cardinal Sins*, which depicted sexual and financial misdeeds in the Archdiocese of Chicago. The press ran several exposés of real-life clerical fraud and sexual exploitation, including the real-life malfeasance on which Greeley based his book. The first child abuse suits began to appear in U.S. courts and, moreover, to be covered somewhat tentatively in the press.

None of these books could have been published in the 1930s or 1940s, at least without setting off a boycott that would probably have closed the publishing house or movie studio concerned, if direct government censorship had not intervened first. Nor could the newspapers have ventured so boldly into exploring the financial exploits of Cardinal Cody, or the early reports of pedophile clergy. Something clearly had changed, beyond the general relaxation of standards regarding what could appear in print. These new developments certainly reflected the influence of Watergate and the consequent vogue for investigative journalism or muckraking. In addition, a generation of legal decisions had strengthened the ability of journalists to report on such powerful institutions, while reducing the range of legal protections available to the churches.

Both political and demographic changes also played their part. In the 1920s, demographic developments permitted the U.S. Catholic Church hierarchy to undertake aggressive measures against anti-Catholic defamation. Following the great migrations at the turn of the century, the main metropolitan centers had a strongly Catholic character; media corporations knew that much of their business depended on the purchasing power of populations who were largely Irish, Italian, or Slavic. In most cities, these groups tended to ally themselves with the Democratic party, an alliance consummated by the triumph of the Roosevelt administration and the New Deal. The strength of the urban Democratic machines indirectly gave the Catholic hierarchy unparalleled power, which in some areas lasted until quite recent years. However, changes in urban population structure in the 1950s and 1960s broke up many traditional Catholic neighborhoods and created new suburban communities, wealthy, well educated, and generally less willing than their urban forebears to observe strict Church discipline. This meant initially that Catholic bishops and archbishops lost much of their power in urban affairs, as well as the automatic veto power over prosecutions and investigations of felonious clerics. Coupled with wider changes in the international Church, the hierarchy faced a severe reduction in its power over the secular world and, more troubling, over its own flocks.

The weakening of internal Catholic solidarity was critical to the new media environment. Before the 1960s, the very vigor of external assaults had reinforced the strength and ideological homogeneity of Catholic culture. The outrageous nature of the obscene stories peddled by the American Protectionist Association and the Ku Klux Klan effectively immunized the Catholic laity against listening to any such story that might arise in the future; they were no more likely to accept a tale of a pedophile priest than of the "secret tunnels" and baby cemeteries. Well into the late 1980s, a newspaper or television station that told even a well-authenticated story of clerical pederasty expected numerous letters complaining of its anti-Catholic bias and threatening boycotts.

However, Catholic attitudes irrevocably changed with the ecclesiastical disputes that followed the Second Vatican Council of 1963–1965, which in North America caused decades of controversy between liberals and conservatives over issues like papal authority, the ordination of women, clerical celibacy, and access to contraception and abortion. Though notionally part of the same Church, the two wings became almost rival sects, each with its own network of news media and institutions, and each prepared to confront the hierarchy openly over issues of principle (Jenkins 1996; McBrien 1992; Lernoux 1989; Lader 1987). In the 1980s, these rival Catholic groups first drew public attention to the alleged epidemic of sexual abuse within the Church, each for its ideological goals While conservatives used the pedophile issue to stigmatize homosexual priests, liberals focused on the same theme to force the hierarchy to confront its alleged hypocrisy over sexual orthodoxies. A liberal paper, the *National Catholic Reporter*, in1985 launched the first exposé of the numerous cover- ups of clerical abuse cases nationwide. This coverage by a Catholic paper permitted secular papers to examine the same topics with less fear of being denounced for anti-Catholic bigotry. For better or worse, the *National Catholic Reporter* coverage opened up the whole "pedophile priest" crisis. Media investigations soon reached epic proportions, with something of a national feeding frenzy between about 1992 and 1994.

In contrast to the midcentury's extreme diffidence about offending the Church, works of the last decade have indulged in the most extreme and damaging stereotypes. Andrew Greeley's best-selling 1993 novel, *Fall from Grace,* concerns a fictional "pedophile priest," a sado-masochist and a multiple child molester, who specializes in the anal rape of ten- to twelve-year-old boys. He is also a cryptosatanist. Though the image is repulsive in itself, the priest receives virtual carte blanche to carry out his crimes from diocesan authorities who care only for the reputation and financial health of the Church. Fantasy author Whitley Strieber's *Unholy Fire* (1992) depicts a boy so traumatized by priestly abuse that, as a Catholic priest himself, he becomes a serial killer.

Explorations of the once unthinkable have not diminished in recent years. In mid-1995, for example, the media gave heavy play to a new film, *Priest,* which frankly explored both homosexual and heterosexual behavior in a group of Catholic clergy. Apart from the obvious objections from Catholic believers, the film attracted obloquy because it was originally scheduled to be released on Good Friday. Meanwhile, Thomas M. Disch's novel *Priest* portrays a cleric as a promiscuous homosexual and child molester who gives hypocritical public statements on the necessity for enforcing strict sexual morality. The coverage of true-life abuse cases continued unabated, and a typical issue of the *National Catholic Reporter* on April 21, 1995, contained several related abuse stories. One was headlined "Man Sues, Charges Abuse and Priest Sex Parties"; "Priestly Discontent Smolders in Winona" explored bitter interclerical disputes in a Minnesota diocese, with some of the participants under suspicion of improper sexual behavior. Nor were the Church's difficulties confined to child abuse, as the article "Male Religious More Alcoholic, Study Finds" indicated. Priests as pedophiles, drunkards, hypocrites, even serial killers: Taken together, an image of the Catholic Church that would have struck the public as inconceivably negative in 1980, let alone 1940. While not wishing a return to the sickly sweet Bing Crosby image of the Catholic priest, it is difficult to deny that the pendulum has swung too far in the other direction.

The Media Awareness Issue

Not all memories of childhood abuse are authentic, and we should treat some of the recent charges against Catholic clergy skeptically. On the other hand, we now have numerous instances of specific allegations verified not only by multiple witnesses but also by the offenders themselves, as well as by internal Church investigations that long remained concealed. Some of these confirmed or probable cases concern offenses that occurred in the 1950s or even earlier, with a great many located in the 1960s. In other words, they occurred at a time when, according to the most thorough review of court records and contemporary media, such activities simply did not and could not occur. We therefore have a clear example of an unbridgeable gap between actual experience and media perception. Though the press reported no "clergy abuse problem" in 1950 or 1965, the behavior itself assuredly existed.

As I have argued here, the disjuncture between reality and reporting may also have contributed to increasing the frequency of the deviant behavior itself, by removing any chance of sanction against offending clergy, who were thus literally beyond reproach. Media attitudes therefore helped create an absolutely criminogenic social environment. The extent to which that environment was exploited would become apparent only decades afterwards.

Notes

1. There was also extensive coverage in the Philadelphia press during January 1925; in the *Catholic Standard and Times*, January 3, 1925; the *Sun Transcript*, January 11, 1925; and the *Public Ledger*, January 11, 1925.

References

Bennett, David H. 1990. *The Party of Fear*. New York: Vintage.

Berry, Jason. 1992. *Lead Us Not into Temptation*. New York: Doubleday.

Black, Gregory D. 1994. *Hollywood Censored: Morality Codes, Catholics, and the Movies*. New York: Cambridge University Press.

Blanshard, Paul. 1949. *American Freedom and Catholic Power*. Boston: Beacon.

Boyle, Hugh. 1933–38. Papers of Bishop Hugh Boyle. Papers Relating to Legion of Decency, Archives of the Diocese of Pittsburgh, Pennsylvania.

Boyle, Patrick. 1994. *Scout's Honor: Sexual Abuse in America's Most Trusted Institution*. Rocklin, Calif.: Prima.

Burkett, Elinor, and Frank Bruni. 1993. *Gospel of Shame*. New York: Viking.

"Catholic Campaign." 1944. *Time* (October 23): 59.

Franchot, Jenny. 1994. *Roads to Rome: The Antebellum Protestant Encounter with Catholicism*. Berkeley: University of California Press.

Greeley, Andrew. 1977. *An Ugly Little Secret*. Kansas City, Mo.: Sheed, Andrews, and McMeel.

Grünberger, Richard. 1974. *A Social History of the Third Reich*. London: Penguin.

Gunther, John. 1951. *Inside USA*. New York: Harper.

Harris, Michael. 1991. *Unholy Orders: Tragedy at Mount Cashel*. Toronto: Penguin.

Higham, John. 1955. *Strangers in the Land: Patterns of American Nativism, 1860–1925.* New Brunswick, N.J.: Rutgers University Press.

Jenkins, Philip. 1996. *Pedophiles and Priests: Anatomy of a Social Crisis.* New York: Oxford University Press.

———. 1995. "Clergy Sexual Abuse: The Symbolic Politics of a Social Problem." In *Images of Issues,* edited by Joel Best. 2d ed. Hawthorne, N.Y.: Aldine de Gruyter.

Kelly, George A. 1981. *The Battle for the American Church.* New York: Doubleday Image.

Keyser, Les J.. and Barbara Keyser. 1984. *Hollywood and the Catholic Church.* Chicago: Loyola University Press.

Kinzer, Donald L. 1964. *An Episode in Anti-Catholicism: The American Protective Association.* Seattle: University of Washington Press.

Lader, Lawrence. 1987. *Politics, Power, and the Church: The Catholic Crisis and Its Challenge to American Pluralism.* New York: Macmillan.

Lernoux, Penny. 1989. *People of God.* New York: Viking.

Mayo, Katherine. 1925. *The Isles of Fear: The Truth about the Philippines.* New York: Harcourt Brace.

McBrien, Richard P. 1992. *Report on the Church: Catholicism after Vatican II.* San Francisco: Harper.

McCabe, Joseph. 1946. *Rome Irreconcilable with Democracy.* Girard, Kan.: Haldeman Julius.

———. 1937. *The Papacy in Politics Today.* London.

———. 1926. *The Truth about the Catholic Church.* Girard, Kan.: Haldeman Julius.

McLoughlin, Emmett. 1963. *An Inquiry into the Assassination of President Lincoln.* New York: Stuart.

———. 1962. *Crime and Immorality in the Catholic Church.* New York: Stuart.

———. 1960. *American Culture and Catholic Schools.* New York: Stuart.

———. 1954. *People's Padre: An Autobiography.* Boston: Beacon.

Micklem, Nathaniel. 1939. *National Socialism and the Roman Catholic Church.* New York: Oxford University Press.

Rossetti, Stephen J. 1990. *Slayer of the Soul: Child Sexual Abuse and the Catholic Church.* Mystic, Conn.: Twenty-Third Publications.

Schwartz, Michael. 1984. *The Persistent Prejudice.* Huntington, Ind.: Our Sunday Visitor.

Seldes, George. 1941. *Lords of the Press.* New York: Blue Ribbon.

———. 1939. *The Catholic Crisis.* New York: Mesner.

Skinner, James M. 1993. *The Cross and the Cinema: The Legion of Decency and the National Catholic Office for Motion Pictures, 1933–1970.* Westport, Conn.: Praeger.

Wilkes, Paul. 1993. "Unholy Acts." *New Yorker* (June 7):62–79.

CHAPTER 8

Clergy Abuse
in Ireland

A. W. RICHARD SIPE

Rome. March 1994. I ask an official of
one of the nine Vatican congregations why Rome has not been more forthcoming and helpful in dealing with the problem of sexual abuse by priests
in the United States.[1] I receive a clear response: "The Vatican does not understand America. Rome does not understand why the American Bishops cannot control the media and the courts." I am assured that Ireland and Italy are
prominent among the areas where bishops are in control.

Media

Ireland. October 6, 1994. A TV special, "Suffer Little Children," airs.

This documentary recorded the forty-year odyssey of Fr. Brendan
Smyth, an Irish Norbertine monk who had sexually molested uncounted numbers of minors—boys and girls—as he traveled his ministerial circuit.[2] Smyth
had been known by colleagues, religious superiors, and bishops as a sexual
abuser of minors for many years. Smyth's local Norbertine superior of twenty-
five years knew of Smyth's activities, as Ailin Quinlan reported on October
19, 1994, in the *Irish Times* ("Smyth Accused of Sex Abuse in West Cork
School") and Olivia O'Leary reported on November 27 in the *Sunday Tribune* ("Bishop Rejects Church's Position"). Reports like that of the *Irish
Independent*'s Stephen McGrath, "Gardai Not Told of Sex Abuse Claims,"
on October 22 and of the *Sunday Tribune*'s Maeve Sheehan, "Church Protected Sex Abusers: Bishops," on October 23 cited the admission by the
Norbertine abbot general in Rome, Fr. Marcel Van deVen, that a number of
Irish Bishops also knew of Smyth's activities.

Repeated complaints resulted in reassignments and periodic furtive attempts at psychiatric treatment. Smyth had been assigned to numerous parish positions in Scotland, Wales, North Dakota, and Rhode Island, according to Eamon Dunphy of the *Sunday Independent* in "Don't Get Caught, the Hypocrite's Commandment, Gave Fr. Brendan Smyth Sanctuary for Decades," December 4, 1994. The then bishop of Providence, Rhode Island, responded to the priest's sexual activities in that diocese by sending him back to Ireland in 1968. This mode of response typified the handling of sexually abusive religious in Ireland and the United States. Smyth served Catholic parishes in the north and south of Ireland with no restriction of his interaction with minors. He had access to children in Catholic orphanages where he had priest friends who welcomed him on monthly visits; his friends "would supply a number of boys for [Smyth's] sexual amusement." One victim, Danny, had been abused by Smyth for many years by the time he was eleven years old. At that time he was transferred to a second Catholic institution, where Smyth visited him. "Danny was soon thrown into the worst period of his short life, facing sexual abuse on a grand scale, suffering painful degradation and humiliation by up to ten other priests, buggery by other boys in the residence, orchestrated and observed by some of the priests in group sex sessions with other boys led by, and again observed by, other priests" (Moore 1995, 32) .

Ireland's Cardinal Cahal Daly knew about Smyth and wrote letters in 1990 and 1992 to one of Smyth's victims and to the victim's family, as Kevin Myers reported in "An Irishman's Diary" in the *Irish Times* on October 21, 1994. Daly offered sympathy, admitted he knew of the priest's activities and had already spoken to his abbot, but professed he could do "nothing more," as he claimed in the *Sunday Independent* on October 16 under the headline, "Dr. Daly Denies Smyth Case Ignored." Daly was attacked by the Irish media for denying his power. Editorials claimed that he could have done what any good citizen could, that is, report the man to the police. There have been calls for the cardinal's resignation, including one from a nine-year victim of Smyth's abuse, according to the *Irish Times*'s Ailin Quinlan ("Smyth Accused of Sex Abuse in West Cork School," October 19).

The Irish civil authorities also knew of Smyth's activities. Smyth was indicted in a Northern Ireland court in 1993; but his superiors had already reassigned him to work as a chaplain in a hospital in the south, Patricia Deevey reported in the *Sunday Independent* ("Haunted by the Spectre of Abuse," October 16). Both Church and state supported the priest's protracted fight against extradition to Northern Ireland on sex abuse charges. Efforts to protect Smyth from prosecution and the Church from scandal were stances so traditional in Irish church-state politics—where bishops could control the courts and media—the maneuvers were taken for granted. Only this time, media exposure led to a political uproar that challenged ecclesiastical control as never before (see, for example, Bruce Arnold, "Church Putting Itself above Criminal Law on Child Abuse" in the *Irish Independent*, October 22, and the Associated Press's "Irish Government Collapses," November 22).

In January 1994, after several months of resistance by the civil authorities on his behalf, Smyth returned to Northern Ireland on orders from Daly and turned himself over to authorities. He was tried and sentenced to four years in prison in June 1994.

Dublin. November 11, 1994. Prime Minister Albert Reynolds proposes to appoint Harry Whelehan president of the Irish High Court.

Attorney General Harry Whelehan had refused repeated requests from the north for Smyth's extradition, as I reported in "Priest Sex Abuse Stirs Political Storm in Ireland" in the *National Catholic Reporter* on December 2. The appointment's timing was crucial, because promotion to the High Court would place Whelehan beyond Parliament's power to question him

Dublin. November 17, 1994. Reynolds's coalition government falls apart and forces his resignation as prime minister.

Dick Spring, the leader of the Labor party and coalition partner, demanded that Reynolds require Whelehan to explain to Parliament his failure to respond to the extradition warrant in the Smyth case. Reynolds refused to withhold the appointment, exonerating Whelehan, a conservative Catholic, from any blame. Hours after Reynolds resigned, however, Whelehan, too, resigned his post of four days, stories the *Baltimore Sun* reported on November 18 under the headline "Irish Prime Minister Quits In Scandal over Priest: 'You Can't Win 'em All,' Reynolds Says."

In addition to opposing the Whelehan appointment, Spring accused Reynolds of suppressing facts to protect Whelehan. After Whelehan's resignation, Reynolds reversed himself and agreed that Whelehan had been to blame. Smyth's abbot, Norbertine father Kevin Smith, had resigned his position on October 23. He and other officials of church and state were blamed for taking part in a cover-up, the *New York Times*'s James F. Clarity reported on November 17 in "Government Coalition Collapses in Ireland."

The October 16 TV documentary had opened the media flood gates. Until this period, fewer than ten cases of abuse of minors by priests had come before the civil courts in Ireland since 1974, although fifty cases had been processed through canon law channels since then. As Andy Pollack pointed out in the *Irish Times* on October 22 in "Church in Ireland Wakes Up to

Clerical Sex Abuse of Children," critics say these figures hint at massive neg-
ligence. Stories that appeared in the press over the next two years revealed a
variety of clerical sexual activity. The print media backed up their stories with
sharp editorial commentary.

Multiple cases of abuse by priests and religious immediately began to
come before the Irish civil courts. A monsignor, the former president of an
Irish Catholic secondary school, pleaded guilty to sexual assault of an eighteen-
year-old hitchhiker. A religious brother pleaded guilty to assaulting three
eleven-year-old girls. A Belfast priest was accused of abusing nine boys, ages
nine to fifteen. A priest was convicted of raping and sodomizing six boys,
nine to eleven years old, as Charles Mallon reported in "Dublin Priest in Child
Sex Abuse Claim" in the *Evening Herald*, October 22, 1994. I personally have
spoken with a man who alleges abuse by a priest now a member of the Irish
hierarchy.

But child abuse is not the only sexual problem of Catholic clergy. Homosexuality within the priesthood is not a topic of easy public commentary
in Ireland or elsewhere, but the media found an opportunity to break that ta-
boo when a Dublin priest collapsed and died of a heart attack on the floor
of a gay bathhouse at two o'clock A.M. According to Pat Buckley in "Crisis
in the Catholic Church" in the *Belfast Telegraph*, December 16, 1994, men
stepped over and walked around the priest's nude body for two hours before
two other priests, members of the gay club, found him at four o'clock A.M.
(see also Toibin 1995). The owner of the club told the media that at least
twenty Catholic priests belonged to the same club.

Buckley, who speculates that 2,500 of Ireland's priests are involved in
sexual relationships with women, founded a support group for women who
have been in such relationships. The group has seventy-five members in
Belfast. Six of the women have borne priest's children, and four have had
abortions paid for by the priests who impregnated them, Buckley reports.
When conservative commentator and popular singer Father Michael Cleary
died, the woman he lived with for twenty years came forward and revealed
that he had fathered her two children. Although the church initially fought
the claims, the truth of the relationship was incontrovertibly confirmed, as
reported by Sam Smyth in "Angry Fr. Cleary 'Wife' Tells All in New Book"
(*Irish Times,* September 20, 1995) and Clare McKeon in "Phyllis Paints Part
of a Bigger Picture" (*Star,* September 26, 1995).

Dublin. March 8, 1995. The Abortion Information Bill passes Parliament by a vote of 85 to 67.

The 1937 Irish Constitution is intimately bound to Catholic teaching.

Irish Church officials helped draft it, and President deValera submitted the draft to the Vatican for what he hoped would be at the least an unofficial or informal ratification. His submission itself confirmed the alliance between the Church and a state that conceded it would do nothing contrary to Church teaching. The gesture also had some diplomatic logic, asking approval for a struggling new republic where 95 percent of the citizens were Roman Catholic and where for a century the clergy had held enormous practical and political sway. Article 44 of the Constitution acknowledges the special position of the Catholic Church as the guardian of the faith professed by the great majority of the citizens (Keough 1995).

The Abortion Information Bill diminished Church power by allowing certain medical centers to provide abortion information while still banning abortion on Irish soil. Official Catholic teaching on abortion is clear and absolute. Church officials considered the bill a slap at both Church and Constitution and condemned it as defiance by the state.

Dublin. November 24, 1995. The Divorce Referendum, allowing legal divorce in Ireland, passes by a narrow margin.

Some thought that the Divorce Referendum contradicted the "Catholic" Constitution. But as John Drennan reported in "Divorce and the Return of Fear" September 10, 1995, in the *Sunday Independent,* and the Associated Press noted in "Nun Challenges Irish Traditions over Right to Divorce" on November 9, many considered a nun historian, Sister Margaret MacCurtin, a hero in the cause of justice for her support of the bill.

It is difficult to gauge the extent to which the priest sexual scandals influenced the outcome of these two measures, although no one argues that the revelations of abuse strengthened the Church's credibility, especially on sexual matters. The 1980s saw a heated debate over the legalization of condoms, which are also condemned by the Catholic Church and whose sale in the Republic was then illegal, but the victory in the battle to sell condoms came before any media revelation of priest sexual abuse (Toibin 1995, 48).

Ireland. February 22, 1996. The TV special *Dear Daughter* airs.

This docudrama portrayed the lives of some children in the state-owned, Catholic Church–managed schools for orphans and disabled or disadvantaged children. Many of the stories from the 1950s and 1960s recounted beatings, humiliations, and sadistic torture as well as sexual assault inflicted on helpless children by some Sisters of Mercy and their employees. As Anne Boylan wrote in "Hell on Earth for the Sin of Being Born," and Mary Ellen Synon reported in "Unmerciful Nun's Tale" in the *Sunday Independent*, February 25, 1996, it was alleged that some victims were as young as six or eight months old. They were strapped "to pottys all day with the result that their rectums would collapse." In Goldenbridge Orphanage, each girl was known by a number, concentration-camp style. The drama portrayed a ten-year-old girl who moved too slowly for the sisters' pace having a kettle of boiling water poured on her leg. It recounted an instance where another girl's beating by a nun required a hundred stitches to repair.

If the media can serve as a vehicle for the prosecution, it can also serve the defense. Sister Xavieria, a seventy-eight-year-old Mercy nun, one of the principals accused in the documentary, appeared on the media in late April to rebut statements that she had been cruel or abusive. She admitted that she had been too strict but denied scalding anyone with boiling water. Some of her former students spoke in her defense: She was strict and undeniably used corporal punishment, but she was also caring and in many cases showed kindness.

Over a hundred cases of physical and sexual abuse were alleged in the investigation of one Catholic orphanage alone. After the broadcast the Sisters of Mercy made a public apology and established a help-line to support former charges who may have been traumatized while under their care. In one month, more than six hundred people called to tell their stories. After the TV presentation the media floodgates again burst, especially via the radio. Caller after caller recounted beatings, cruelty, and abuse endured both at the orphanages and at school beyond orphanage walls. Men as well as women spoke of being abused as children or of being raped when young. In the last six months of 1995, eight hundred men contacted the rape crisis centers in Ireland. During 1995 ten thousand callers reported alleged child abuse to Childline. Half of the allegations involved sexual abuse. They implicated fathers, mothers, brothers, cousins, uncles, priests, and nuns

The educational and religious systems in Ireland echo the home and vice versa. Media exposure gives substantial credence to Anson Shupe's thesis: "Incidences of clergy malfeasance [are] imbedded in a knowable web of interrelated events that are not as individualist as they must seem to the victims who first experienced them" (1995, 23)

The suddenness and social-political impact of media revelations between 1993 and 1996 of multiple sexual abuse by Roman Catholic priests and religious in Ireland also adds substance to Tom Inglis's analysis: "It is the media that have shattered the myth that it is bad luck to criticize the priest. It is the media that have broken the tradition of not criticizing the church and its teachings in public. It is the media that have forced the church into giving a public account of itself. It was the media and particularly television which brought to an end the long 19th century tradition of Irish Catholicism" (1987, 12).

The Roman Catholic hierarchy in counterattack has blamed the media for the political-religious crisis in Ireland. "Dr. Connell Attacks Politicians and Media" announced the *Irish Times* on September 21, 1995, over a report by Andy Pollack: Archbishop Connell of Dublin had excoriated the media and the legislature for "permissive propaganda that attacks family tradition, Catholic moral values, and promotes a materialistic view of life and hostility toward Catholic standards." In October 1995, Cardinal Cahal Daly, the head of the Irish hierarchy, added his own severe reprimand of the media for its coverage of clerical scandals and tried to undercut the credibility of news reports by implying that the accounts of sexual abuse by priests were based not on fact but on "innuendo, insinuation, hint and suggestion." These attacks recall Cardinal Bernard Law of Boston, who called down the wrath of God on the media for its reporting of the Father James Porter case in 1991 and 1992. The implication was that the media had created the crisis.

The Catholic Church has tried hard to divorce individual clergy malfeasance from any systemic element, in particular the system of mandatory celibacy for priests of the Latin Rite, a sacred and untouchable topic on which the pope himself has forbidden discussion. From a sociological point of view, the ecclesial power and economic structure of the church depend on a male, unmarried clergy. When one Irish bishop, Brendan Comiskey, recommended opening the questions of mandatory celibacy and a married priesthood for debate, he was reprimanded by his cardinal and called to Rome to explain his suggestion of debating questions considered sealed and infallibly irreversible by the Vatican, a story that first appeared in the *Tablet* in London on June 17, 1995, and was reported by Peter Murtagh as "Loneliness of the Long-Distance Bishop" in the *Sunday Times*, September 24, 1995, and as "I Acted but Too Slowly" by Claire Grady in the *Irish Independent*, February 29, 1996.

Comiskey's proposal resulted in personal attacks and media coverage that exposed embarrassing details of his personal life. This time the media coverage seemed to be fueled by Church sources who sprinkled their accounts with innuendo, insinuations, hints, and suggestions, as Gene Kerrigan reported in "Comiskey Gets 90 Per Cent Support in Poll," in the *Sunday Independent*, July 23, 1995. The title of the article, however, which referred to a poll of Irish citizens, showed that public sentiment was on Comiskey's side.

One thing is clear: Sexual activity by priests violates celibate practice as defined by canon law. Researchers independent of the media have demonstrated that celibacy is not a well-kept vow. Studies of the practice of celibacy among Catholic priests in South Africa, the United States, and Spain estimate priest sexual activity between 46 and 60 percent. A 1995 study of the Catholic clergy in Spain claims that 60 percent are sexually active. The author alleges that 7 percent of the total clergy population are involved sexually with minors. An additional sample of 354 sexually active priests in Spain showed 53 percent involved with adult women, 21 percent with adult men, 14 percent with minor boys, and 12 percent with minor girls (Rodriguez 1995).

The bishops of Ireland have sought coaching and advice from the U.S. Church's experience with clergy sexual abuse, a focus of media attention in that country since 1985. Father Stephen Rossetti, director of St. Luke Institute, a treatment center in Maryland for clergy with sexual and psychiatric problems, spent several weeks educating the clergy and bishops in Ireland. On January 30, 1996, the Irish hierarchy promulgated a strong policy statement that calls for full cooperation with the police and the legal system, as the London *Tablet* reported February 3, 1996.

However, the most prominent feature of the Church's counteroffensive against clergy sexual abuse is not reform, but a measured attack on the media with claims of "priest bashing," "church bashing" or "Catholic bashing" at any exposure of priestly malfeasance. For instance, Dr. Dermott Clifford, archbishop of Cashel, led an unsuccessful effort to get the Irish Council of Priests to condemn *Intercom* and *The Furrow*, both prominent Catholic intellectual journals, Fergal Keane reported in "Church Losing Its Former Influence" in the *Sunday Times* on November 28, 1994. Additional elements in the formula for responding to accounts of sexual malfeasance by Catholic priests are: (1) to protest that it is a societal problem, not merely a problem of the Catholic Church; (2) to assert that the number of abusers in the priesthood is no greater, or even less, than in other groups of society; (3) to maintain that abuse of minors by clerics is simply a case of a few bad apples, unrelated to institutional structures, which thus have no responsibility for it; (4) to admit that the hierarchy should apologize to the victims and their families, reassuring them that it is not their fault; and (5) at the same time, to fight legal claims against the Church with every means possible, including the humiliation of victims and accusations against them of instigating the abuse. This strategy is not unlike that of other benevolent institutions accused of malfeasance, for instance, the Boy Scouts of America (Boyle 1994, 314). The Church's public relations offensive is directed by Jim Cantwell in Ireland; the U.S. strategy was employed as a policy from the early 1990s by Monsignor Frank Manascalco, director of communications of the United

States Catholic Conference. Another propaganda unit in the United States, the Catholic League, headed by William Donohue, uses the same tactics and urges boycotts of media entities that expose priestly malfeasance. For instance, in 1995 Donohue urged a boycott of Disney Inc. for releasing the movie *Priest*; in 1996 he called for a boycott of HBO for airing a special, *Priestly Sins: Sex in the Catholic Church*. Both media presentations had been viewed in England and Ireland without significant resistance.

Myth

Ireland revels in myth. The obscurity of its origins (Was it really settled by Phoenicians?), its lyrical and poetic traditions, the romanticism of the Emerald Isle perpetuated by vast numbers of emigrés and people who claim Irish heritage—sixty million people possess Irish passports—plus a glorious mystical history and dramatic oppressions, all conspire to shape and color the myth of holy Ireland. Here is an island oasis of peace where all are united in the holiness of religion, social warmth, and acceptance of the magical (O'Halloran 1994). The dark streaks and somber stories found in works by Irish authors and poets only reemphasize the basic wonder of a special people, much as biblical accounts of sin enhance the truth of the main thrust of the theme—"You are a chosen people" (Cahill 1995).

Now that the media have broken the silence and shouted the secrets woven into the fiber of the myth, no one can predict what permanent effect the current crisis of credibility will have upon Church and state power in Ireland. But many of the factors being exposed beneath the Irish myth have been well known for a long time; Irish authors also embrace and perpetuate a strong strain of realism (Greeley 1972; Breslin 1973; Ardagh 1995). The onslaught of media reports between 1994 and 1996 of sexual abuse by priests and religious in Ireland were less revelations than confirmation of hundreds of thousands of peoples' observations and experience—and permission to talk about their observations openly. As Fintan O'Toole, religion editor of the *Irish Times*, wrote under the headline "Lessons for the Church in Bishop's Painful Experience" on September 29, 1995, "At the level of raw experience, hundreds of thousands of people in Ireland have known for most of their lives that there is a problem of paedophilia within the church." Secrecy and fear of scandal are fostered at the local level, but they are imbedded in canon law and the oath each cardinal makes to the pope. Bishops, superiors, victims, and families have been influenced by these attitudes and have fostered and perpetuated them.

Three books—bestsellers in Ireland between 1983 and 1991—recorded the physical and sexual atrocities endured by children in orphanages and schools under the care of Catholic religious. *Fear of the Collar* is an autobiographical account of life at Artane, the famous industrial school run by the Christian Brothers, where "[e]very brother carried a black jack. It was made of two long pieces of leather, two inches wide and sewn together by a boot maker, . . . some brothers asked to have keys, lead or metal sewn into the bottom part . . . when you were slapped with it across the open hand you could really feel the full force of it" (Touher 1991, 47). The author tells how he was stripped naked, beaten and held across a brother's lap. In that position the brother held the boy's penis in his hand. After the beating the brother hugged and caressed the boy all over, promising to protect him in the future. This mode of sadomasochistic bonding was common and pervasive in Irish culture from 1850 onward. Paddy Doyle's autobiography, *The God Squad*, published in 1988, received the first Christy Brown Award for Literature. It is a tale of trauma and terror told without recrimination or self-pity; some of the nuns who care for him as an orphan from the age of four are kind, warm, and loving, but others are cruel and sadistic, with tragic, lifelong crippling effects for the writer. Mannix Flynn describes unsentimentally childhood in Ireland under the critical eye and harsh discipline of priests and Christian Brothers in his first novel, *Nothing to Say*, published in1983. It too has the ring of authenticity and reflects a tradition of abuse far deeper than most people care to admit.

My point is quite simple: All the revelations in the media about physical and sexual abuse in Ireland have not only been well known but also recorded with completeness and accuracy, although some have been coded under the cloud of censorship in the Irish literary tradition. James Joyce is the prime example.

Joyce's work, especially the *Dubliners* and *A Portrait of the Artist as a Young Man*, illustrates the reality of child abuse and its effects on the lives of Irish people and Irish society at the turn of the century.[3] Over the years Joyce has frequently been treated as a symbolist, or as a psychological realist, reducing the images in his stories to representations of states of mind or psychic processes. But this view contradicts Joyce's own aesthetic, according to which characters, events, locations, and things are *both* real and symbolic. Joyce grounds his work in an actual Dublin, as well as in specific time and according to appropriate modes of discourse—slang, sermons, song lyrics, the language of advertising. All these impel us to consider the gnomon outlined in "The Sisters" as an authentic record of social conditions in Ireland in the last decade of the nineteenth century.

Children in Joyce's Dublin are beaten as a matter of custom. "Counterparts" ends with the brutal beating of a little boy by his father. In "Ivy Day in the Committee Room," an old man remembers nostalgically how he used to beat his son, now grown too big for beating. In *A Portrait,* Steven Daedalus is unjustly beaten by a priest with a pandybat; this incident reappears in the "Circe" section of *Ulysses.* But far from being condemned, the infliction of pain on Irish children is approved by the Church and the family as "the right way to bring up children" ("Ivy Day"). Sometimes beatings shade into sadomasochism. "An Encounter" describes a strange man fixated on whipping schoolboys. His fantasies excite him so much that he masturbates in front of the narrator and his friends.

The significance of "An Encounter" lies in its metaphoric similarities and metonymic links to "The Sisters," the gnomon for the rest of the book (Weir 1994). The narrator of the first two stories in *Dubliners* is a thirteen-year-old boy. In "The Sisters" the boy experiences the death of his tutor, Father Flynn. In "An Encounter" he meets a sex abuser when he skips school. The metonymic links between the two stories were understood by the Irish censors, who delayed the publication of the book. These stories, written in 1902, were only published in 1917 under protest and when the author had made compromises because of censorship. But both men's black-green coats, yellow teeth, and sexual orientation—homosexuality and pedophilia—are coded in the stories (Jackson and McGinley 1993). "An Encounter" can deal with sex more directly because the old man is not identified as a priest. Father Flynn was removed from office for an offense known but only alluded to by the adults in the story as "simony," that is the selling of something sacred or profiting from the sale of a sacred service. A reference to the "breaking of an empty chalice" clearly suggested the priest's offense to be sodomy, symbolism understood even by Joyce's publisher.

The implications that Father Flynn had been a child abuser are multiple: Old Cotter remarks that he would not want a boy of his talking too much with a priest like Flynn; there is a reference to "Persia," a code for homosexuality; and a statement, "They say it was the boy's fault." Joyce also refers to Bruno Latini, a priest scholar from Dante's youth whom he meets in canto 15 of the Inferno in a space reserved for sodomites. Dante is assured that this section of hell houses many clergy and scholars of great fame, including a bishop (Gallagher 1996, 33–36). A suppressed reference to sodomy in connection with Father Keon appears in a later story ("Ivy Day"), and parallel accounts and direct references to the fact that priests beat children appear in *Portrait* and *Ulysses*.

A subtext that runs throughout Joyce is also part of Irish reality—the idea that women carry the moral message and, through their obedience, protect priests and religious (Inglis 1987, 4; MacCurtain 1987; Mahoney 1993). In Joyce's Ireland, the priests and the church set the example for women and the entire family to be complicit in the oppression of children, adolescents, and young adults. "The Sisters," for example, tells of the adult world's incomplete efforts to hide an unseemly truth about Father Flynn from the narrator, a thirteen-year-old boy. The mystery seems deliberate and enforced, like the conspiracy of silence recorded by Paddy Doyle or a state secret perpetuated against the population. Another adult authority, Mrs. Mooney of "The Boarding House," uses silence to encourage her daughter, Polly, to carry on a sexual relationship with her lodger in order to land a good Catholic husband. The mother of the little boy in "Counterparts" is in church while he is beaten. Clearly the entire family in *Dubliners* is involved in the abuse, but the priest's abuse of children represents the prototype. The children of Joyce's Dublin, beaten, browbeaten, and seduced, learn their lessons well: silence (about the abuse they have suffered), violence (toward those weaker than themselves), respectability, paralysis, and "simony" in the priesthood (read "sodomy").

Again my point is simple: Sexual and physical abuse inflicted, encouraged, or tolerated by the Church was a well-known characteristic of the power base and subtext of Irish myth over the past hundred and fifty years. The potato famine of 1846 marked a key shift in Church power and abuse toward children. Those who talk about the famine as a holocaust have a strong case. The government of occupation was exporting food while one million people starved to death in one year. Another two million died of starvation by 1851. The original population of eight and one half million people was reduced by death and emigration to three and a half million by 1861, a population that has remained stable since.

Priests gained ever more power from the 1829 Catholic Emancipation onward, because they were allowed an education. They also gained leadership, because there was no Catholic ruling class in Ireland. Priests gained additional power after the famine, because they were given control of the national school system (Lyons 1971, 6–9). "In 1850 there were about 5,000 priests, monks and nuns for a Catholic population of 5,000,000 [North and South]; in 1900 there were over 14,000 . . . to administer to approximately

3,500,000 Catholics. And this vastly increased figure takes no account of the steady flow of Irish Missionaries overseas" (Larkin 1967, 857)

The corporal punishment of children was reinforced by the introduction in 1867 of English law that subjected children as young as seven to criminal prosecution, Margaret MacCurtain has pointed out: "After the famine, brutality came into the Irish countryside." Corporal punishment of children flourished in the religious controlled schools and at home. It would be a pretense to claim that the connections between the 1846 famine, priestly power, and physical and sexual violence against children are obscure or academic constructs (MacCurtain 1991).

Microcosm

Ireland–United States. May 7, 1992. Bishop Eamonn Casey of Galway is exposed as the father of a seventeen-year-old boy. Annie Murphy, the mother, is American.

The relationship between the U.S. and the Irish Roman Catholic Churches is not incidental. And the media revelation of an Irish bishop's violation of his vow of celibacy had both practical and symbolic consequences for the shift in priestly image and power in both countries, as Ray Mosley reported in the *Chicago Tribune* November 12, 1995, under the headline "Crisis of Confidence Rocks Irish Catholic Church." The Catholic Church in the United States had been struggling for a decade with media exposure of clergy sexual abuse, when another facet of celibate violation—the exploitation of women—hit the newspapers, radio, and TV talk shows. As the story unfolded, it exposed the Church in the United States to questions of broader scope about priests' celibate observance. In Ireland the story prepared the way for the media handling of the Smyth case. Bishop Casey had asked Annie Murphy at the time of her pregnancy to give their baby up for adoption. She refused. Social workers and others in the United States were not slow to speculate that the persistent opposition of the United States Catholic Conference and the National Conference of Catholic Bishops to make birth records available to adoptees was in part an attempt to save some priests and bishops from exposure and embarrassment. It may be no coincidence that a great number of Irish orphans were adopted by Americans before the Second World War.

Everyone concedes that the problem of priest sexual abuse is not of recent origin. A number of the allegations reported in the U.S. media stemmed from abuse perpetrated one to three decades earlier. It is relevant to review the ethnic structure of the U.S. Catholic Church from a point in time (1960–

1970) when the image of the priest was at its zenith and no media dared speak of sexual violations by clergy. Irish Americans represented 17 percent of the U.S. population, yet 54 percent of priests were Irish American or Irish, while 85 percent of archbishops and 75 percent of bishops were Irish American. More than any other country, Ireland influenced U.S. Catholic seminary education, spirituality, practice, and organization (Dosh 1972).

Ireland's limited population and geography make it a suitable microcosm for the study of priest sexual abuse and celibacy observance/violation. Ireland has special implications for understanding Catholicism and church structure in the United States and throughout the world (O'Donoghue 1995). Media exposure in Ireland in effect is national in extent. The Irish Catholic Church has four archdioceses and twenty-two dioceses, and fifty-four bishops who since 1989 have placed an embargo on information about the number of priests and seminarians in their country, as Michael J. Farrell reported in "Feisty New Ireland Leaves the Church Panting to Keep Up" in the *National Catholic Reporter* on July 29,1994. It is widely speculated that the 2,652 Catholic churches in Ireland are financially secure and that all dioceses are profitable enterprises, according to Liz Allen in "What Is the Church Worth?" in the *Irish Independent* of October 7, 1995.

The United States has 148 dioceses, 33 archdioceses, more than 300 bishops and archbishops, and 49,000 active priests for a Catholic population of sixty million. Over the past twenty years, the media has recorded approximately 800 priests and brothers implicated or accused of sexual abuse of minors; one registry of abusers records 923 alleged priest perpetrators (*Survivors Connections*1996). According to various court depositions, approximately 1,300 priests and religious have been treated for psychosexual disorders in the past twenty years. Relatively few of these cases have come to national attention. Estimates of the percentage of U.S. priests involved in sex with minors varies from a low of 1.2 percent to a high of 10 percent. Priest-sociologist Andrew Greeley estimated in 1993 that 5–7 percent of priests in the United States are abusers; I estimated in 1976 that 6 percent of priests in the United States involve themselves with minors.

Because sex with minors is illegal both in Ireland and in the United States, it holds a special place among celibacy violations. Precisely because its criminal character demands public attention and legal redress, sexual abuse of minors by a priest opens the door to hitherto unaddressed questions about celibate observance. How is celibacy really practiced by those who profess it? Further, media exposure reinforces debate about the whole range of questions about celibate/sexual observance and teaching of the Church, including mandatory celibacy for the clergy, the ordination of women, a married clergy, premarital sex, masturbation, remarriage after divorce, and homosexuality. Most important it raises systemic questions about the relationship between celibacy and power. The intimate connection between Irish and American Catholicism suggests a number of questions that can be addressed in the current crisis:

1. Is there a correlation between ethnic origin and clergy abuse?
2. What is the rate of sexual abuse/activity by priests in Ireland versus the United States?
3. How many sexual abusing priests in the United States, England, and elsewhere, were born or educated in Ireland?
4. Is the proportion of known sexual abusive Irish-born or Irish-educated priests greater or less than their representation in the indigenous clergy pool? (US, UK, missions)

Whatever the result of studies in progress or future studies in this area, the painful problems Catholics face will not go away by themselves or be productively resolved without the best efforts of all who care about religion and the Catholic Church. Ireland is a paradigm of the current crisis in the universal Church and therefore will receive more rather than less attention in the future.

New York. October 3, 1992. Irish singer Sinead O'Connor tears up a picture of Pope John Paul II during a performance on *Saturday Night Live.*

Sinead O'Connor demonstrated dramatically how aware Irish artists continue to be of the scope and significance of abuse in Ireland and its connection with historical facts and institutions. O'Connor was seriously abused by her own mother, she claims, with the encouragement and support of priests. She executed a powerful protest against child abuse during her appearance on the popular U.S. late-night show *Saturday Night Live.* She sang Bob Marley's song *War,* whose words are drawn from a speech in which Haile Selassie declared that in order to save children we must stop racial war. O'Connor sang instead, "We must stop abuse" as she ripped up a photograph of Pope John Paul II. The gesture was one of the most powerful protests on media record. Millions of people who had not seen the program heard about it. It became legendary. A joke circulated widely in Ireland: Pope John Paul II during his "Urbi et Orbi" Christmas blessing from the balcony of St. Peters "ripped up a picture of Sinead O'Connor."

The singer's acerbic gesture cut close to the bone of truth—that ecclesiastical authorities should be held accountable for the abuse within their ranks. James Joyce's writings held up the same mirror and ripped into the clerical image in a similar manner in the early 1900s. Both artists were deprived of universal popular approval. The producers of *Saturday Night Live* distanced themselves from the gesture the following week by claiming they had no foreknowledge of the singer's intentions. In effect, the gesture has been censored: It is the only clip that NBC holds inaccessible. O'Connor paid an immediate price for her protest when she was confronted with a well-organized booing section at a concert in Madison Square Garden on October 16. However, the great majority of the concert audience applauded her. The prophetic nature of her gesture was understood by vast numbers of Catholics both in Ireland and the United States. Abuse by clergy is not merely a problem of individuals—perpetrators or victims. It has systemic roots that influence and perpetuate it. One woman who works as an advocate in a U.S. Catholic diocese—mother of five, grandmother of a dozen—responded in a representative way: She applauded when she heard of O'Connor's protest.

O'Connor's song *Famine* pinpoints the relationship between the Irish famine and broad social problems of addiction, self-destruction, and child abuse (she claims Ireland has the highest rate in the European Economic Community). The song blasts Irish myth at the same time that it vibrantly represents it. When I spoke to historian MacCurtain about the Irish artist's articulation of the truth of clergy abuse (like Joyce before her), she responded, "The oppressed always sing" (cf also Grey 1994). Artists, traditionally revered in Irish culture, have in the age of TV the opportunity to see their message magnified and sometimes distorted by the media.

Certainly the media is a major player in brokering power by its ability to transmit images, true or false, to vast numbers of people who previously may have doubted their own perceptions or experience. This is what has happened both in the United States and Ireland in regard to the crisis of sexual abuse by priests. It will take a great deal more research to determine exactly the general public response (or responses) to such clergy malfeasance.

A Final Note

Anthropologist Claude Levi-Strauss once compared ethnography to geology, because in both disciplines seemingly unimportant surface phenomena can reveal fundamental structures beneath. A look at the surface of Irish society after the famine reveals a number of such anomalous features: Attendance at Sunday mass grew from 30 percent to 90 percent; numbers of clergy increased significantly; the age of marriage was postponed, resulting in large numbers of unmarried adults; the Church took control of education; a high incidence of alcoholism became endemic; and the culture sustained a pattern of child abuse.

Although statistics are lacking, credible accounts of Irish society before the famine show that about five thousand priests and religious served a population in excess of eight million. By 1900, fourteen thousand priests and religious served three million. In the 1830s Irish women commonly married at sixteen and men at eighteen or twenty; by James Joyce's day, Irish women married in their late twenties, while two-thirds of Irish men were unmarried at the age of thirty. Homelessness was not a problem in Ireland before the famine. Rural children received education from ad hoc "hedge schools" before the famine; by the end of the nineteenth century, Church control of education was all but absolute. The true scope of child abuse is only now being validated as it is openly confronted, but from all indications it is stunning in its frequency and severity.

I believe these phenomena reveal a deep structure of systemic abuse of children handed down from generation to generation and structured by priests and nuns. This structure arose in reaction to, and as a result of, the experience of the famine and its social and economic consequences: millions of deaths, with the attendant feelings of guilt and fear among survivors; the bankruptcy of institutions other than the Church; the consolidation of Church power; the flood of emigrants and depopulation of the countryside. All of these exacerbated alienation from Britain and culminated in revolution. Two other factors seem important: the not always wholesome backdraft of money and sentiment from the United States and the isolation of Ireland from modern Europe. Other peoples have faced similar devastations. The Jews come first to mind, but gypsies, Cambodians, Armenians, African Ibo and Tutsi, and Native Americans have undergone slaughter and have faced—in some cases still face—societal dislocations.

Only an awareness of an ideology of the problem will allow Ireland and the Church to escape what Padraic Pearse called (1922, 5) "the murder machine."

Notes

1. Vatican congregations are part of the system of departments, *discasteria* of the curial Church administration in Rome. Each is headed by a cardinal prefect who oversees or safeguards various teachings, functions, or personnel in the worldwide Church.
2. I was in Ireland during October 1994 when the Brendan Smyth affair broke in

the media, which afforded me the opportunity to conduct interviews with a wide range of people. In addition to personal interviews with priests and victims, I reviewed three hundred media presentations between October 1994 and June 1996. Four main themes have been addressed in this two-year period: (1) The Brendan Smyth affair and child abuse among priests, brothers, and nuns in Ireland; (2) a range of celibacy violations by priests, from affairs with women to homosexual life-styles; (3) Bishop Brendan Comiskey's call for a discussion of celibacy and the possibility of a married priesthood and the aftermath of his speaking out; and (4) the questions of divorce and abortion and Irish law.

3. I am indebted to my colleague, Dr. B. C. Lamb, for his collaboration on a long essay on sex in Joyce's *Dubliners*. I have incorporated here a few of our conclusions.

References

Ardagh, John. 1995. "Ireland and the Irish: Portrait of a Changing Society." *New York:* Viking.

Boyle, Patrick. 1994. *Scout's Honor: Sexual Abuse in America's Most Trusted Institution*. Rocklin, Calif.: Prima.

Breslin, Jimmy. 1973. *World without End, Amen*. New York: Avon.

Cahill, Thomas. 1995. *How the Irish Saved Civilization: The Untold Story of Ireland's Heroic Role from the Fall of Rome to the Rise of Medieval Europe*. New York: Doubleday.

Dosh, Millicent Adams. 1972. "Irish Cultural Influence on American Catholic Leadership." California State College. Mimeograph.

Doyle, Paddy. 1988. *The God Squad*. London: Corgi.

Flynn, Mannix. 1983. *Nothing to Say*. Dublin: Ward River.

Gallagher, Joseph. 1966. *To Hell and Back: A Modern Reader's Guide to Dante*. Liguori, Mo.: Triumph.

Greeley, Andrew M. 1972. *That Most Distressful Nation: The Taming of the American Irish*. Chicago: Quadrangle.

Grey, Mary. 1994. "Liberation Theology and the Bearers of Dangerous Memory." *New Blackfriars* (November).

Inglis, Tom. 1987. *Moral Monopoly: The Catholic Church in Modern Irish Society*. New York: St. Martin's.

Joyce, James. 1993. *James Joyce's Dubliners: An Annotated Edition*. Edited by John Wise Jackson and Bernard McGinley. London: Sinclair-Stevenson.

———. 1964. *Portrait of the Artist as a Young Man*, New York: Viking.

———. 1961. *Ulysses*. New York: Random House.

———. 1954. *Dubliners*, New York: Modern Library.

Keough, Dermot. 1995. *Ireland and the Vatican: The Politics and Diplomacy of the Church State Relations, 1922–1960*. Cork, Ireland: Cork University Press.

Larkin, E. 1967. "Economic Growth, Capital Investment, and the Roman Catholic Church in Nineteenth Century Ireland." *American Historical Review* 2 (April): 856–858.

Lyons, F.S.L. 1971. *Ireland Since the Famine*. London: Weidenfeld and Nicholson.

MacCurtain, Margaret. 1991. "Women, Education, and Learning in Early Modern Ireland." In *Marriage in Ireland*, edited by Art Cosgrove. New York: Columbia University Press.

———. 1987. "Moving Statues and Irishwomen." *Irish Studies* (summer):139–147.

McEnany, Annemarie. 1995. "Fr. Cleary 'Son' Court Bid Goes Ahead." *Irish Independent* (September 25).

———. 1994. "Pervert Priest: More Victims Come Forward." *Evening Herald* (October 19).

Mahoney, Rosemary. 1993. *Whoredom in Kimmage: Irish Women Coming of Age*. Boston: Houghton-Mifflin.

Moore, Chris. 1995. *Betrayal of Trust: The Father Brendan Smyth Affair and the Catholic Church*. Dublin: Marino.

O'Donoghue, John. 1995. "The Irish Church: Beyond the Bleak Landscape." *The Furrow* (March):135–143.

O'Halloran, Ruth L. 1994. "How Catholic Are the Irish: Less Conventional, More Committed." *Commonweal* (March 11).

O'Toole, Fintan. 1994. *Black Hole, Green Card: The Disappearance of Ireland*. Dublin: New Books.

Pearse, Padraic H. 1922. "The Murder Machine." In *Collected Works of Padraic H.*

Shupe, Anson. 1995. *In the Name of All That's Holy: A Theory of Clergy Malfeasance*. Westport, Conn.: Praeger.

Survivor's Connections. 1996. Newsletter. Vol. 4 (1): 4.

Toibin, Colm. 1995. "Dublin's Epiphany." *New Yorker* (April 3):45.

Touher, Patrick. 1991. *Fear of the Collar: Artane Industrial School*. Dublin: O'Brien.

Weir, David. 1994a. "A Womb of His Own: Joyce's Sexual Aesthetics." *James Joyce Quarterly* 31, 3 (spring):207–231.

CHAPTER 9

The Moral Bankruptcy
of Institutionalized Religion

JEANNE M. MILLER

*M*y firsthand experiences dealing
with an incident of sexual abuse of my son and several other altar boy companions by a Roman Catholic priest ultimately catapulted me into the role
of advocate for thousands of victims of clergy sexual abuse. Once I dared to
speak publicly about the Church's best-guarded secret and most devastating
scandal, other victims who had lived for decades with the secret of their clergy
sexual abuse began speaking out. What continued to astound me was the familiar ring in every disclosure of abuse, and the indifference shown by the
perpetrating cleric and his religious superiors. Altogether, this is the story of
the outrageous operations of a hierarchical patriarchy that in the name of God
abusively wielded its power from the top down as its means of damage control. It is about the powerless laypeople at the bottom who became victims
vainly looking up to their church leaders for the salvation and the compassion they preached.

A Chicago native, I grew up in its suburbs. My parents, both alcoholics, were real estate brokers. We moved from house to house, sometimes just
down the block, and often two or three times in a year. My parents divorced
when I was twelve years old. Two years later, my mother committed suicide.
Subsequently, my maternal grandparents sent me off to convent boarding
school in Clinton, Iowa.

I was educated exclusively in Catholic schools. In those pre–Vatican
II days, Catholic parents were bound by a religious duty to send their children to Catholic school no matter what hardships the steep tuition caused
them. Throughout my turbulent childhood, the nuns and priests at school gave
me a stability and structure that home life lacked. They taught everything in

terms of black and white. Something was either wrong or it was right, true or false. Every virtuous act had its reward, while every sin had its consequence. They provided the care, concern, and compassion I needed to survive. Their teachings gave me comfort; some things in life were perpetual and reliable. In short, these nuns and priests were my family.

Catholicism teaches that every moral and religious question has an answer. When I was in school, the Catholic student's source of doctrine and dogma was *The Baltimore Catechism*. The Catholic religion had found it increasingly difficult to promote and perfect a uniform institutionalized religion in the nineteenth century, when most people were uneducated and illiterate. In 1884, responding to what they perceived as a crisis of faith in Catholicism, Catholic bishops gathered in Baltimore in the Third Plenary Council, where they developed and authorized the *Catechism*. The bishops' ambitious goal was to establish a uniform code of dogma that all Catholics would be required to know, and in light of mass illiteracy they devised this method of rote memorization. The *Catechism*, published in 1885, comprised a series of questions and answers that every Catholic and convert was required to memorize.

This *Catechism* methodology of teaching Catholic dogma survived until the 1970s. From first grade, I was drilled daily on the *Catechism*. At forty-nine years old, I can still remember it. It began: "Who made you?" Answer: "God made me." Second question: "Why did God make you?" Answer: "God made me to love, honor, and serve him in this world." The *Catechism* was not open to question or interpretation. If a student expressed doubt, he was chastised as an agnostic, which was a very bad disease of the soul. When the nuns had no logical explanation for a "truth" such as the Immaculate Conception, one could be saved only by accepting it "on faith."

The nuns asserted that divine revelation had made known to us that these certain doctrines were infallibly true as declared by our holy father in Rome from the chair of St. Peter. Everything was carved in stone. Nothing was left to question. The nuns were adamant about compliance with stringent identifiable rules. There was no margin of error for deviation from the rules. A Catholic was either in the state of grace destined for heaven, or he was in the state of sin relegated to eternal damnation in a fiery hell. There was nothing in between. One's salvation from his failings could be found only in the confessional, in confidential and intimate contact and conversation with a priest. A priest was viewed as God on earth.

We regularly sang "We Are Climbing Jacob's Ladder." It was the nuns' segue into religious vocation lectures. They would remind us of our Christian responsibility to listen for our religious vocations, because "many are called but few are chosen." According to the nuns, God had extended a religious vocation to at least one child in every family. I had only an older brother who was quite unorthodox. By process of elimination, I surmised early on in grade school that the religious vocation in my family must be mine.

The nuns taught that, absent a religious vocation, Catholics had a duty to achieve the highest state of virtue on "Jacob's Ladder." It was quite a sophisticated, but concrete, ordering of states of life. From the top down it comprised (1) ordained priesthood, (2) unordained religious life (nuns and brothers), (3) single life of virginity, and (4) married life. To choose the loathed nonvirgin single life was to choose to live in a state of sin. Priests were "like Christ." while unordained religious were "next to Christ." The single virgin or married person was "under Christ." Because priesthood excluded females, the best I could do in the hierarchical ranking of virtuosity was to become a nun.

To the extent that Catholic school provided any amount of sex education, girls and boys apparently received conflicting messages. Girls were taught that their sexual drive heats up slowly, like turning on an electric iron. A male's sexual drive lights up instantly, like striking a match. He has virtually no control over his passion once ignited. Thus, because a female has time to think before responding, it was always her responsibility to stop sinful sexual activity. The nuns developed extravagant ways for girls to avoid exciting these "sex-crazed" boys. At exclusively female sessions, they instructed us that when we were in the company of a boy, we were never to wear pearls, lest the boy see the reflection in them down our blouse; never wear patent leather shoes, lest the boy see the reflection in them up our skirt; never sit at a table with a white tablecloth, lest the boy be reminded of bed sheets; always carry pebbles on a rainy day to throw into puddles to cause ripples, lest the boy see the reflection in the water up our skirt should we have to pass over the puddle.

Boys, on the other hand, were taught that women are teasers and temptresses. If a boy wanted to avoid sin, he must avoid girls, a message reinforced by the segregation of boys and girls in school. There was a boys' side of the classroom, the hallway, the school entrance, and there was a girls' side. Teens were altogether segregated. No Catholic high school was coeducational. The message was clear: Sex was dirty. We were to save sex for someone we married.

The foregoing were universal Catholic truisms, teachings, and procedures. My background is virtually identical to the religious education experience of every Catholic before 1970, and that initiation into the hierarchical system produced the mind-set of children who became vulnerable to the sexual proclivities of Roman Catholic clergy. It is the mind-set with which many, including myself, naively entered parenthood, only to unwittingly thrust their children into the arms of perpetrators. It was a mind-set that confused sexuality with sin, suppressed normal human development, and stunted the emotional and sexual maturity of those who entered religious life.

Aside from being the most virtuous state of life that I, as a female, could obtain, convent life attracted me because it offered a serenity and security absent from my turbulent home life. Boarding school had given me a preview of religious life, and the calling I was certain I had lingered after high school graduation. In 1966, I entered a convent in Dubuque, Iowa. Although religious sisterhood provided a comforting camaraderie and emotional protective shield my family never could, it also restricted me from any meaningful ministry to the Church. It was an ethereal life. I was assigned to laundry detail in the winter and the community's radish patch in the summer. Indeed, I was out of touch with reality. My most challenging feats were keeping veils white, producing gargantuan radishes, and withstanding the hours on end on my knees praying and scrubbing floors. I owed more to the Church for being my support. I believed my religious convictions could better serve the Church in the real world. So, on Independence Day, July 4, 1967, standing on the edge of the convent bluff watching the Mississippi River pass below, my white veil blowing in the wind, I decided to reenter the world.

I resumed college in Chicago, then married. Not knowing anything about birth control, except that its practice was evil, my husband and I quickly produced four babies. We were deeply committed to Catholic action and parish life. My husband became a discussion leader for the teen religious education program, and I became a master catechist and retreat coordinator. We thrust all four of our children into church involvement, urging them to volunteer in parish activities and requiring them to register for religious programs. Our two sons became altar boys. That was the beginning of the end of my naive blind faith. Soon I would learn about the moral bankruptcy of institutionalized religion.

The rude awakening came in the summer of 1982, just weeks after our associate parish priest treated my thirteen-year-old son and three companion altar boys to two fun-filled days of waterskiing at his lake cottage. I was thrilled that Father had taken an interest in our son and delighted that my son even wanted to be with the priest. I had a sense that this, our oldest son, was the one in my family nest whom God had chosen for the priesthood. I thought that exposure to the priest would help my son define his goals and keep him on the straight and narrow. I thought wrong. His exposure to Father was of a kind I could not have conceived.

Weeks after the outing, a parent of another boy who had attended the outing informed us that her son had revealed that Father had provided his young guests with alcohol and shown them pornographic movies. Father had also undermined our authority by telling the boys that we parents were hypocritical because we swore and drank but did not permit them to do so. She told us that Father had made sexual passes at our sons. To demonstrate his confidence in their maturity, she reported, Father had allowed our thirteen-year-old sons to drive his car and his speedboat. The boys knew that Father had his authority from God. We, the parents, had taught them that.

This news, coupled with our awareness that our son's personality had altered since the outing, concerned us. Since returning from the outing, our son had responded defiantly to anything we said to him. He had spent much of his time alone in his room rather than with his friends. Thus, in that July of 1982, immediately upon hearing this report, we confronted Fr. Walter Somerville, the pastor of our parish church, St. Edna's, in Arlington Heights, Illinois, with our concerns. We wanted him to quiet our fears by telling us we were wrong. Instead, the pastor told us that Father had a problem with young boys and recommended that we report the incident to the Chicago Archdiocesan Priest Personnel Board.

It was difficult to comprehend: "Father"—a trusted friend, a respected vicar of the Church, popular with families, charismatic leader of youth—*molesting children*. More shocking still was the broader scandal that evolved as I sought accountability and resolution from Church leaders. As I climbed the rungs of the institution's hierarchy, I learned of clerics so arrogant in the abuse of power that they saw themselves as impervious to the law.

Following up on our pastor's advice, all four sets of parents initiated a complaint with the Chicago archdiocese, but the Priest Personnel Board was a brick wall. Its members and other Church leaders whom we subsequently spoke with evaded our reports by shutting themselves off behind archaic allegiances and dealing with the matter internally, with no due process for anyone. They steadfastly refused all of our requests to provide therapeutic counseling for the boys and to place restrictions on the priest. Clerics from the archdiocesan chancery explained that taking any restrictive actions might be "wrongly" construed as an admission of guilt and/or liability. They said their lawyer—of the now-defunct law firm of Reuben & Proctor—would not permit this. On hearing of attorney involvement, one set of parents stopped pursuing accountability from the Church, stating that "even if the allegations were true, no one challenges a priest."

After repeated failures to obtain an appropriate response from the archdiocese, the three remaining sets of parents initiated a criminal complaint with the local state's attorney's office. However, criminal law enforcement officials were reluctant, and ultimately refused, to prosecute a priest. There were political considerations. It was an election year. The popular Joseph Bernardin had just been appointed on July 10 to lead the archdiocese (Bernardin was installed on August 25 and created cardinal on February 2, 1983), and, it seemed, no one wanted to alienate the Catholic vote.[1] With a criminal investigation going nowhere and no help from the archdiocese, on December 24 we were finally forced to file a civil suit against it and the priest, *Doe v. Catholic Bishop of Chicago and Mayer* (82 L 24923), hoping to prevent him from molesting other children. Another set of parents now resigned from the effort, stating that they felt guilty about suing the Church.

For two years, my husband and I and the remaining single mother who initially reported the abuse to us fought through the courts to have Father restricted from his ministry with children. On March 30, 1983, we met with the archdiocesan chancellor, Fr. Richard Keating (now bishop of Arlington, Virginia), in the basement boiler room of St. Theresa's rectory, Palatine, Illinois, who told us that if we pursued the matter we could be excommunicated for violating canon law. It was a horrible threat. My belief system had been undermined, but my religion was still all-important to me. I was about to retreat until I realized that my beliefs belonged only to me and that this institution was powerless to deprive me of what was mine alone.

Finally, after endless stalls by Church attorneys and legal wrangling, after mortgaging our house, spending our savings, and even selling my jewelry to finance the lawsuit, on March 12, 1984, we accepted a settlement of $15,000, less than half of what we had put into legal fees, with the contingency that Cardinal Bernardin meet with our families and sons. (Cardinal Bernardin had never attempted to contact us personally.) The settlement promised nothing more. We reasoned, however, that the archdiocese's investment of $15,000, along with a request from the cardinal himself at our court-ordered meeting on April 4, 1984, to settle the matter and to "trust him," was a strong indication that the archdiocese would never again allow this priest to harm another child, much less be allowed to continue to take young boys to his lake cottage. We were wrong.

Despite the archdiocese's financial settlement of the civil litigation, Church leaders acted no more responsibly or with any more accountability than they had before the suit. They simply transferred the priest to a new parish. Although the cardinal supposedly placed the priest under supervision and a mandate that he not be alone with children under the age of twenty-one without another adult present, the pastor of the new parish was dying and bedridden.[2] This recalcitrant priest to all outward appearances remained unrestricted and unsupervised, and he freely continued to escort young teenage boys to his lake cottage. He was eventually transferred three times—to St. Stephen's in Des Plaines, Illinois, St. Dionysius in Cicero, and St. Odilo's in Berwyn—as new allegations sparked police investigations in each parish.

The experience of standing up for my moral convictions cost me far more than money. I lost my best friend, who could not forgive me for challenging the Church. Even more shattering, I lost my marriage. Following this experience, my husband had reconstructed his life. We were both struggling to recover, but we took different paths. After a marriage of twenty years, in the end, we barely knew each other. My husband plunged back into parish life, but I could not. I recoiled from the power structure that I perceived devalued children, admitted no guilt, took no responsibility, and had never responded in moral or pastoral terms. I enrolled at Mundelein College and earned a master's degree in creation theology, delving into the basis of my belief system, and rebuilt my faith life in my own terms, independent of an oppressive institution. Unable to bridge our rift, my husband and I divorced.

Moreover, the crisis had taken its toll on the parish community, which had been a vibrant center of lay ministry. In the wake of abuse, the circles of victimization ripple outward. Upon hearing a victim's allegation, people—be they family, parish, or local community—find themselves forced to choose sides, to believe either the accuser or the priest. In either case, the process tears apart families and divides parishes. In our case, parishioners fell on both sides of the battle lines. Many left the parish. Those who stayed resented us, the pastor who encouraged our resolution of the matter, and other parish staff members who extended care and compassion to our injured children. The pastor retired under the strain of critics who thought him weak for not supporting his fellow priest. Six staff members either resigned or were fired by the archdiocese for "conspiring" to rid the parish of Father. Archdiocesan Personnel Board members insisted that the parish staff instigated our families' complaint in order to rid themselves of Father because of a personality conflict among them. (Fr. Thomas Ventura, vicar of priests of the Archdiocese of Chicago, expressed this opinion on behalf of the archdiocese in a settlement discussion held in early March 1984, adding, "You have your truth and we have ours.")

As Father moved on through a series of parishes, I plunged into a manuscript about the traumatic struggle with the cardinal's lawyers and chancery staff. In 1987, *Assault on Innocence* was published under the pseudonym Hilary Stiles. Using fictional names for key figures but otherwise sticking to the legal record, it detailed my experience of fighting the Roman Catholic Church, its hierarchy, and its lawyers in civil court. Its publication led to my appearance over the next few years on dozens of national radio and television talk shows, where I advanced my message: Bishops must stop reassigning child molesters and start reaching out to the victims and their families. In response, individuals in the audiences began divulging their secret, personal stories of clergy sexual abuse and the self-serving stratagems of Church leaders. Often, others watching these programs at home would be waiting outside the studio by the end of a program to tell me about their own or a loved one's story of clergy sexual abuse. Before long, it became apparent that my story was tragically typical of a serious and pervasive problem with institutionalized religions.

In the summer of 1991, I received the inevitable news: An ex-priest friend called to tell me that the cardinal had just personally removed Father from his current parish after the archdiocese received a report from neighbors who had spotted him nude with two males, ages fourteen and twenty, on the roof of his rectory garage. The removal was swift, clean, and quiet. No one but archdiocesan personnel had identified the boys involved. Parishioners were simply told that Father resigned "for personal reasons," as the *Chicago Tribune* reported on October 25 in "Ex-Arlington Heights Priest Faces New Sexual Allegations" by Andrew Fegelman and on October 26 in "Panel to Examine Priests in Sex Cases" by Michael Hirsley. I needed to locate the boys' families. I knew from personal experience what they were going through, and I wanted to connect with them in order to keep the vow I had made to the cardinal at our court-ordered meeting nearly a decade earlier: "If ever you allow this man to harm another child, I will be there with the record so that you will never be able to deny you are the person responsible for that child's harm."

Realizing that I could never find the families, I devised a way that they could find me. For years I had contemplated establishing a victims' network through which people could report their abuses; be listened to, cared for, encouraged, and advised; and could find others like themselves. A network of numbers—a visible indicator that the problem involved not just a few unlucky people here or there but a nation. I knew from the talk-show feedback I had gathered that the problem was pervasive. I had been too busy with work and with school. Now the time was ripe to establish the network: Victims of Clergy Abuse Linkup, Inc., which first became known by its acronym, VO-CAL, and later as The Linkup.[3]

I turned to my television news contacts. Reporters uninterested in reporting my ten-year-old lawsuit or unsubstantiated allegations about Father's recent sexual misconduct were enthusiastic about a clergy victims' advocacy group. I had provided our local NBC News outlet not only with copies of our 1982 lawsuit against Father but with copies of four other cases involving allegations of sexual misconduct by four other Chicago priests that were on public record in the Circuit Court of Cook County.[4] Reporters contacted the archdiocese to inquire about the status of the pending cases and to ask what it was doing about the problem of clergy sexual misconduct.

In an effort to minimize the scope of the Chicago problem, Cardinal Bernardin called a press conference on October 10, 1991. He offered a panel of six professionals in the areas of law and psychiatry to the media as proof positive that the Chicago archdiocese was responsibly handling the few alleged incidents of child sexual abuse by its priests. At the conclusion of the presentation, an archdiocesan spokesperson, Auxiliary Bishop Raymond Goedert, asserted that Chicago had no sex abuse problem among its priests. Reporters questioned why the archdiocese would have such a large professional staff for a nonexistent problem. That evening, many local television and radio stations led the news with the story of the Chicago archdiocese's clergy sex abuse crisis and highlighted the five Chicago cases, including our 1982 civil suit against Father and the Archdiocese of Chicago. NBC News introduced VOCAL as the first and one-of-a-kind clergy sexual abuse network and provided my phone number.

The next morning, I received phone calls from several parents of school children at Father's most recent parish, St. Odilo. They had united and made their demands to the cardinal. He or his representative must immediately present himself to them to explain why he placed Father in their parish knowing he had a history of sexual abuse, why he had failed to warn parishioners of Father's history, and why the archdiocese lied to them about the reasons for Father's departure. In response, the cardinal was sending his Pastoral Intervention Team to the parish to meet with the parents of school children there on October 16, 1991. The parents requested my presence at the meeting to "keep them honest." No one I spoke with knew the identity of the boys on the roof.

The Pastoral Intervention Team comprised the professionals whom the archdiocese had presented at the press conference. The same priest who had been sent to us as a pastoral counselor a decade earlier in an effort to thwart our lawsuit, Fr. Andrew McDonough, introduced to the assembly Auxiliary Bishop Raymond Goedert, who had called me on November 11, 1986, and met with me for three hours four days later to discuss the dissatisfaction with the archdiocese's mishandling of our complaint against Father I had expressed in my book. On this occasion, neither cleric recognized me sitting in the front seat before him. The bishop explained to the parish parents that Father could not have been a threat to their children. He was certain no child had been harmed because the lawsuit ten years ago was merely the result of one mother's overreaction to an innocent situation. He said that the mother eventually dropped the lawsuit because she had no claim. I could barely breathe when I rose to reintroduce myself to these men and to explain to the parents who I was in connection with the previous lawsuit against Father, and that the lawsuit had not been dropped, but settled.

The bishop's story quickly changed. He told the parents that after our lawsuit, Father underwent psychiatric evaluation. He was found to be "merely narcissistic." The bishop asserted that the psychiatrists assured the archdiocese that he was not a threat to children. As a precaution, however, the cardinal had placed a mandate on Father. He was not to be alone with anyone under the age of twenty-one without another adult present. The bishop explained that when Father was seen alone with the twenty-year-old boy, he was removed from the parish because he had violated the mandate. No mention was made of the presence of the fourteen-year-old boy on the roof, and the bishop emphasized that the twenty-year-old was not a minor. Nonetheless, the bishop explained, the young man was under twenty-one, and therefore the mandate had been violated, justifying Father's removal from the parish. Parents were livid because they had not been told anything about the mandate. They wondered aloud how compliance with this "mandate" was to be enforced if no one in the parish but Father knew it existed. Several reported that they had permitted their minor sons to go with Father to his lake cottage. On occasion, Father had gathered all the eighth-grade boys at the rectory to teach them sex education. Among the several topics he raised was "fisting." He often coached children for confirmation alone in the confines of the rectory.[5]

At a subsequent St. Odilo parish meeting on October 22, 1991, called to discuss issues raised by Father's removal, a distraught thirteen-year-old girl nervously approached the microphone and announced that Father had sexually abused her while coaching her for confirmation. A grand jury indicted Father on December 4 for molesting her, as Andrew Fegelman reported in

the *Chicago Tribune* on December 5, in "Priest Indicted on Sex Charges."
Finally, Father was tried, convicted, and sentenced in February 1993 to three
years in prison for child molestation.[6] The family of his latest victim and
many parish members were angry with me for not stopping him sooner.

Once the story of Father's removal and indictment on charges of child
sexual abuse hit local television, the aftershocks escalated into more stories
about more Chicago priests. The visible and vocal nature of The Linkup and
the growing number of other advocacy organizations for victims of clergy
sexual abuse created a public relations disaster for institutionalized religions
of every denomination. The Linkup gained momentum as national media began focusing attention on the nationwide problem. Churches felt the reper-
cussions in diminished financial contributions.[7] Their knee-jerk reaction was
to engage in damage control through denial and minimization. Religious leaders blamed the victims for "scandalizing the church" by their allegations, and
they indicted the media for sensationalism. (Pope John Paul II's letter of June
11, 1993, to U.S. bishops regarding the "scandal" that victims have created
by their disclosures of clergy abuse echoed the U. S. bishops' longstanding
position [Pope John II, 1993].) But they soon discovered that these tactics
could not contain the truth. Scores of disclosures followed by successful
criminal prosecutions and civil lawsuits testified that religious leaders had
been involved in a conspiracy of silence and cover-ups that reached back for
decades.

As I lambasted the cardinal in national news interviews for his extended
tolerance of these priest perpetrators' behavior, he sought a truce, telephon-
ing me at my office on November 25, 1991. He asked my assistance in for-
mulating policies and evaluating the Isaac Ray Center, a Chicago-area
diagnostic and treatment center to which he was referring his pedophile
priests. At his request, I met with Cardinal Bernardin at his residence that
day and on January 25, 1992. He gave me his private home number, and we
called each other often between that November day and September 22, 1992.
During our meeting in November, the cardinal asked me to meet with the
Isaac Ray Center staff to assess its sex offender treatment program.

One month earlier, and only two days after Father's latest victim had
publicly disclosed her molestation, the cardinal named an auxiliary bishop
and two lay Catholics to review all Chicago priests' personnel files. As Hirsley
reported in his October 26, 1991, *Chicago Tribune* article "Panel to Examine Priests in Sex Cases," on the commission were Hon. Julia Dempsey-Quinn
of Cook County Juvenile Court, an associate judge; John Madden, former
chair of the advisory council of the Illinois Department of Children and Fam-

ily Services; Auxiliary Bishop John R. Gorman, a licensed clinical psychologist and vicar general of the Archdiocese of Chicago As Cardinal Bernardin announced in a news conference on June 15, 1992, the commission ultimately recommended forming a review board and drafting a formal written policy for the handling of allegations of clergy sexual abuse. In July, the cardinal formed the recommended board, with a full-time director. Upon the board's recommendations, the cardinal ultimately disabled at least twenty-nine archdiocesan priests—twenty-two of them publicly—from active parish ministry because of admitted sexual misconduct with minors, as Leon Pitt and Daniel Lehmann noted in "How Sexual Abuse Allegations Are Handled" on December 12, 1992, in the *Chicago Sun Times.*

In the midst of this activity, in the fall of 1992, The Linkup held its first national conference at the Woodfield Hilton Hotel in Arlington Heights, Illinois, October 16–18, on the theme "Breaking the Cycle of Silence." A. W. Richard Sipe, a former priest and author of *A Secret World*, a study of celibacy in the priesthood, began his speech with, "My friends, welcome to Wittenberg"—the city where Martin Luther in 1517 hammered his theses on the cathedral door, launching the Protestant Reformation (Sipe 1992). At the end of this keynote address, a woman rose among the audience of three hundred, sobbing, "Where do I direct my rage at the priest who abused me in a convent?" she asked. "The first kiss of a young woman should not come from a middle-aged priest." The father of a thirteen-year-old boy who was sodomized by his pastor stated that after that incident, "the lights went out in my child's eyes." Three years later, the boy was still in residential treatment with no assistance or compassion from the priest's superiors. The mother of a twelve-year-old girl who over a period of years was repeatedly raped by her pastor in the family's home said that when she learned of the abuse, she "knew our lives would never be the same. We were so devastated that I wondered if we could ever be happy again."

More than retribution, victims indicated that "justice" could only come through resolution and reconciliation. For them, resolution involved honesty. It would require that the perpetrator and his superiors acknowledge the offenses, take moral responsibility for them, and establish and enforce appropriate measures to ensure that no one would be harmed in the future. Punishment was not an issue for most victims. Indeed, everyone who spoke about having taken legal action said they had done so only as a last resort, after Church leaders failed and refused to respond appropriately to their requests for resolution.

Surprisingly, victims were expressing a need to reconcile with the

Church. Like me, many had imagined the church and its representatives as their family, a symbolism long encouraged by the Church. God was our "father"; Jesus was our "brother" because he was the "son of God." Mary embodied universal motherhood. Together, Jesus, Mary, and Joseph were our model "holy family." The Catholic Church was our "kingdom on earth," our nurturing "spiritual family." This was the Church whose representatives on earth taught us the values, morals, and principles that governed our behavior and beliefs. This was the family that ultimately failed us by ostracizing us for speaking up and demanding accountability. Nonetheless, we were grieving its loss. In its absence we felt empty, unconnected and alienated from God. Most of us felt compelled to reconcile with this family because, consciously or unconsciously, we still saw it as the only conduit through which we could obtain spiritual redemption. Ironically, despite the abuses, we could not shake the need and desire to reunite with it. We needed—demanded—that the representatives of this family live up to our dashed expectations. We still needed to know that its members cared. We still needed to know that all its teachings were not a fraud because, if they were, we had nothing left to believe in.

Having identified the passionate need among victims to feel cared about and connected with the Church, I asked Cardinal Bernardin to demonstrate his articulated pastoral concern by presenting himself to The Linkup's first national conference as its keynote speaker. When he agreed to deliver this address, The Linkup began promoting his appearance as a healing highlight of the conference. Feedback from registrants evidenced a general enthusiasm for the cardinal's appearance and admiration for his courage.

About two weeks before the conference, a hand-delivered letter arrived from the cardinal advising me that he had decided to cancel his appearance when my mild criticism of some aspects of his policy reforms appeared in the *Chicago Tribune*.[8] The cardinal wrote that he believed his appearance would be counterproductive for both of us. At the opening of the conference, I read his entire letter aloud from the podium in lieu of his keynote address. The attendees gasped and cried in disappointment. I explained, "It's not as though the Church did not come to you tonight but, rather, the Cardinal did not come to his Church."

The conference was like a homecoming. Even though most of the attendees were strangers to each other, a feeling of kinship cloaked the event. These men and women, driven to tell their stories, had now found each other and, for the first time, felt heard and understood. People who for years or, in some cases, decades feared reprisal for speaking a cleric's name in vain bonded as kindred spirits; in their numbers, they found courage to demand their religious leaders be accountable. They discovered among themselves a new community to replace the one that had betrayed them.

Observing and listening to the attendees clarified for me as never before that sexual abuse involving clergy has its own dynamic. The word "betrayal" surfaced time and again as victims spoke of the way they have come to view pastors, priests, and bishops. Talking to one another, victims searched for patterns to help them understand how their abuse occurred. One pattern that surfaced indicated many victim families had once had exceptionally strong ties to the Church or individual priests. These ties, it seems, facilitated trust and close contact. Some wondered aloud whether predator priests chose families like those, who might seem less likely to turn suspicious or accusatory.

Many who had carried this secret burden into adulthood told of how, since their abuse, they had acted out in obsessive behaviors such as sexual promiscuity, drug and alcohol addiction, and obesity. Some had become sexually frigid. Many were not able to develop or sustain any meaningful intimate relationship. Some male victims of male clergy and female victims of female clergy remained confused over their sexual identity decades after a single abusive act.

Emotions flared as attendees spoke of the guilt they carried through the years. Frequently, victims had blamed themselves long before they blamed their assailants. Many parents of children abused by clergy chastised themselves for the implicit trust they had placed in the perpetrator. More than one parent spoke of having regularly welcomed the offending cleric into their home, of having made him nearly a member of the family. Several parents spoke of how Church attorneys had named them as codefendants in suits brought on behalf of their children. The strategy was, apparently, to intimidate them by naming the parents as codefendants with the Church for allegedly having failed to exercise adequate parental care in entrusting their child to the offending cleric. In one case involving a twelve-year-old boy, the allegation alone resulted in the parents' ineligibility to proceed in their pending adoption of a new baby from Catholic Charities. Victims spoke of various other intimidating strategies employed by church officials or their attorneys to ward off allegations of sexual misconduct, such as threats of excommunication from the Church or civil countersuits.

The conference speakers who had dealt with the problem of clergy sexual abuse in their professional capacities testified to the long history and pervasiveness of clergy sexual abuse as well as the universal reluctance of the various religious institutions to appropriately respond to it. Rev. Thomas P. Doyle, canon lawyer, former Vatican embassy official in Washington, D.C., and current Catholic chaplain in the U.S. Air Force, spoke about how, in 1985, he, attorney Ray Mouton, and Rev. Michael R. Peterson, M.D., had confronted the National Catholic Conference of Bishops (NCCB), warning them in a written report of the magnitude of the priest sex abuse crisis in the Catholic Church of America, and the Church's massive potential exposure to liability(Doyle, Mouton, and Peterson 1985). The report concluded that the problem had reached epidemic proportions and projected that the Catholic Church would have paid $1 billion in litigation damages by the year 2000 unless the bishops took immediate action.

Doyle told the conference that the bishops chose to ignore the report, after which he resigned from the Vatican embassy and enlisted in the U.S. Air Force. He said that the Roman Catholic Church is "still reacting rather than acting" on the problem and "is still trying to work damage control to save its patrimony." Like the conferees, Doyle said, he had been disillusioned by the moral bankruptcy of these Church representatives, but he had not lost his faith. He said that now he goes right to the top (meaning God) for spiritual support and doesn't dilute his faith through dependence on the institutional Church (Doyle 1992).

Jeffrey Anderson, an attorney from St. Paul, Minnesota, who spoke at the conference, specializes in clergy sexual abuse cases and claimed at the time to represent 150 victims in twenty-three states. In his presentation, he stated that there were cases in every one of the nation's 188 Catholic dioceses. His statistics revealed that since 1982, four hundred to five hundred cases had been or were being litigated, that out-of-court settlements were ranging upward from $300,000, and that the Catholic Church alone had already paid out more that $500 million in settlements and fees to sexual abuse victims and their families (Anderson 1992). Anderson's figures appeared consistent with the Archdiocese of Chicago's 1992 published budget with expenses of $1.1 million connected to charges of clergy sexual misconduct involving minors. The Chicago archdiocese's 1993 budget projected $2.8 million in legal fees and settlement expenses for the sexual misconduct of its priests. (These figures had been published as part of a major archdiocesan campaign to raise money to offset a projected $12.6 million overall deficit.)

Sociologist Andrew Greeley, a Chicago archdiocesan priest and long-time critic of the Catholic Church's lack of response to the clergy sexual abuse problem, supported Anderson's statistics in his own presentation. Greeley blamed a "privileged class" Church structure that rewards loyalty, sometimes punishes individual idealism, and "imposes no standards of appropriate pro-fessional behavior on its members." As a result, Greeley stated, "priests can do anything they damn please to people, and feel pretty confident that they can get away with it. . . . The sexually maladjusted priest has been able to abuse the children of the laity and thus far be reasonably secure from pun-ishment. There is no power of church or state that is willing to force priests to be accountable for their behavior." After quipping that "even the outfit—mob, syndicate, Cosa Nostra, call it what you want—has sanctions," Greeley drew prolonged applause when he said, "Every priest in the country who does not take action against the problem is, I would argue, morally responsible for it" (Greeley 1992).

The Linkup's first national conference received extensive international publicity. The group soon grew into an international organization serving thousands of victims of clergy sexual abuse and their families from not only the United States but England, Ireland, and Australia. With a public relations disaster in the making and financial ruin looming, institutionalized religions found the situation too volatile to ignore. They now recognized that victims demanded action and were willing to go to civil authorities to get it, that they would persist in holding their respective religious institutions accountable to practice as they preached.

Consequently, bishops and religious leaders of various denominations decided to demonstrate some cooperation with victims. Many sought me out for consultation, stating that they wished to draw on the expertise I had gained as a victims' advocate. Believing in their sincerity, I participated in many church-sponsored meetings, think tanks, and bishops' subcommittee hearings. Church leaders said all the right things. They expressed a desire to know and understand what victims needed for recovery. They espoused compassion for the victims. They pledged assistance to victims and their families. They pub-licly announced their commitment to resolving the problem. Some even re-solved to report allegations of child sexual abuse to civil authorities and cooperate with resulting criminal investigations. Many religious leaders de-veloped formal written policies that seemed responsive to victims' needs.

For one think tank, Fr. Canice Connors, director of St. Luke Institute (which treats abusers), empaneled a thirty-two-member group of nationally renowned therapists, theologians, canonists, victims, and "recovering" pedo-phile priests. He asked me to participate on behalf of victims of clergy abuse. We would meet February 22–23, 1993, in St. Louis, Missouri, to draft rec-ommendations to present to the NCCB's annual June meeting.

This think tank got off to a rocky start when, contrary to what Fr. Connors had implied when soliciting our participation, he explained that our activities were underwritten not by the NCCB but by an anonymous donor and that there was no guarantee that the NCCB would accept the group's recommendations. Further, no agenda existed, and this would be a one-shot deal—no returns to the drawing board, no future discussion. It was astonishing that an anonymous sponsor could ensure that our recommendations would pass up the hierarchical chain of command. Hearing that the bishops had made no investment in the process sent my emotions plunging. But I had agreed to participate without any real expectations, thinking that whatever developed, we were laying a paper trail that down the line the Church could not deny.

At the conclusion of the think tank, Fr. Connors explained that he knew the proper way to communicate with bishops. He said that our recommendations were too straightforward. If we expected the bishops to read them at all, we could not sound like we were telling them what to do. Fr. Connors announced that he and his comrades would edit the recommendations and submit them to us for approval before delivering them to the NCCB. In the meantime, he said, the draft recommendations should remain confidential. In the opinion of think-tank participants, the recommendations needed to be presented in the form we had submitted. I immediately published our version in The Linkup's newsletter, for which I was quickly admonished in a letter from Fr. Connors.

Fr. Connors submitted his revisions to the think-tank participants in March with an invitation for our feedback. Some of the participants I spoke with expressed profound displeasure over the dilution of our recommendations. I informed Fr. Connors that I wanted my name removed from the recommendations before submission to the bishops because these were not the recommendations I had helped develop. Nonetheless, eventually, an even tamer version than the one we were shown was presented to the NCCB in June over a full roster of our names (Secretariat for Priestly Life and Ministry 1993).

As I watched Fr. Connors on national television make "our" presentation to the bishops, I was overcome with anger at the compromises he had made and presented on our behalf (Connors 1993). The moment was well orchestrated. Following Fr. Connors's presentation, Bishop John Kinney of Bismarck, North Dakota, rose to address his colleagues. He stated, "I want to make sure that all of us bishops understand the depth and seriousness, the pain and the agony of this problem and why it strikes at the very heart of the church's trust level and credibility level." He announced the formation of the NCCB's Ad Hoc Committee on Clergy Sexual Abuse, designating himself as chair (Kinney 1993).

The following week, I received a telephone call from Bishop Kinney's secretary inviting me to Washington at once to meet with Bishop Kinney to discuss victims' issues. Despite my skepticism as to how productive such a meeting would be, I agreed to go. At that meeting, on July 19, 1993, I told Bishop Kinney how Fr. Connors had presented the bishops with a diluted version of the think tank's recommendations. I suggested another think tank composed of victims and Bishop Kinney's ad hoc committee of bishops. Bishop Kinney asked me to send a written proposal to him with alternative dates and a location. He said it was urgent.

Immediately upon my return to Chicago, I contacted Abbot Timothy Kelly of Saint John's Abbey in Collegeville, Minnesota. He said he would be pleased to offer the Abbey as a think-tank site and provided possible dates for the event. I then put together a detailed written proposal and sent it by Federal Express to Bishop Kinney; the package was later returned to me unopened. In subsequent communications, the bishop told me that, in lieu of a think-tank meeting, he wanted me and other Linkup representatives to return to Washington for another three-hour session. It seemed to me counterproductive to fly to Washington for a session that would only reiterate or rehash what the bishops already knew. They had many psychologists, doctors, and lawyers to help them understand and appropriately address this problem. I believed our participation in another such meeting would only serve to legitimize the NCCB's inaction by allowing it to publicly claim it was meeting with victims' representatives and addressing the issue, while it actually stalled any real progress. I believed bishops and victims needed several days together on neutral territory to get to know each other in a spontaneous exchange of information and ideas. However, although Bishop Kinney's expressed the desire at our meeting in July to empathize deeply with the pain of victims, he rejected my proposal.

In August 1994, The Linkup held its "Healing toward Prevention" conference at Saint John's University, with no representatives of the bishops' ad hoc committee present. The keynote speaker, Benedictine sister Joan Chittister, a social psychologist, summed up the universal experience with patriarchal religious institutions: "Patriarchy is power run amok, run aground, run over the defenseless and the powerless. . . . A patriarchal system wants its women and children docile, demur, and disturbingly dependent—under control and under authority, and under someone somewhere" (Chittister 1994).

It is too early to know whether religious leaders are attempting to work toward a real solution to the problem of clergy sexual abuse or are merely engaged in a public relations campaign. In 1993, every Catholic diocese in the United States had adopted policies for dealing with reports of clergy sexual misconduct, according to a statement made by Mark Chopko, NCCB general counsel, to the think tank in St. Louis. Whether they implement these is another question. For example, even after Cardinal Bernardin announced the Chicago archdiocesan policy, which requires his cooperation with law enforcement authorities, archdiocesan attorneys invoked a legal privilege to quash a subpoena of Church employment records.[9] Citing statutory priest-penitent privileges between the cardinal, his clergy aids, and the perpetrator priest, the archdiocese refused to turn over allegedly incriminating personnel files to the Cook County prosecutor. The subpoenaed employment files were those of priests whom the cardinal himself had publicly named for removal from their ministries for admitted sexual misconduct with minors. Following a review of the files in camera, the court ruled for the archdiocese, maintaining that the documents were covered by the privilege and, therefore, unobtainable for purposes of prosecuting the offending priests, according to Michael Hirsley and Terry Wilson in "Priest Files Can Remain a Secret— Archdiocese Protected in Abuse Cases" in the *Chicago Tribune* on November 17, 1992.

In other cases, religious leaders have created random exceptions to their own rules. For instance, only a few years after Chicago's Cardinal Bernardin received national public praise for his unprecedented hard-line opposition to clergy sexual abuse, he defied his own explicit, unconditional written policy that prohibits the return to ministry of any priest who has engaged in sexual misconduct with minors. In October 1995, Cardinal Bernardin reassigned an offending priest to his parish following psychiatric treatment. In this case, Cardinal Bernardin cited as his reason for making an exception the overwhelming willingness on the part of parishioners to extend "Christian forgiveness and reconciliation" to the priest. The parochial cycle had brought these parishioners back to their Catholic conditioning. Their compliance with Catholic tenets of forgiveness and faithfulness to the institution and what it dictates led them to welcome Fr. John Calicott back to Holy Angels Church after his removal for the admitted molesting of several teenage boys, as Bob Secter and Paul Galloway reported in "Church Takes Risk of Forgiving" on October 15, 1995, in the *Chicago Tribune*.

What appears virtually certain is that demands for accountability must proceed from the bottom up to effectuate change. Victims of clergy sexual abuse, weary of words and restless for resolution, have abandoned hope for pastoral relief from their religious leaders and have, for the most part, turned to civil authorities to punish the guilty. But clearing the clergy of child molesters will not occur until all lay members of institutionalized religions refuse at any cost to tolerate them and the morally bankrupt Church leaders who perpetuate the problem.

Notes

1. This was the expressed opinion of Detective Portia Wallace, Lake County Sheriff's Department, when, in 1982, based on her investigation of our case, she recommended the criminal prosecution of Father Robert Mayer for child sexual abuse to the state's attorney. He declined. She reiterated this opinion publicly on October 18, 1992, in her address to VOCAL's (Victims of Clergy Abuse Linkup) first annual national conference.
2. This mandate was first disclosed by Auxiliary Bishop Raymond Goedert at a parents' meeting at St. Odilo Church, Berwyn, Illinois, on October 16, 1991, after Father Mayer's removal from that parish.
3. Victims Of Clergy Abuse Linkup, Inc. d/b/a "VOCAL" was incorporated on September 19, 1991. The assumed name was changed to "The Linkup" on May 17, 1993.
4. Status of cases in 1991: Fr. William Cloutier (pending civil suit), Fr. Robert D. Friese (convicted in 1989), Fr. Robert Lutz (pending civil suit), Fr. Robert Mayer (1982 civil suit settled in 1984), and Fr. Henry Slade (pleaded guilty/convicted in 1990).
5. These facts were later confirmed by the sworn testimony of witnesses at the 1992 criminal trial of *People of the State of Illinois v. Robert E. Mayer.*
6. On December 11, 1992, Father Mayer was convicted on four counts of criminal sexual abuse for fondling the thirteen-year-old girl in St. Odilo Church rectory, as reported on December 12 in the *Chicago Sun Times* by Leon Pitt and Daniel Lehmann in "Ex-Berwyn Priest Guilty in Sex Case" and in the *Chicago Tribune* by Terry Wilson in "Ex-Berwyn Priest Convicted of Sex Abuse." As Wilson reported in the *Tribune* on February 6, 1993, in "Priest Gets 3 Years for Sex Abuse," Mayer was sentenced to a three-year prison term.
7. The Archdiocese of Chicago's published 1992 budget disclosed an overall deficit of $6.4 million and forecasted "equally bleak" figures for 1993. Expenses directly attributable to charges of clerical sexual abuse involving minors were $1.1 million in 1992, with $2.8 million projected for 1993, according to Andrew Herrmann in "Catholics' Cash Crisis" in the *Sun Times* on September 24, 1993. In fact, the Archdiocese of Chicago ended fiscal 1993 with a hefty overall deficit even after closing several of its schools, according to *Sun Times* reporter Herrmann in "Church Deficit Reaches $4.5 Million in Fiscal '93" on January 12, 1994.

8. Also see Michael Hirsley's column in the *Chicago Tribune* of October 16, 1992, "Cardinal Missed an Opportunity," criticizing Bernardin's cancellation of his appearance at the VOCAL Conference.
9. On September 21, 1992, Cardinal Bernardin approved his appointed board's written policy, "Clerical Sexual Misconduct with Minors: Policies for Education, Prevention, Assistance to Victims and Procedures for Determination of Fitness for Ministry." In a press release dated September 21, 1992, Cardinal Bernardin stated, "These new policies are designed to accommodate the needs of all these people whose lives have been changed forever by these tragic encounters. *I accept the clinical data which suggest that once it has been demonstrated that a priest is an abuser, he should never again return to parish ministry or any ministry which might place a child at risk*" (italics mine).

References

Anderson, Jeffrey R. 1992. "Visiting the Sins of the Fathers upon the Church: A View from the Victims' Lawyer." Speech presented to the first annual VOCAL National Conference, Arlington Heights, Ill., October 17.

Chittister, Joan. 1994. "Sexual Abuse and the Abuse of Power." Speech presented to the second annual VOCAL National Conference, Collegeville, Minn., August 4.

Connors, Canice. 1993. "Subcommittee Head Introduces Think Tank Recommendations." *Origins: Catholic News Service* 23, 7 (July 1):105–107.

Doyle, Thomas. 1992. "How Did We Get Here from There?" Speech presented to the first annual VOCAL National Conference, Arlington Heights, Ill., October 17.

Doyle, Thomas P., Ray Mouton, and Michael R. Peterson. 1985. "Executive Summary." Presented to the annual meeting of the National Catholic Council of Bishops. Washington, D.C. August.

Greeley, Andrew. 1992. "Clerical Culture and Pedophilia." Speech presented to the first annual VOCAL National Conference, Arlington Heights, Ill., October 17.

Kinney, John. 1993. "NCCB Establishes Committee on Sexual Abuse." *Origins* 23, 7 (July 1):104.

Miller, Jeanne M. [Hilary Styles, pseud.]. 1987. *Assault on Innocence: For the First Time . . . The Untold Story of Pedophilia.* Albuquerque: B and K.

Pope John II. 1993. "Letter from Pope John II." *Origins* 23, 7 (July 1):102–103.

Secretariat for Priestly Life and Ministry. 1993. "'Recommendations of the "Think Tank" on Child Sexual Abuse, St. Louis, February 21–23, 1993,' as presented to the NCCB annual meeting in New Orleans, Louisiana, on June 17, 1993." *Origins: Catholic News Service* 23, 7 (July 1):108–111.

Sipe, A. W. Richard. 1992. "Sexual Abuse by Priests—Why?" Paper presented to the first annual VOCAL National Conference, Arlington Heights, Ill., October 17.

"Think Tank Produces Recommendations." 1993. *The Missing Link: Newsletter of The Linkup* 1, 2 (April):6–10.

PART III

Models for the Study of Clergy Malfeasance

CHAPTER 10

Disclaimers and Accounts in Cases of Catholic Priests Accused of Pedophilia

JAMES G. THOMSON, JOSEPH A. MAROLLA,
AND DAVID G. BROMLEY

*T*he priest abuse scandal in the Roman Catholic Church in the United States began to surface in 1983. Over the last decade the scandal has broadened, with a seemingly endless string of pedophilia cases involving scores of young children discovered and disclosed. In a number of instances priests have been criminally prosecuted and sentenced to long prison terms; others have been remanded for mental health treatment. Although sexual violations of various kinds have occurred across a number of religious groups (e.g., Jacobs 1989; Shupe 1995), what distinguishes the current Catholic cases analyzed here is that they involve sexual encounters between priests and children under the age of majority, often in their teen and preteen years. Most of the abuse has involved young boys, but there have been cases of abuse of young girls as well.[1] Scattered reports have surfaced of similar incidents involving clergy in other churches, but incidents involving non-Catholic clergy most often consist of extramarital affairs between adult women and ministers.

The child sexual abuse scandal constitutes an extreme case of deviance. The priests involved have violated their personal vows of celibacy and chastity; they have engaged in predatory homosexual activity in many cases, against which the Church they represent preaches; they have deliberately concealed the sexual violations that they committed; and they have violated the moral trust reposed in them by the Church, their fellow priests, and the families whose children they exploited. Most centrally to the analysis here, these priests have engaged in sexual activity with children (see Beal 1992; Provost 1992). Moral condemnation of pedophilia is virtually universal and impassioned, and efforts by individuals or groups to rationalize or defend such behavior meets strenuous resistance (de Young 1984, 1988, 1989). In addition to the nature of the acts themselves, the significance of these priests' actions is compounded by the status they occupy within the Catholic tradition. Priests are the immediate intermediaries between parishioners and the Church, trustees responsible for parishioners' spiritual lives and spiritual welfare.

Disclaimers and Accounts in Contemporary Priest Abuse Cases

In this chapter we examine the types of narratives priests construct in initiating sexual relationships with children and in explaining their conduct when the violations are exposed. Given the number and seriousness of norms that these priests are violating and their lofty moral standing, the ways they explain their conduct becomes an interesting sociological issue. We divide the narratives that priests and their spokespersons develop into two broad types. First, priests must formulate prospective interpretations, or *disclaimers*, for their behavior toward the children with whom they are sexually involved. These explanations are constructed within the perpetrator-victim relationship and are concealed from others by various means. Second, upon public exposure of the sexual relationships, priests and their spokespersons are compelled to offer retrospective interpretations, or *accounts*, for their conduct. As we look at both types of explanations and the relationship between them, we find that retrospective accounts are significantly influenced by and must be understood in the context of prospective disclaimers.

Not surprisingly the data on priest abuse cases are limited. Many local cases are not nationally reported, journalistic reports often are fragmentary or focus on issues other than defendant disclaimers and accounts, and the Catholic Church routinely has demanded sealed records as a precondition for out-of-court settlements. We gathered most of the narratives presented here from four recent books and 257 press reports on priest abuse cases. The most fruitful sources were books authored by journalists, which were based on cases that had reached a conclusion and contained considerable detail about events and explanations. In some cases, however, we find disclaimers and accounts in other sources, such as news conferences, trial testimonies, and victims' accounts. Journalistic narratives in particular are biased in favor of public statements that yield sensational stories; they systematically exclude stories that are handled privately or are more mundane and unexceptional. Given the nature of the sources, we must exercise caution in generalizing broadly from these data. At the same time, we have conducted an extensive review of scholarly and journalistic sources, which constitute virtually the only accessible data sources. We should also note that narratives constructed over a period of time typically are more complex than the analytic account categories employed here, and actors are likely to use multiple disclaimer and account types (Schoenbach 1990).

Disclaimers

A disclaimer is "a verbal device employed to ward off and defeat in advance doubts and negative typifications which may result from intended conduct. Disclaimers seek to define forthcoming conduct as not relevant to the kind of identity challenge or re-typification for which it might ordinarily serve as the basis" (Hewitt and Stokes 1975, 3). Disclaimers, in other words, are offered to "cushion" an anticipated reaction when some behavior is about to be discovered. There are five types of disclaimers. Persons use *hedging* disclaimers when they have a tentative commitment to a forthcoming line of action and are uncertain about the probable response to their actions. In this circumstance they express willingness to consider and negotiate alternative perspectives. People use *credentialing* disclaimers when they are committed to a line of action that they know will be discrediting. They thus offer qualifications or credentials that legitimate the line of action they are proposing. Similarly, people use *sin license* disclaimers when they are committed to a line of action that they anticipate will evoke a negative response, but in this case they seek to depict a situation in which generally recognized rules may be suspended without discrediting themselves. People come up with *cognitive* disclaimers when they anticipate that others may doubt that there is a shared understanding of the "facts of the situation" on which they are operating; they use such disclaimers to reassure others of such agreement. Finally, people issue *appeals for the suspension of judgment* when they anticipate that their statements or actions may produce a negative emotional reaction. They ask others to suspend their response until the meaning of the line of action is clarified.

Virtually all of the explanations priests offered to children in the incidents we examined are *credentialing* disclaimers. In most cases their authoritative statements take the form of simply asserting divine approval for the proposed relationship. For example, "Sex is okay," a priest told one girl. "This is the way God would have it" (Burkett and Bruni 1993, 74). In some instances divine approval is paired with a stipulation that the relationship should remain secret: "Father Jay told the boy; 'This is between you and me. This is something special. God would approve'" (Burkett and Bruni 1993, 67). Children clearly are often shocked when priests first approach them. The credentialing disclaimers provide a means for moving beyond this disorientation and potential resistance. One victim recounts: "One day he went into the bedroom and all of a sudden he came out with his pants down around his knees and I freaked out . . . I was shakin'. He said, 'It's not wrong. God made the body to be beautiful—for each of us to share it'" (Berry 1994, 128). Some episodes do involve considerably more planning and complex interpretations. One victim remembers that the priest organized the sexual encounters with him and another boy named Morris as therapeutic penance:

> Ed's abuse began as a condition of absolution. The youth confessed to impure thoughts and to the sin of pride. Father Terrence directed him to learn self-control. The lesson was simple, Ed alleges: the priest would masturbate Morris, or lie on top of him rubbing their groins together, but would stop just shy of Ed's ejaculation. "Desensitization," Father Terrence called this penance. "No matter how you go to the altar, as a priest or to marry, this will help you," Ed remembers Father Terrence telling him. "You are special. You are pleasing to God. But you have a corruptible side you must learn to control." (Burkett and Bruni 1993, 76)

In one case the priest employed a sin license. According to a December 12, 1993, story in the *Fort Wayne [Indiana] Journal-Gazette* by Ron French, "Shattered Trust: Pain Endures for Victim of Alleged Clergy Abuse": "'He'd talk about unconditional love,' Schrader [the victim] said. 'He said too many people love conditionally.' And so although Schrader was uncomfortable with the sexual relationship, he felt that 'it fit with what he [the priest] was saying about unconditional love, . . . if you're going to unconditionally love, you need to express it." Finally, in one incident credentialing was combined with a sin license disclaimer. In this case the priest not only asserts that his female partner has been chosen by God but also seeks to suspend the relevant normative context by asserting that he needs assistance because he is ignorant of sexual matters. "She recalled the beginning of the abuse . . . 'I was told that I had been chosen by God to help him with his studies of sex because he was responsible for helping adults and he didn't know anything about it'"(Berry 1994, 128)

It is not surprising that credentialing disclaimers predominate in priests' constructions of sexual relationships to their youthful partners. Proposing sexual relations and offering to negotiate the relationship, attempting to reach agreement on the nature of the situation in which they are involved, or asking the children to suspend judgment would each probably cause confusion or resistance that the priest would then have to surmount through some other disclaimer or line of action. The credentialing strategy places the priest firmly in control of the situation; it asserts a legitimate basis for the connection that then can be veiled from outside observation. That illicit sexual relationships with children have occurred in substantial numbers over a long period of time without being discovered outside the Church hierarchy suggests that this strategy has generally succeeded.

Accounts

Numerous typologies of accounts have been formulated (Sykes and Matza 1957; Schoenbach, 1980, 1990; Tedeschi and Reiss 1981; Semin and Manstead 1983). We base the analysis here on Scott and Lyman's widely used typology, which defines an account as "a statement made by a social actor to explain unanticipated or untoward behavior—whether the behavior is his own or that of others, and whether the proximate cause for the statement arises from the actor himself or from someone else" (1968, 46). Scott and Lyman divide accounts into two broad types, *excuses* and *justifications*. From their perspective, "An excuse is an admission that the act in question was bad, wrong, or inept, coupled with a denial of full responsibility. A justification is an admission of full responsibility for the act in question, coupled with a denial that it was wrongful" (1970, 93). Excuses thus are accounts constructed with the objective of mitigating the actor's responsibility for the act in question; justifications are intended to normalize the act in question.

Justifications

Scott and Lyman define six types of justification. *Denial of injury* accounts construct events so as to minimize the negative and maximize the positive consequences of contested behavior. *Denial of victim* accounts define victims as deserving harm as a result of having injured the actor, being enemies of the actor, or holding membership in devalued groups. *Condemnation of condemners* accounts rationalize contested actions by comparing them to uncensured acts by others that are equal to or greater than the actor's own normative violations. *Appeal to loyalties* accounts deem contested conduct appropriate in terms of higher allegiances to which the actor is committed. *Sad tale* accounts reconstruct the actor's biography in highly disadvantaged terms that explain current behavior. Finally, *self-fulfillment* accounts lay claim to personal growth, health, or conscience as a legitimate rationale for contested conduct.

In the priest abuse cases we examined, almost every instance involved *denial of injury* accounts.[2] In one case a priest included in his account a statement referring to self-fulfillment. Father Ritter asserted his right to personal fulfillment, avowing that even divine disapproval would not override his right to pursue his own identity. He stated: "You know, I decided twenty years ago, if God didn't like me the way I was, that's His problem" (Sennott 1992, 30). However, this account differs markedly from virtually every other justificatory statement.

The priests or their spokespersons have employed several strategies to elevate the moral standing of the deviant behavior. One approach insists that the sexual contact is consensual. For example, a therapist/columnist specializing in treatment of priests accused of sexual abuse wrote in a Catholic magazine: "We are not involved with the dynamics of rape but with the far subtler dynamics of persuasion by a friend. As we speak to and about the victims we must be aware the child sometimes retains a loving memory of the offender" (Connors 1992). In this account the denial of injury is buttressed by characterizing the incident as involving *persuasion* rather than *coercion* and by further asserting that the child involved in fact harbors no hostility toward the priest.

In another account, journalist Jason Berry (1994, 11) records the statement of a diocesan vicar responsible for the conduct of priests. The vicar makes a comparable characterization of the sexual relationship as "misguided affection" but seeks to mitigate the damage by juxtaposing indiscretion or poor judgment in this incident with the catastrophic consequences for the priest's career. "The diocese had received a report some time ago, Larroque continued, terming it 'a case of misguided affection. . . . We're talking about ruining a man's career,' said Larroque, referring to the implication of charges against a priest."

A third strategy is to moderate claimsmaking by emphasizing the "extraordinary importance" of the work in which the priest and his colleagues are involved, a mission that should not be jeopardized by a single behavioral "failure": "It is probably better to say I failed. If I had to give a reason for my own personal failure it is probably hubris. . . . What happens to me, ladies and gentlemen, is not really very important. I decided long ago that I did not care about that. What happens to the kids is very important. The work we do here is of extraordinary importance" (Sennott 1992, 273). Justice for the victims and the vital mission of the institution thus are placed in opposition. Vigorously prosecuting the offender might cripple or destroy the institution, thereby sacrificing "the kids."

Finally, the harm involved in sexual abuse may be minimized by shifting the behavior to a category with at least subcultural legitimacy and by carefully distinguishing the traits of acceptable and unacceptable sexuality. For instance, in a legal statement one priest distinguishes between sexual intercourse and what he calls a "reserved embrace": "'I may have had a reserved embrace,' he admitted in a deposition in 1992. . . . Sexual intercourse, he said, doesn't occur unless a man clutches a woman with passion and ejaculates into her. Yes, he had lain atop Susan. Yes, he put his penis in her vagina. But there was, 'no passion, no kissing, no nothing,' he said. And he had not ejaculated" (Burkett and Bruni 1993, 87–88).

What is most striking about justification accounts, of course, is their clustering in the denial of injury category. Other types of justification accounts apparently are unavailable or difficult to construct for this type of violation. Priests and their allies can hardly accuse the young boys with whom they have sexual liaisons of deserving harm. They would also be understandably reluctant to group themselves with the other categories of deviants with which comparisons are most likely to be drawn, such as incestuous fathers, sexual predators, and homosexuals. Likewise, given the high moral calling to which priests are pledged, it would be difficult to rationalize sexual relationships with children with an appeal to higher principles. Even were priests to make a case for the "sexual liberation" of children, they could not be the liberators. Given priests' pledge to the spiritual welfare of their parishioners and to sacrificial life-styles, self-fulfillment could not be accorded a higher priority than the welfare of children. Priests might conceivably reconstruct their biographies to explain their conduct, an accounting strategy often employed by psychotherapists accused of inappropriate sexual intimacy (Pogrebin, Poole, and Martinez 1992). However, since priests' personal lives are so completely enmeshed in the Church, such a strategy would almost inevitably involve an attack on the Church or admission of their own incompatibility with the priestly role. Priests seeking to mitigate claimsmaking against them seem to have few justification options beyond damage control. Asserting that the acts they have committed are not as heinous as public depictions of them in the media or prosecutorial rhetoric may be their best available option.

Excuses

Scott and Lyman identify four types of excuse accounts. *Accident* accounts seek to mitigate responsibility by asserting that the actor cannot control environmental events. Actors may misinterpret events, be unable to foresee impending events, become distracted, lack skills and abilities requisite to deal successfully with occurrences, or have insufficient time to respond. *Defeasibility* accounts aver impairment of mental capacity as a result of mental disorder, intoxication/addiction, or psychological duress. *Biological drives* accounts identify biological attributes such as sexual passion, sexual orientation, or criminogenic tendencies as the source of contested behavior. Finally, *scapegoating* accounts seek to shift responsibility for contested behavior to the participation, duress, or provocation of another actor.

Three types of excuse accounts dominate in the cases we examined. Accident accounts usually are presented by Church representatives with the objective of defending the Church rather than the individual priests. These accounts assert the impossibility of absolutely preventing individuals with psychological disorders from entering the priesthood. In some cases these errors are blamed on the absence of effective screening techniques. In this effort Church officials are supported by Church-affiliated clinicians responsible for treating offenders (e.g., Berry 1994, 208) For instance, the bishop of Baton Rouge blamed his ignorance on the priest's deliberate, skillful deception: "'My mistake,' said Frey, '[was] not being able to recognize the depth of [Gauthe's] mental illness. His personality was such that he skillfully masked his condition'" (Frey 1986).

A second type of excuse account is scapegoating, also largely employed by Church administrators. In these accounts Church officials imply, with varying degrees of specificity, that individuals or groups are using the abuse scandal for their own nefarious purposes. The issues of responsibility and harm are turned around, with the accused presented as a victim of a kind of conspiracy to discredit the offender. The controversy thus results not from the actions of the accused but from the evil intentions of named or unnamed enemies, calling the motives of the accusers into question. In some cases the alleged enemies remain anonymous. For example, an editorial in the *Lafayette [Indiana] Sunday Advertiser* for June 16, 1985, issued this advice under the headline "In the Gauthe Affair: The Catholic Church Is Not on Trial!": "Let's offer a special prayer for the resolution of the affair that has rocked the

Acadiania community and ask the forgiveness of any unscrupulous individuals who for one reason or other attempt to blacken the reputation of our entire religious community."

Sometimes enemies are more clearly defined. In the now famous Covenant House case, one of Fr. Bruce Ritter's staff said to a reporter, "I think it was outrageous and disgusting for the District Attorney to outfit this kid with a wire to try to entrap Father Ritter" (Sennott 1992, 265).

Another strategy for scapegoating involves alleging that the charges against the Church are being pursued so vigorously precisely because of the Church's high moral standards. A letter from Pat Hayes to the editor of the *Springfield [Illinois] State Journal-Register* on December 13, 1993, published under the headline "Priests Should Not Be Stigmatized by the Few," blames the problem on the low moral character of the public in general and the mass media in particular: "[H]ow the media glorifies scandalous stories, but they do so because of the public's love affair with dirt. . . . I have to wonder about the potential contagiousness of allegations, a contagiousness that is only being encouraged by sensationalistic media and a 'let's sue' atmosphere that is cheered on by some of the most ridiculous and inciteful advertising I've ever seen." Attacking the Church through the conduct of wayward priests becomes a cynical means for undermining its calls for moral standards to which the larger society does not wish to adhere: "Archbishop Daniel Pilarczyk [said] 'I think our culture in general sees this as a chance to get a little bit even with the Church in the context of unpopular prophetic things the Church says about society. Maybe it's really a kind of implicit acknowledgment of the relevance that people, even unconsciously, find in the Church'" (Burkett and Bruni 1993, 199). In this account the vendetta is portrayed as part of a larger conflict, with the individuals accused merely victims of the Church's crusade to foster sexual morality. Condemnation of the priests helps undermine the Church as a bastion of morality.

In some instances Church spokespersons even question the motives of the victims making claims against the Church. A bishop wrote in a newspaper column: "[O]ne can ask; if the victims were adolescents, why did they go back to the same situation once there had been one 'pass' or suggestion? Were they cooperating in the matter, or were they true victims?'" (Harris 1990, 16). However, in most instances accounts simply assert psychological disorder, often in rather perfunctory terms. This was the tack taken by North America's most notorious priest-pedophile, Fr. James Porter: His illness made him abuse a minimum of several hundred victims, many repeatedly (Burkett and Bruni 1993, 18). One source of defeasibility specified, which fits with current explanations for abusive behavior, is the priest's own abuse as a child: "A certain proportion of priests . . . abuse children not because they are sexually starved, but because their 'love-maps'—their objects of sexual desire—have been vandalized in childhood experiences of their own" (Greeley 1993, 45).

In these defeasibility accounts priests tend to emphasize the potency of their emotional feelings, which often become more powerful once they are expressed. One priest refers to the "enormous stress on him, which is why, he believes, his desires caught him so off guard. Horsing around with a parish altar boy for a Mass well done, he patted him on the rear. . . . The more he touched them, the harder it became to control his gestures. 'It opened up a hunger,' he says. 'Now fantasy was not enough. It's like—how does a person go back to masturbation when he's had intercourse?'"(Burkett and Bruni 1993, 93). The offender's experience of desire is depicted as an inexorable progression from thought to physical satisfaction. The overpowering nature of the feelings and their growing strength are important in these accounts, for priests frequently abused a succession of children over an extended period of time. Loss of control may account for a single episode; a more elaborate accounting is necessary for extended abuse. The potency of his feelings becomes such an explanation to the extent that the priest is unable to resist them.

Church-affiliated professionals offer support for this interpretation. For example, in a professional paper both a canon and a civil lawyer use anecdotal evidence to argue that offenders have no control and therefore accrue a lower level of personal liability: "We are dealing with compulsive sexual habits which the priest may temporarily suspend in the face of legal or canonical pressure, but not in all instances. There are many examples wherein sexual abuse took place very soon after the confrontation between the priest and his Ordinary (bishop) had taken place. The priest must clearly be seen as one suffering from a psychiatric disorder that is beyond his ability to control" (Mouton and Doyle 1985). Making sexual abuse a psychological disorder offers the Church an explanation that relieves the individual priest of responsibility and avoids the stain on the Church's reputation that accompanies a moral interpretation (Freidson 1970). Thus to the extent that pedophilia is an undetectable disorder, this account reduces the responsibility of both priest and Church.

One more development of the defeasibility account mitigates priest responsibility even further. Using the medical model, Church psychiatrists separate behavior from character:

> Diagnosing a person as a pedophile says something about the nature of his sexual desires and orientation. It says nothing about his temperament, or about traits of character (such as kindness vs cruelty, caring vs uncaring, sensitive vs insensitive, and so on). Thus a diagnosis of pedophilia does not necessarily mean that a person is lacking in conscience, diminished in intellectual capabilities, or somehow "characterologically flawed." One needs to evaluate independently the nature of an individual's sexual drives and interests, as opposed to what the person is like in terms of character, intellect, temperament, and other mental capacities. (Berlin and Krout 1986, 14)

Separating behavior from character is important to both the Church and the priest. The stigma for both is reduced if conduct rather than moral essence is at issue. The Church is less culpable for failing to detect behavioral disorders than for failing to recognize low moral character, and priests can be treated for specific disorders but not for flawed moral essence.

As with justification accounts, excuse accounts sometimes have several themes. For example, one priest who asserts long-term defeasibility bordering on biological drives argues that the Church's structure caused his condition to manifest itself, mitigating his own guilt by transferring responsibility to the institution and his peers: "I sought that feeling out after that. I began to look for and depend upon affection from younger persons. There had been so many needs that had been unmet and so many disappointments and so many pains and so many rejections that it didn't matter. . . . After 20 years of parish life, I guess I felt that nobody gave a damn about me" (Burkett and Bruni 1993, 85).

Excuse accounts vary more than justification accounts. Accident and scapegoating accounts are employed primarily by Church officials who use them to defend the institution rather than individual priests. The Church improves its moral positioning by arguing that it cannot possibly detect every case of behavioral disorder, particularly when priests deliberately conceal such attributes, and by contending that opponents are using the few incidents that have escaped detection to discredit an institution that in fact is a moral exemplar. For their part, priests appear most likely to choose related biological and defeasibility accounts that attribute their conduct to loss of control. Where they offer more than perfunctory illness accounts, priests tend to emphasize a process of spiraling out of control after the initial transgression, which offers an interpretation that explains a pattern of long-term violation.

Preliminary Observations

The analysis of narratives explaining priest sexual abuse led us to two general conclusions. First, we can better interpret narratives as a sequence than as separate elements. We have illustrated this point by exploring the relationship between prospective disclaimers and retrospective accounts. Second, we must examine narratives in their social structural context as well as their symbolic context. This dimension of narrative construction is not the focus of our analysis here, but we can offer some preliminary observations.

Developing the kind of explanatory narratives for behavior we examine here is an extended process that begins when the actor pursues a contested line of conduct. Most sociological research has focused on the account construction process. We believe that it is theoretically important to analyze both (1) the prospective explanations (disclaimers) through which actors initiate lines of action that may be contested and that may alter the actor's identity in a negative fashion and (2) the retrospective explanations (accounts) through which actors justify or excuse acts evaluated as deviant in an effort to minimize sanctions and defend personal identity. Whatever the ultimate sources of priests' motivation in initiating sexual relationships with minors, the evidence here indicates that priests find it important to assert a rationale and identity as central elements of the process.

Disclaimers largely cluster in the credentialing category. Priests draw on their spiritual authorization in most instances to legitimate the lines of action they are about to take. Particularly in dealing with children, this strategy maximizes the priest's capacity to orchestrate the interaction, reduces the necessity for more difficult, complex negotiation, and creates the basis for sealing off external disclosure. Virtually all priests select this solution as a way of asserting priestly authority, integrating the priestly role with conduct that norms define as incompatible with and violative of that role.

This type of disclaimer pattern arguably has clear links not only to the priests' behavioral objectives but also to a specific organizational context. Priests can employ the credentialing disclaimer in large measure because of their high moral/spiritual status. Devoted Catholics, particularly children, are unlikely to challenge their authoritative pronouncements. Further, the priest role is located within a religious organization that entrusts to priests' care the spiritual welfare of parishioners. In organizations granted trustee status, normative violations are adjudicated internally with limited, if any, external oversight (Bromley 1995). As findings from a number of priest abuse scandals make clear, Church officials were well aware of pedophile priests, deliberately concealed their identities and activities, and in a number of cases simply transferred priests out of one parish to a new, unsuspecting parish when sexual violations were discovered. That priests could use a credentialing disclaimer to initiate and sustain sexual relationships with a succession of youth over an extended period of time in the same and different locations becomes highly improbable outside of this structural context.

Justification accounts that diminish wrongfulness are considerably less common than excuse accounts. Where justifications are offered, they are almost invariably denial of injury accounts. Priests have little alternative but to attempt to mitigate the seriousness of their infractions by emphasizing the consental nature of the sexual encounters; characterizing the behavior as misguided, an indiscretion, or reflecting poor judgment; or shifting the behavior to a less stigmatized category. Priests often incorporate into these accounts statements inviting comparison of the limited number and severity of the incidents to the vital larger mission of the Church or the priest. Such comparisons place the injury in a larger framework that tends to diminish relative harm and discourage prosecution that would unduly damage the priest or the Church. In short, priests concluded that damage control in the form of minimization of injury is their most viable course.

Excuse accounts are far more common than justifications as priests and their spokespersons acknowledge wrongfulness but deny culpability. Given the rapidly growing number of scandals and the frequent presence of numerous victim-witnesses offering corroborating testimony, neither priests nor the Church can easily refute the charges. Rather, institutional representatives seek to disavow responsibility through accident and scapegoating accounts. Both shift the focus of attention from the child to the Church as victim, in the first case accidentally and in the latter case as part of a deliberate campaign (both tend to infuriate victims and their families). Church officials offer an accident excuse account based on the impossibility of identifying psychologically disordered priests either because diagnostic procedures are fallible or because priests deliberately camouflage these personality characteristics. Alternatively, Church spokespersons contend that opponents paint a far grimmer portrait of Church untrustworthiness than a few individual violations warrant. In this version, the Church is being attacked precisely because of its principled character, which raises moral standards to a level that most individuals would prefer not to meet. Both the accident and scapegoating accounting strategies are premised on a "bad apples" theory that assumes the existence of few abuse cases. The Church has attempted to create this reality through an institutional strategy of not responding to victims and of private settlements that require the sealing of all records as a precondition. As the number of revelations has mounted and the concerted efforts by the Church to deny victim claims and conceal incidents come to light, both accounting strategies have become less tenable.

For their part, individual priests almost unanimously employ defeasibility accounts. There are scattered references to biological drives, but the primary theme is psychological disorder. These excuse accounts try to explain, first, having engaged in prohibited relationships at all but also the succession of illicit relationships over an extended period of time. One major problem that such defeasibility accounts face is that because priests consciously used their priestly authority (credentialing disclaimer) in initiating and sustaining sexual relationships with children, they need to account not only for a sexual encounter but also for a highly organized pattern of behavior and legitimation. This requires a stronger defeasibility claim than they might need to account for a single, momentary lapse. In essence these priests must argue that the planning and disclaiming in which they engaged are elements of the disorder, but this means pleading to a much more serious condition. Nonetheless, defeasibility accounts offer the best chance for priests to continue in their occupational/spiritual roles, for the issue becomes their behavior rather than their moral character, with at least a possibility of rehabilitation. The Church can also come to the defense of the priests for these same reasons.

The results of disclaimers and accounts we report here underline the significance of symbolic formulations in the organization of deviant behavior. Actors must prospectively construct motives and identities that permit them to engage in a deviant line of action, and they must do so in a way that minimizes the likelihood of resistance and stigmatization. Likewise, when violations are exposed, individuals are pressed to formulate accounts that will place their conduct in a symbolic context that minimizes sanctions and damage to individual identity. The data on priest sexual abuse presented here illustrate how explanations for action formulated at the prospective stage limit the degrees of freedom and shape the nature of accounts at the retrospective stage. Further progress in interpreting these symbolic strategies requires placing disclaimers and accounts in a relational context. In the case at hand, it is evident that major normative breaches are difficult to negotiate symbolically when violators are called to a final reckoning.

Notes

1. Although we will probably never know the true extent of such activity, Sipe (1990) estimates that 2 percent of U.S. priests suffer from pedophilia and another 6 percent are attracted to older minor children.
2. This analysis focuses on priest-pedophile behavior. However, there have been cases of nuns engaging in similar activities, and they have resorted to comparable accounts.

References

American Psychiatric Association. 1994. *Diagnostic and Statistical Manual of Mental Disorders*, 4th ed., rev. Washington D.C.: American Psychiatric Association.

———. 1987. *Diagnostic and Statistical Manual of Mental Disorders*, 3rd ed., rev. Washington D.C.: American Psychiatric Association.

Beal, John. 1992. "Doing What One Can: Canon Law and Clerical Sexual Misconduct." *The Jurist* 52:642–683.

Berlin, Fred S., and Edgar Krout. 1986. "Pedophilia: Diagnostic Concepts." *American Journal of Forensic Psychiatry* 7 (1):13–30.

Berry, Jason. 1994. *Lead Us Not into Temptation: Catholic Priests and the Sexual Abuse of Children*. New York: Doubleday.

Bromley, David. 1995. "The Politics of Religious Apostasy." Paper presented at the annual meeting of the Society for the Scientific Study of Religion, St. Louis.

Burkett, Eleanor, and Frank Bruni. 1993. *Gospel of Shame: Children, Sexual Abuse, and the Catholic Church*. New York: Viking.

Connors, Canice. 1992. "Priests and Pedophilia: A Silence that Needs Breaking?" *America* 166 (May 9):400–401.

de Young, Mary. 1989. "The World According to NAMBLA: Accounting for Deviance." *Journal of Sociology and Social Welfare* 16 (1):111–126.

———. 1988. "The Indignant Page: Techniques of Neutralization in the Publications of Pedophile Organizations." *Child Abuse and Neglect* 12:583–591.

———. 1984. "Ethics and the 'Lunatic Fringe': The Case of Pedophile Organizations." *Human Organization* 43 (1):72–74.

Freidson, Eliot. 1970. *Profession of Medicine: A Study of the Sociology of Applied Knowledge*. Chicago: University of Chicago Press.

Frey, Gerard. 1986. "Bishop Denied Gauthe Cover-up, Won't Give up Job." *Lafayette [Ind.] Sunday Advertiser* (February 2). Quoted in Berry 1994, 145.

Greeley, Andrew. 1993. "A View from the Priesthood." *Newsweek* (August 16):45.

Hamilton, V. L. 1978. "Who Is Responsible? Toward a Social Psychology of Responsibility Attribution." *Social Psychology* 41:316–328.

Harris, Michael. 1990. *Unholy Orders: Tragedy at Mount Cashel*. New York: Viking.

Hewitt, John P., and Randall Stokes. 1975. "Disclaimers." *American Sociological Review* 40:1–11.

Jacobs, Janet. 1989. *Divine Disenchantment: Deconverting from New Religions*. Bloomington: Indiana University Press.

Money, John. 1972. *Man and Woman, Boy and Girl*. Baltimore: Johns Hopkins University Press.

Mouton, F. Ray, and Thomas P. Doyle. 1985. *The Problem of Sexual Molestation by Roman Catholic Clergy: Meeting the Problem in a Comprehensive and Responsible Manner. Internal report to the National Council of Catholic Bishops.* Washington, D.C.

Murphey, Michael. 1986. "Priest Faces Second Felony Charge." *Spokane Spokesman-Review* (March 4) as quoted in Berry 1994, 165.

Pogrebin, Mark, Eric Poole, and Amos Martinez. 1992. "Psychotherapists' Accounts of Their Professional Misdeeds." *Deviant Behavior* 13:229–252.

Provost, James. 1992. "Some Canonical Considerations Relative to Clerical Sexual Misconduct." *The Jurist* 52:615–641.

Schoenbach, Peter. 1990. *Account Episodes: The Management or Escalation of Conflict.* New York: Cambridge University Press.

———. 1980. "A Category System for Account Phases." *European Journal of Social Psychology* 10:195–280.

Scott, Marvin B., and Stanford M. Lyman. 1970. "Accounts, Deviance, and Social Order." In *Deviance and Respectability: The Social Construction of Moral Meanings,* edited by Jack Douglas. New York: Basic.

———. 1968. "Accounts." *American Sociological Review* 33 (1):46–62.

Semin, A. S., and S. R. Manstead. 1983. *The Accountability of Conduct: A Social Psychological Analysis.* New York: Academic.

Sennott, Charles M. 1992. *Broken Covenant.* New York: Simon and Schuster.

Shupe, Anson. 1995. *In the Name of All That's Holy: A Theory of Clergy Malfeasance.* Westport, Conn.: Praeger.

Sipe, A. W. Richard. 1991. *The Secret World: Sexuality and the Search for Celibacy.* New York: Brunner/Mazel.

Sykes, Gresham, and David Matza. 1957. "Techniques of Neutralization: A Theory of Delinquency." *American Sociological Review* 22:664–670.

Tedeschi, J. T., and M. Reiss. 1981. "Verbal Strategies in Impression Management." In *The Psychology of Ordinary Explanations of Social Behavior,* edited by Charles Antaki. New York: Academic.

CHAPTER 11

How the Problem of Malfeasance Gets Overlooked in Studies of New Religions: An Examination of the AWARE Study of the Church Universal and Triumphant[1]

ROBERT W. BALCH AND STEPHAN LANGDON

*D*uring the siege of the Branch Davidian community in Waco, Texas, the national news media frequently speculated about parallels between the Branch Davidians and other new religious movements. Which, they wondered, would be the next Waco? The group mentioned more often than any other was the Church Universal and Triumphant, a New Age community in Montana near the northern entrance to Yellowstone National Park. The main basis for the speculation was the Church's extensive network of underground bomb shelters, supposedly heavily armed. Because of the publicity, Church members worried that they too might be targeted for an assault by the Bureau of Alcohol, Tobacco, and Firearms (BATF), a concern shared by many in the academic community.

The ashes from the Waco conflagration had barely cooled when, in the summer of 1993, James Lewis, founder of the Association of World Academics for Religious Education (AWARE), organized an interdisciplinary study of the Church. The Church's leader, Elizabeth Clare Prophet, approved the study because she wanted to show that the Church had no dark secrets. The study team included sociologists, anthropologists, psychologists, religious scholars, an attorney, and a former police detective. Balch was invited to take part in the study because he had visited the Church before and was already somewhat familiar with its beliefs and practices. Langdon was included at Balch's request because he had conducted a six-month participant-observer study of the Church for a senior thesis at the University of Montana (Langdon 1997).

During our initial phone conversations with Lewis and his wife, Eve Oliver, we were led to believe the AWARE study was intended to be a thorough investigation of the Church. Several scholars had been selected to investigate specific topics, such as the Church's history, beliefs, demographics, child rearing practices, and the psychological characteristics of its members. The police detective on the team had been chosen to investigate the charge that Church members were stockpiling illegal weapons. Other scholars, ourselves included, were invited to develop their own projects. We were told that the interdisciplinary make-up of the research team would insure that the Church would be examined from a variety of perspectives. However, these same conversations made us wonder just how thorough and objective the study would be.

From the outset we believed the AWARE study would turn out to be an apology for the Church rather than a thorough investigation. Our suspicions grew out of our initial discussions of the study with Lewis and Oliver. Balch was told the purpose of the study was to head off "another Waco" by showing that the Church was not a dangerous cult, but simply an alternative religion whose members were normal, intelligent, law-abiding citizens. Although Balch agreed that the Church was not dangerous, it appeared that the study's conclusions already had been reached. Langdon got the same impression. He was told that Church members were "wonderful people" and that the study would "exonerate the Church" of the charges against it. Based on Langdon's research, we knew the charges included psychological coercion, abuses of power, questionable economic practices, financial exploitation of members, and illegal weapons purchases. However, except for the gun controversy, no provisions had been made to look into these issues. Our misgivings were heightened as we watched the study unfold. The study's design virtually assured that if malfeasance existed within the Church, it would not be discovered.

Our intention is not to discredit the Church or malign the scholars who took part in the AWARE study. Instead we want to raise questions about the way social scientists study alternative religions because we believe the AWARE study, aside from its interdisciplinary nature, is more typical than exceptional. We find it ironic that social scientists have devoted volumes to corruption in conventional institutions, such as law enforcement and business, while generally ignoring charges of malfeasance in new religions. We believe the oversight reflects a widespread belief in the social scientific community that unconventional religions need to be defended against religious intolerance. However, we believe the more fundamental problem is how studies of new religions are designed and executed. A good research design can minimize the effects of bias and insure the collection of thorough, objective, reliable information, while a poor one can result in an unfounded attack or a blatant apology.

Based on our observations of the AWARE project, we will argue that social scientists need to adopt a more critical perspective when studying new religions. We believe the study of new religious movements could profit immensely from research designs that combine traditional sociological methods with the model of investigative journalism. The investigative approach should be used to assess the validity of accusations against new religions, while standard sociological methods can help us understand why malfeasance is common in some groups but is absent in others. Unfortunately, the AWARE study lacked this critical perspective. As a result, the study gave the appearance of clearing the Church of the charges against it, when in fact most of those charges were never investigated (Lewis and Melton 1994).[2]

The Church Universal and Triumphant

The Church Universal and Triumphant is one of several new religions known as "Ascended Master activities," which include its predecessors, Theosophy and the I AM movement (Melton 1992). Ascended masters are thought to be enlightened beings who, upon balancing their karma from previous lifetimes, have ascended to a higher spiritual realm where they watch over human affairs. The masters include Jesus, Buddha, Krishna, El Morya, St. Germain, Mother Mary, the Chinese goddess Kuan Yin, and dozens more. Church members believe the masters deliver their teachings through "dictations" received by Elizabeth Clare Prophet, fifty-seven, known to her followers as the Messenger.

The Church has a complex, syncretic belief system that blends Christianity with ideas from Eastern religions. Every individual is thought to possess a divine spark known as the "I AM presence." The Church teaches that each soul has the potential to become one with God by tuning into the I AM presence through a demanding process of self-mastery. Its belief system incorporates karma, reincarnation, astrology, alchemy, gnosticism, and elements of Catholicism, such as belief in saints and angels.

The masters teach various methods to help seekers along the path toward ascension. The best-known is decreeing. Decrees are high-speed prayers and affirmations used to balance karma and invoke the intercession of the masters on behalf of humanity. Although decreeing resembles Buddhist chanting and reciting the rosary, anticult writers have capitalized on the apparent oddness of the practice to support their claims that the Church uses mind-numbing brainwashing techniques.

The Church dates from 1958 when Mark Prophet founded the Summit Lighthouse in Washington, D.C. Prophet, a former evangelical Christian, claimed he had been anointed as the Messenger by the master El Morya. In 1963 he married Elizabeth Clare Wulf, who became the Messenger after Prophet died in 1973. Mrs. Prophet declared her husband had ascended to become the master Lanello and in 1974 she changed the group's name to the Church Universal and Triumphant. In 1986 she moved the Church's headquarters from California to Montana, where the Church now owns approximately 24,000 acres of land adjacent to Yellowstone Park.

The Church does not divulge membership figures, but it claims to have two hundred centers in forty countries. Current membership estimates reported in the media run as high as fifty thousand worldwide, but according to ex-members, less than ten thousand is more realistic. Members tend to be middle-aged and middle-class, and most have at least some college education (Jones 1994). Former Catholics are heavily overrepresented, and most members have considerable experience with New Age religions. At the time of the AWARE study, at least a thousand members lived in Montana.

The Church's structure can be represented by a series of concentric circles. The outermost ring consists of Keepers of the Flame, whose only commitment is subscribing to the monthly Church publication, *Pearls of Wisdom*. The next ring consists of Keepers of the Flame active in a local Church center but not formally initiated into the Church. Communicants, those who have been initiated in a ceremony similar to Catholic confirmation, make up the third ring. They have agreed to abide by various conduct rules, such as decreeing every day and giving 10 percent of their income to the Church. Members who are "on staff" comprise the next ring. These members work full-time for the Church and typically live in Church-owned residences. Staff members adhere to a strict code of conduct that prohibits drinking, smoking, drug use, and sex outside of marriage. They typically attend daily decree sessions and write confession letters to Mrs. Prophet several times a year. Dating relationships must be approved by Prophet, and married couples are expected to follow additional rules governing their sexual activities.

The innermost circle consists of Prophet, her board of directors, and her most trusted confidants. Here all decisions affecting the Church are made. The members closest to Prophet are referred to as the "white fire core," reflecting their devotion to the Messenger. Most core members joined the Church when Mark Prophet was still alive and have been on staff for at least fifteen years. At the time of the AWARE study in 1993, Prophet was president of the Church, and her husband, Edward Francis, was vice president and business manager.[3]

Ever since the days of Summit Lighthouse, the Church has been embroiled in controversy. Besides the usual charge of mind control, the Church has been accused of using high-pressure scare tactics to coerce members into donating money, keeping secret files on members, and violating the priest-penitent relationship by using confidential confession letters to humiliate dissidents. Church officials have vehemently denied these charges, claiming that the Church has been singled out for attack because of its unconventional beliefs.

No issue, however, incited as much controversy as the Church's "shelter cycle" in 1989. In a 1986 dictation, the master St. Germain declared that members should prepare for possible nuclear war with the Soviet Union by building bomb shelters. The largest shelter, capable of housing 756 members, was built in the Mol Heron Valley, which environmentalists claimed was prime grizzly bear habitat. During construction a fuel tank ruptured and thousands of gallons of diesel fuel leaked into the ground. Shortly before the fuel spill, Edward Francis and another member, Vernon Hamilton, were arrested and convicted of using false names to buy assault rifles. Although Elizabeth Clare Prophet denied any knowledge of the purchase and Francis publicly apologized to Church members, the incident exacerbated fears that the Church was a dangerous cult.

Despite the bad press resulting from these incidents, the Church slowly managed to win supporters among local residents, who found members to be ordinary people, good customers and employees, and honest business owners. Then in 1993 the Branch Davidian community went up in flames.

An Overview of the AWARE Study

Most of the study took place during the Church's summer conference between June 25 and July 4, 1993. About 2,500 people attended, with nearly all the activities concentrated in several huge tents erected for the occasion. In the largest, which held about two thousand people, the speeches and dictations occurred. Other tents housed the cafeteria, a bookstore, an activity center for children, and listening rooms where non-English-speaking members could watch events in the main tent on closed-circuit TV with simultaneous translations into Spanish, Portuguese, and French. The theme of the conference was healing the environment, and the featured speakers were nationally known experts on environmental issues. The most important events, however, were the dictations, which occurred every day throughout the conference.

Members of the research team had been promised unrestricted access to Church activities and archives, and the doors truly seemed open to us. We toured the Church's 756–person bomb shelter, which hardly anyone except staff members had seen, and we were allowed into the high-speed decree sessions preceding the dictations, normally closed to outsiders and even to new members. Several scholars were allowed to read and copy large portions of the Church's extensive files. Two psychology graduate students administered a battery of psychological tests to a sample of conference participants, and one of the sociologists on the team distributed a long questionnaire about members' beliefs, activities, backgrounds, and demographic characteristics. To facilitate our research, the Church had set aside a mobile home, the "Hospitality Trailer," where we could conduct interviews, watch events on closed-circuit TV, and meet to share information.

One participant claimed that only three new religions in the country—Scientology, the Unification Church, and the Hare Krishnas—had been subjected to as much scrutiny. The Church Universal and Triumphant presumably was about to become the fourth most thoroughly studied new religion. However, that was not to be.

The AWARE Team in Action

As soon as we arrived at the conference site it became obvious that the study lacked a coherent plan. In fairness to Lewis and Oliver, much of the disorganization was inevitably a reflection of the urgency of the situation in light of the Waco debacle. It seemed imperative to begin the study as soon as possible, but this required members of the research team to put other projects on hold and fly to Montana on short notice. It also meant that the participants had little time to familiarize themselves with the Church's history and beliefs before arriving. Most were unable to stay for more than a few days, and because of conflicting schedules, the research team never had a chance to meet beforehand as a single group to exchange ideas and agree on a research design. The result was that most participants were unfamiliar with the Church's belief system and knew little about the controversies surrounding the Church. To our knowledge, no effort had been made to acquaint members of the AWARE team with either the Church's beliefs or the charges against it.

The lack of familiarity with the Church surfaced even before the research team assembled in Montana. When Balch requested a copy of the questionnaire designed for conference participants, he found that it revealed numerous misunderstandings about the Church's structure and beliefs. For example, the questions failed to distinguish between Keepers of the Flame, Communicants, and staff members, and it confused receiving dictations with the popular New Age practice of channeling. In the Church's belief system, dictations are messages from the ascended masters that are delivered only through Prophet, whereas channeled information is thought to come from less evolved spiritual entities who speak through ordinary people. Were it not for Langdon's eleventh-hour advice to the person who had designed the survey, the respondents might not have taken it seriously.

It quickly became clear that there would be few opportunities to share information during the data-collection phase of the study. Shortly after we arrived at the conference, one member of the research team proposed that we meet every evening in the Hospitality Trailer to discuss our observations. But that never happened, primarily because most members of the team were housed about thirty miles away and were dependent on a Church shuttle bus for transportation. Although we did have daily morning meetings at the Church's restaurant, we never received an agenda or any leadership, so our meetings proved thoroughly unproductive. We met once to decide on a final version of the conference questionnaire, but this was the only meeting where any concerted effort occurred.

Considering the limited time members of the research team had to spend at the conference, one might suppose that they would devote the better part of each day to learning as much about the Church as possible. However, several people took a day off to visit Yellowstone Park, and others spent much of their time hanging out in the Hospitality Trailer. Instead of observing dictations firsthand, some members of the team chose to watch them on closed-circuit TV because it was cold in the main tent. It was also surprising to see that much of the discussion in the Hospitality Trailer had nothing to do with the Church. For instance, several members of the team spent the better part of an afternoon discussing child abuse charges against The Family, another controversial new religion being studied by AWARE (Lewis and Melton 1994; Balch 1996). Even Church members noticed how superficial the investigation was. One of our hosts, a high-ranking staff member, told Langdon: "They don't want to talk to us. They just want to sit in the trailer and bullshit."

Lack of Attention to Critical Issues

We do not mean to imply that the AWARE study failed to yield any worthwhile information. The questionnaire and psychological tests produced valuable profiles of the conference participants (Jones 1994; Sowards, Walser, and Hoyle 1994). A field study of the children at the conference proved especially insightful (Shepherd and Lilliston 1994; Lilliston and Shepherd 1994). And DeHaas (1994) conducted a thorough investigation of the Church's public image problems in the local area.[4]

For the most part, however, the AWARE study failed to dig into the issues that made the Church so controversial in the first place. Three were highlighted in 1992 when the Internal Revenue Service revoked the Church's tax exempt status. The first charge involved excessive commercialism. Records showed that the Church ran several profit-making enterprises, including Summit University Press, the Royal Teton Ranch, the Cinnabar General Store, the Ranch Kitchen restaurant, Chamuel Records, a mobile-home park, and two subdivisions where members could lease residential property. Lanello Reserves, a for-profit company registered in California, traded gold and silver, and during the shelter cycle it also sold survival food to members, grossing over $1 million in 1988, according to Natalie K. Phillips's article, "CUT: A For-Prophet Company," in the *Bozeman Chronicle* of March 25, 1990. Most of the Church's money came from donations, which ex-members claimed were frequently solicited through high-pressure fear appeals. Yet, to our knowledge, no one on the research team took any interest in the Church's economic practices.

The IRS also charged that Church funds had been used to pay a $521,000 civil penalty against Prophet. This involved a suit against the Church alleging several instances of clergy malfeasance. In 1986 Gregory Mull, an architect and former staff member, won a $1,563,300 judgment against the Church in the Superior Court of Los Angeles, California, on the grounds that he had been coerced into signing a $32,000 promissory note (*Church Uni-*

versal and Triumphant, Inc. v. Gregory Mull). The judgment against Prophet was part of the settlement. Mull claimed he was so impoverished after being expelled from the Church that he had to forage for food in supermarket dumpsters. Randall King, Prophet's former husband and one-time president of the Church, testified that one of Mull's confession letters, in which he had reported homosexual experiences, had been circulated among staff members and was used to make him an object of ridicule. Although one of the scholars mentioned the Mull trial at the beginning of the study, no one tried to find out if such abuses still occurred.

The principal IRS charge against the Church involved weapons. The IRS claimed not only that the Church stockpiled arms, but that it demonstrated a twenty-year pattern of concealing these activities from its members. As the *Billings Gazette* reported in "Papers Detail CUT Arms Deal" on July 1, 1993, the IRS also charged that the arms violations by Edward Francis and Vernon Hamilton were "undertaken by and attributable to CUT, Inc." Although these allegations were reported by Montana's largest newspaper while the AWARE team was at the conference, no one investigated whether Church officials regularly deceived members, or if Francis and Hamilton had been acting individually or on behalf of the Church. One member of the study, a retired detective, visited more than twenty-five shelters looking for secret compartments where weapons might be hidden, but he found nothing. One reason for skepticism, however, as the *Gazette* reported in the July 1 article, is that evidence compiled by the U.S. Department of Justice suggests that all weapons had been secretly removed from the shelters after the BATF raid on the Branch Davidians.[5]

In addition to the IRS charges, the research team failed to investigate other controversies. One notable oversight was the shelter cycle. In his 1986 dictation about nuclear war, St. Germain urged members to spend every available penny preparing for the holocaust, and in 1989 he proclaimed the odds of nuclear war as greater than the chances of a death in the family. In response, hundreds of members moved to Montana and incurred enormous debts building shelters and buying survival gear. Many accumulated thousands of dollars in credit card charges, which they later were unable to pay. Faced with bankruptcy, many members defected and some allegedly suffered mental breakdowns. During the peak of the crisis, some children ran away from home, seeking refuge with families outside the Church. None of these issues was investigated by anyone on the AWARE team.[6]

Had Anyone Read Goffman?

In *The Presentation of Self in Everyday Life*, Goffman (1959) describes how group members engage in "teamwork" by cooperating to prevent the "leakage" of potentially discrediting "back-stage" information. To his embarrassment, Balch had learned the hard way just how important it is to keep Goffman's "dramaturgical" model in mind when studying new religions.

Based on several visits to a religious commune known as the Love Family, during which he had stayed in members' homes and had taken part in numerous activities, Balch confidently told students in one of his university classes that the Love Family was one of the few contemporary communes that had managed to avoid the problems of corruption and drug abuse. Just three months later, Balch learned that the community was breaking up because of those very same problems.[7]

Balch's subsequent research (1988, 1995) revealed that the Love Family's leader, Love Israel, had pushed the community to the brink of bankruptcy to support a debilitating cocaine habit and an increasingly self-indulgent lifestyle. However, most of Love's followers were completely unaware of the problems because for years members of the inner circle had concealed information about Love's private life from ordinary members, and even from each other. The teamwork that protected Love from criticism is remarkable because the Love Family was an intimate, communal society with only about two hundred adult members, many of whom lived in Love's house and saw him nearly every day.

Based on our knowledge of the Love Family, we understood the methodological implications of Goffman's insights: If potentially discrediting information about malfeasance can be hidden so effectively from members, one can only imagine how well secrets can be kept from visiting scholars, especially when their fieldwork lasts only a few days.[8]

One problem with the AWARE study was its timing. The investigation took place during the Church's biggest conference of the year, when staff members understandably would have been concerned about making a good impression, even without outside investigators. In addition, the conference participants probably were more committed than typical members because attending the conference required a substantial financial investment. Besides registration fees ($195 per person to preregister or $225 at the door), participants had to pay for meals, lodging, and transportation. During a group interview we conducted with some younger staff members, our informants pointed out that we were not meeting ordinary members, but those who were "on fire." Everyone in the interview agreed that we were not seeing every-day life in the Church.

Nor were we meeting people who might have provided us with mean-ingful glimpses behind the scenes. With few exceptions, the conference par-ticipants had no first-hand knowledge of life on staff, and staff members themselves generally were too busy working on the conference to take time for interviews. A few interviews were conducted, but most were not the kind one would expect to reveal evidence of malfeasance. For example, Lilliston and Shepherd interviewed teachers about the Church's educational system, and other scholars conducted a long interview with a member who had suc-cessfully resisted a recent deprogramming attempt. Aside from detached ob-servation, the main contact most of the scholars had with the Church came through a handful of Church officials who had been designated to serve as our hosts.

Studies of new religions (Balch 1995; Butler 1983; Johnson 1992; Latkin 1991) suggest that structural conditions that free leaders from social control encourage corruption. These include an inner circle of highly pro-tective devotees, norms discouraging the expression of doubt and negativity, and an ideology of unquestioning submission. However, the only systematic data collected by the AWARE team focused on issues that were, at best, only marginally related: Church history and beliefs, community relations, child rearing, and members' personal-biographical characteristics. No strategy had been devised to find out if malfeasance existed in the Church or to identify conditions that might contribute to it.

It was obvious to us that someone should have been designated to in-terview defectors, especially former members of Elizabeth Clare Prophet's inner circle. Although sociologists tend to dismiss ex-member accounts as unreliable (Lewis 1989; Solomon 1981), Balch had concluded from his pre-vious research on new religions that defectors are more trustworthy than so-ciologists like to believe. In a field study of a UFO cult (now known as Heaven's Gate), for example, Balch (1985) found few inconsistencies between the observations recorded in his field notes and the stories ex-members told him about the same events several months later, and his study of the Love Family demonstrated that ex-member accounts could be corroborated by checking stories against each other (Balch 1988, 1995; see also Zablocki 1996). Yet the AWARE study did not include defectors. Given the impromptu nature of the project, nobody, including us, had the time to locate and inter-view a cross-section of ex-members.[9]

Even if there had been time, however, no one on the research team expressed any interest in interviewing defectors. We were surprised at how readily the scholars appeared to accept as true whatever our hosts said. For example, after Prophet and Edward Francis gave speeches describing the Church's response to the IRS gun charges, a member of the research team told Prophet that her remarks had been "just perfect," and another applauded Francis for the "believability of the speech."

Pressures toward Partisanship

Our assessment of the AWARE study is that it suffered from the problem of *groupthink*. Janis (1972) borrowed the term from George Orwell's novel *1984* to describe a conformist mode of thinking that develops in groups of likeminded individuals where the desire to maintain congenial relationships takes precedence over critical analysis. In groupthink, subtle pressures to conform inhibit expressions of skepticism, and anyone bold enough to question the prevailing viewpoint is likely to be ostracized, resulting in an illusion of unanimity.[10]

Some of the conditions contributing to groupthink are (1) the illusion of invulnerability; (2) belief in the inherent morality of the in-group; (3) stereotypes about the out-group; (4) shared rationalizations for questionable actions; (5) strong pressures to conform; and (6) self-censorship by members holding alternative opinions. In our opinion, all these conditions were present in the AWARE study.

The Illusion of Invulnerability

The illusion of invulnerability refers to the shared belief that the group cannot fail. Everyone on the research team knew that the study was being conducted by an outstanding group of scholars. We had been granted unprecedented access to Church files and activities, and the team appeared well suited to take advantage of the situation because almost everyone had extensive experience with unconventional religions. As one person put it, the AWARE study would "leave no stone unturned." A few members of the team seemed to have inflated conceptions of their ability to find out what was really going on in the Church. One claimed to have an "amazing" talent for detecting lies and half-truths, and the detective charged with investigating the gun controversy prided himself on his sophistication about weapons and cults.

Belief in the Inherent Morality of the Group

Although Lewis and Oliver had described the study to us as an objective investigation, the events at Waco gave it an added twist. Based on statements we heard in the Hospitality Trailer, we believe most members of the research team saw themselves as defenders of religious liberty. We were told that the purpose of the study was to "dispel myths" about the Church and to prevent "another Waco." The Church was called a "stigmatized" religion whose members were "not bad people." Several people on the team expressed the belief that unconventional religions needed to be protected from government oppression. One claimed that the government was out to "get the Church," and another told Langdon that "the federal government is becoming the thought police, and freedom of religion is what the Constitution is all about."

Stereotypes about the Out-Group

Despite the actions of the BATF and FBI in Waco, the real enemy for the AWARE scholars appeared to be the Cult Awareness Network (CAN), a nationwide anticult organization. Not once during the study did we hear anyone on the research team give any credibility to CAN's allegations against the Church. Instead, to quote two members of the research team, CAN could not be trusted because it had "axes to grind," and its perceptions of new religions were "independent of empirical realities."[11]

Rationalizations for Questionable Actions

According to Janis, group members construct justifications for their actions that enable them to ignore contrary evidence. Although we believed the flaws in the AWARE study should have been obvious, members of the research team were able to explain away the problems: The scholars may not have known much about the Church before the study, but they learned once they got there. The study may have been brief, but most studies of new religions are based on short visits. Defectors may have been left out of the study, but they could not be trusted anyway. Groups conceal information from outsiders, but the AWARE scholars were experts at finding out what new religions are really like. As a result of these rationalizations, we believe AWARE team members overlooked or downplayed the study's flaws.

Pressures to Conform

Throughout the investigation, we both observed and experienced subtle pressures not to raise critical questions about either the Church or the study itself. For example, when Balch persisted in asking questions about the study during one of his initial conversations with the project director, he noted that the director became irritated and seemed impatient to get off the phone. In another instance, after touring the Mol Heron shelter, we asked our guide a question about the gun controversy. Our host gave us an exasperated look, as if to say, "How many times do I have to answer this question?" Our guide had given only a perfunctory reply before someone on the study team cut off the questioning by saying, "Well, Tim, we have grilled you again." Another member of the team followed up with the comment: "We do appreciate your candor. It's quite clear that you are giving us sincere answers." With that statement, the discussion ended and the group dispersed for the afternoon.

The difficulty we had raising questions was compounded by the attendance by one or more Church members at every formal meeting of the research team and at many of our informal discussions in the Hospitality Trailer. The constant presence of Church officials put a damper on the open expression of any information contrary to the Church's public image.

Perhaps the most subtle pressure to keep from asking hard questions came from the research team's indebtedness to the Church (Barker 1983; Glazer 1972; Horowitz 1983). Not only had the Church opened its doors to us, but our registration fees had been waived, and we were provided free meals, lodging, and any books we wanted from the conference bookstore. Our hosts, gracious and genuinely likeable people, allowed us to see and do more than any of the regular participants at the conference. After being treated so well, it was hard to challenge our hosts with difficult questions.[12]

Langdon, one of the few who did challenge them, paid a price for being outspoken. After he continued to raise questions about issues that were not being investigated, some members of the research team (ironically) began to question his objectivity. It appeared that he had been labeled a CAN sympathizer.

Self-Censorship

Janis claims that the ultimate result of the pressure to conform is an illusion of unanimity, because members who question the wisdom of the group's actions are reluctant to voice their concerns. In fact, we found it difficult to keep raising objections about the way the study was going because hardly anyone else seemed to have a problem with it. For example, during our interview with the younger staff members, we heard stories about the "fanaticism" of some staff members, the "many eyes, many ears" within the community that put a damper on individual expression, the surveillance and record keeping conducted by the Church's personnel department, a secret "security" section in the Mol Heron shelter, and the abuse of privileges by high-ranking staff members. To our discredit, we failed to mention these issues because other members of the research team seemed to be growing impatient with our questions.

In fairness, we need to add that three of the scholars (Cathy Wessinger, Gordon Melton, and Connie Jones) did come to our defense when our objectivity was questioned, but not until after the study was completed did we discover, in private conversations, that other members of the research team also felt dissatisfied with the study. Unfortunately, their reservations did not come to light until it was too late to do anything about them because the study never provided a forum for truly open discussion.

The Aftermath of the Study

The results of the AWARE project were published a year later in an edited volume entitled *Church Universal and Triumphant in Scholarly Perspective* (Lewis and Melton 1994). In his introduction, Lewis stated that the goal of the AWARE project was "to produce an interdisciplinary study of the Church that would be the first major study of this movement by an outside group of neutral academics (p. xi)." Lewis rejected the anticult view that social scientists who study new religions are "naive and gullible":

> "Many scholars of stigmatized religions, myself included, have a secret fear that they will one day examine a controversial religious group, give it a clean bill of health, and later discover that they have defended the People's Temple, or worse. This anxiety causes us to be, if anything *more* skeptical than the average observer" (p. viii; original emphasis).

With few exceptions, the findings were thoroughly positive. The Church belongs to a long tradition of metaphysical thought; its demographic profile resembles a church's more than a cult's; its members are intelligent, well educated, and psychologically normal; the Church does a good job of raising its children; and its relationships with neighbors in surrounding communities have improved steadily as the locals have come to know Church members as individuals.

In a review for *Journal of Church and State*, Davis (1995, 158) praised the book for its objectivity: "Overall, this volume helps to provide some long-overdue, academically objective perspectives on the church. While the authors generally conclude that most critics' charges against the church are false and undeserved, they are not reluctant to offer appropriate criticism of some aspects of the church's life." The only "major omission" the review mentioned was "an in-depth treatment of the intellectual, relational, and experiential worlds of the church's adult members."

The Church's newspaper, the *Royal Teton Ranch News*, also congratulated the research team for being "scrupulously objective" in an article headlined "Reality Wins over Perception: Church Is Entering Mainstream" in April 1994. Over a two-year period, the paper published interviews with several of the AWARE scholars, all overwhelmingly positive.[13] The scholars were quoted as describing the Church as a "healthy" community (in "Church Has Rich Life: Antithesis of Anti-Cult Stereotypes" in August 1993), whose members are "just like the Methodists and the Baptists" (in "Church Members Make the Grade as a Denomination" in February /March 1995) but who have been stigmatized in the press by "myths" and "gross exaggerations" ("Saved by the Facts," November 1994).

However, at least some of those "myths" may be true. Not until the end of the study did anyone on the research team get a glimpse of the Church's backstage life. Ironically, it was Eve Oliver, one of the AWARE study's organizers, as she told Balch over the telephone November 16, 1995. During a chance conversation with a disaffected member, Oliver discovered a well of discontent within the Church. Oliver's informant later arranged a meeting with about thirty other disaffected members. Besides Oliver and Lewis, two other members of the AWARE team were present. Among the alleged abuses that came to light was a recent incident in which a popular Church minister had been publicly humiliated by having two of her confidential letters to Elizabeth Clare Prophet read before an assembly of Church members, after which she was removed from her role as a minister. Unfortunately, by the time Oliver learned about this, most of the AWARE scholars were gone, and the allegations were never investigated.[14]

The AWARE Study in Retrospect

As we stated earlier, our purpose is not to slander the Church or to question the integrity of our fellow researchers. Instead we hope to provoke scholarly debate about the way controversial religious groups are studied. Although we realize that new religions are frequently victimized by false and misleading allegations, we also know that sometimes the charges against these groups turn out to be true. This is where the model of investigative journalism can be useful. Even when allegations of malfeasance fly in the face of conventional academic wisdom or promote the goals of angry apostates and anticult groups, they need to be investigated thoroughly and objectively. We believe the best way to defend new religions from persecution is to provide convincing proof that the charges against these groups are truly baseless. To do this, those allegations need to be investigated more thoroughly than they were in the AWARE study.

However, we believe the real purpose of social scientific research should not be to defend or criticize, but to *describe and explain* social phenomena. From the standpoint of sociological theory, it should not matter if some new religions turn out to be corrupt or abusive. What is most important is our ability to identify those features of social organization that promote or discourage corruption. However, without reliable means of documenting malfeasance, any attempts to explain it are likely to fail.

Researchers should keep Goffman in mind whenever they study new religions. His dramaturgical model demonstrates that virtually all groups have secrets to hide. Police officers band together to protect each other against charges of brutality and corruption; academic departments soft-peddle rumors of in-fighting during accreditation reviews; and family members stop arguing when neighbors come to visit. We believe Goffman's work has several important implications for the study of new religions. First, scholars who study alternative religions need to be familiar with the charges against them before they begin collecting data. Second, they should not take members' claims at face value, however reasonable they seem. Third, they need to interview defectors and other critics to get different viewpoints, although here too they must be aware of hidden agendas. Finally, whatever the source of information, statements presented as fact need to be corroborated and verified with independent evidence.

To deal with the problem of groupthink, the directors of collaborative projects need to establish a norm of free and open communication. Before data collection begins, members of the research team should meet to discuss their preconceptions about the group, as well as related moral issues, such as First Amendment rights. Team members should also agree on the nature of the research design. During the study itself, regular group discussions should be held so researchers can describe their findings and question each other about their observations and insights. Throughout these discussions, the project director should take the devil's advocate role to make sure that minority opinions are considered.

These steps cannot guarantee thoroughness and objectivity, but we believe they can help us avoid many of the pitfalls that plagued the AWARE study.

Notes

1. We are indebted to Professor Catherine Wessinger, a participant in the AWARE study, for her comments on an earlier draft of this paper. While we have incorporated many of her suggestions, we are solely responsible for the information and opinions in this chapter. We also thank Martha Heller, Sociology Editor at Rutgers University Press, for her painstaking efforts to clear up ambiguities in our description of the AWARE project.

2. In a letter to Heller, Balch, and Shupe (July 21, 1997) commenting on an earlier draft of this paper, Lewis stated that the AWARE study was not intended to investigate charges of malfeasance. We agree completely. This is one of our objections to the study.

   In addition to notes we took on the Church during the study, we kept a detailed record of every aspect of the study which we observed first-hand or heard about from Church members or our fellow researchers. Our notes include our initial telephone conversations with Lewis and Oliver. All statements in quotation marks are direct quotes, not paraphrases.

   In his letter to Heller, Balch, and Shupe, Lewis questioned the ethics of our transforming members of the research team "into objects of study." However, it is customary for field researchers to keep a record of how their studies take place, and it is a fundamental norm of science that research methods should be open to public scrutiny. We believe such scrutiny is crucial in studies of controversial religious groups because social scientists are in a unique position to influence public opinion and the outcome of court cases involving alternative religions.

3. In July 1996 the Church announced that Prophet was stepping down from the presidency to devote her time to writing and teaching. Church leaders elected Gilbert Cleirbaut, a professional management consult and ten-year member, as their new president.

4. DeHaas conducted her investigation independently of the AWARE team after the conference, so nothing in this paper applies to her study.

5. The IRS restored the Church's tax exemption in 1994 after the Church agreed, among other things, to sell any weapons it owned and pay income taxes on money it earns from its businesses.

6 In fact, Lewis had encouraged the scholars who had not been assigned particular tasks to develop their own projects, so these issues could have been investigated. Yet, except for the weapons issue, no effort was made to acquaint members of the research team with the charges against the Church. Aside from Melton, Langdon was the most knowledgeable, but he had to return to his job in Maine. Balch was in the best position to do a subsequent investigation because he lived less than 300 miles from the Church. After the conference he did begin a study of staff members, which he hoped to broaden to include defectors who had worked on staff before leaving the Church, but family matters forced him to curtail the project.

7. Although most members defected, the Love Family survived and is prospering again, but as of 1997 it had only about forty adult members, compared to about two hundred in 1980.

8. We do not mean to imply that we had direct evidence of malfeasance in the Church. We did not. Our information was based on media reports, which varied considerably in their thoroughness and objectivity. With few exceptions we did not know how valid the accusations in these reports were, and even though Gregory Mull's allegations had been substantiated in court, we had no evidence that similar abuses still occurred.

9. For a while there was a plan to include a sample of ex-members in the questionnaire survey, but that was dropped when it appeared that the only expedient way to locate defectors would be to get their names from the Church. Even if ex-members had been included, the survey questions were not designed to uncover structural problems that contribute to malfeasance.

10. We are indebted to Victor (1993) for demonstrating the applicability of groupthink in academic settings. Victor used the concept to analyze conformity pressures in the subculture of therapists and academicians who specialize in the treatment of satanic ritual abuse survivors.

11. CAN recently was put out of business in a lawsuit and rights to its name were purchased by a member of Scientology, so it no longer can be considered an anti-cult group.

12. A related issue is the question of who funded the study. We were told the project was being supported by AWARE with the help of "private donors." It later became apparent that most of the participants' expenses were being covered by the Church, but this never was made clear to members of the study team. From our perspective, the significant issue in the AWARE study was the indebtedness that grew out of personal contacts with members. For example, at times when writing this paper, we both felt that we were betraying the Church because its members had been so warm and helpful to us.

13. Balch declined to be interviewed on the ground that he wanted to maintain his impartiality. Langdon was not asked for an interview.

14. Oliver later encouraged Balch to conduct a study of ex-members for a second volume about the Church, but not until after she and Lewis had a falling-out with Church officials. In 1996 Balch and several of his students met with several defectors and disaffected members on the verge of leaving the Church. Unfortunately, by the time of the meeting, Balch was involved in another study, and he was unable to find students with the time or financial resources to do a systematic study of ex-members.

References

Balch, Robert W. 1996. Review of *Sex, Slander, and Salvation: Investigation The Family/Children of God*, edited by James R. Lewis and J. Gordon Melton. In *Journal for the Scientific Study of Religion* 35:72.

———. 1995. "Charisma and Corruption in the Love Family." In *Sex, Lies, and Sanctity: Religion and Deviance in Contemporary North America*, edited by Mary Jo Neitz and Marion S. Goldman. Vol. 5 of *Religion and the Social Order*. Greenwich, Conn.: JAI.

———. 1988. "Money and Power in Utopia: An Economic History of the Love Family." in *Money and Power in the New Religions*, edited by James T. Richardson. Lewiston, N.Y.: Edwin Mellen.

———. 1985. "'When the Light Goes Out, Darkness Comes': A Study of Defection from a Totalistic Cult." In *Religious Movements: Genesis, Exodus, and Numbers*, edited by Rodney Stark. New York: Paragon House.

Barker, Eileen. 1983. "Supping with the Devil: How Long a Spoon Does the Sociologist Need?" *Sociological Analysis* 44:197–205.

Butler, Katy. 1983. "Events Are the Teacher." *CoEvolution Quarterly* (March): 112–123.

Davis, Derek H. 1995. Review of *Church Universal and Triumphant in Scholarly Perspective. Journal of Church and State* 37:157–158.

DeHaas, Jocelyn H. 1994. "The Mediation of Ideology and Public Image in the Church Universal and Triumphant." In *Church Universal and Triumphant in Scholarly Perspective*, edited by James R. Lewis and J. Gordon Melton. Stanford, Calif.: Center for Academic Publication.

Glazer, Myron. 1972. *The Research Adventure: Promise and Problems of Field Work.* New York: Random House.

Goffman, Erving. 1959. *The Presentation of Self in Everyday Life.* New York: Doubleday.

Horowitz, Irving Louis. 1983. "Universal Stands, Not Uniform Beliefs: Further Reflections on Scientific Method and Religious Sponsors." *Sociological Analysis* 44:179–182.

Janis, Irving L. 1972. *Victims of Groupthink.* Boston: Houghton Mifflin.

Johnson, Benton. 1992. "On Founders and Followers: Some Factors in the Development of New Religious Movements." *Sociological Analysis* 53: S1–13.

Jones, Constance A. 1994. "Church Universal and Triumphant: A Demographic Profile." In *Church Universal and Triumphant in Scholarly Perspective*, edited by James R. Lewis and J. Gordon Melton. Stanford, Calif.: Center for Academic Publication.

Langdon, Stephan. 1997. "Shelter from the Storm: The Church Universal and Triumphant and Their Shelter Phase." Senior thesis, University of Montana.

Latkin, Carl. 1991. "From Device to Vice: Social Control and Intergroup Conflict at Rajneeshpuram." *Sociological Analysis* 52: 363–377.

Lewis, James R. 1989. "Apostates and the Legitimation of Repression: Some Historical and Empirical Perspectives on the Cult Controversy." *Sociological Analysis* 49: 386–396.

Lewis, James R., and J. Gordon Melton, eds. 1994. *Sex, Slander, and Salvation: Investigating The Family/Children of God.* Stanford, Calif.: Center for Academic Publication.

———. 1994. *Church Universal and Triumphant in Scholarly Perspective.* Stanford, Calif.: Center for Academic Publication.

Lilliston, Lawrence, and Gary Shepherd. 1994. "Psychosocial Functioning and the Experiential World of Children in the Church Universal and Triumphant." In *Church Universal and Triumphant in Scholarly Perspective*, edited by James R. Lewis and J. Gordon Melton. Stanford, Calif.: Center for Academic Publication.

Melton, J. Gordon. 1992. *Encyclopedic Handbook of Cults in America*. New York: Garland.

Shepherd, Gary, and Lawrence Lilliston. 1994. "Children of the Church Universal and Triumphant: Some Preliminary Impressions." In *Church Universal and Triumphant in Scholarly Perspective*, edited by James R. Lewis and J. Gordon Melton. Stanford, Calif.: Center for Academic Publication.

Solomon, Trudy. 1981. "Integrating the 'Moonies' Experience: A Survey of Ex-Members of the Unification Church." In *In Gods We Trust.*, edited by Thomas Robbins and Dick Anthony. New Brunswick, N.J.: Transaction.

Sowards, Bruce A., Michael J. Walser, and Rick H. Hoyle. 1994. "Personality and Intelligence Measurement of the Church Universal and Triumphant." In *Church Universal and Triumphant in Scholarly Perspective*, edited by James R. Lewis and J. Gordon Melton. Stanford, Calif.: Center for Academic Publication.

Victor, Jeffrey S. 1993. *Satanic Panic: The Creation of a Contemporary Legend*. Chicago: Open Court.

Washington, Peter. 1995. *Madame Blavatsky's Baboon*. New York: Schocken.

Zablocki, Benjamin. 1996. "Reliability and Validity of Apostate Accounts in the Study of Religious Communities." Paper presented at the annual meeting of the Association for the Sociology of Religion, New York City, August 17.

CHAPTER 12

Criminology's Contributions to the Study of Religious Crime

PETER IADICOLA

$\mathcal{T}$he subject of clergy malfeasance shares definitional difficulties with older phenomena in criminology and deviance. Therefore, it is worth establishing a conceptual background for analyzing this newer concern.

Controversies in the Study of Elite Crime

In the study of crime, three essential controversies define the field and set the parameters for investigation. The first focuses on how we define crime, the second on the criminal agent (individual or organization), and the third on defining the crime problem (masses vs. elites).

Definition of Crime

The dominant position in criminology argues that crime is defined in terms of the *legal code*. Without law, there is no crime. From this perspective, criminologists are bound by the definition established by the recognized order—in a democratic system, the citizenry. In a democracy, all citizens essentially have the power to make the laws directly, or indirectly through elected representatives. Thus, the legal code defines the agreed-upon normative order.

The opposing position argues that if we adopt the definition of crime found in the legal code, then we are accepting the definition only of those most powerful in determining the law—elites and controlling interests. In a stratified social system, this definition may not represent the interests of those who have the least ability to define law.

A minority position in the field promotes a comparative definition of crime that is more universal, emphasizing human rights and their violations (Schwendinger and Schwendinger 1975).

Issues of personal bias and the imputation of values in the research process are part of this debate. The position on bias aligned with the dominant, legalistic definition of crime maintains that the study of crime must proceed from a presumed value-free position. Mainstream criminology takes the position that this is precisely the reason that law must be the basis for defining crime. Adopting the legal definition of crime minimizes researcher bias. Crime is a socially objective phenomenon designated by law. To define crime in any other way allows the prejudice of the researcher to enter the inquiry.

The common position of more critical approaches in the field is that *all* definitions of crime represent value premises or biases. Researchers choosing to define crime in terms of the legal code merely abdicate the use of their own value premises and assume the premises of those dominant in the society who define crime.

Further, the usual pattern in criminology is that those who study conventional, or "street," crimes (those listed in the Uniform Crime Reports of the U.S. Department of Justice) focus on the individual as the agent. Those who study crime by the elite tend not to be restricted in defining crime by the legal code, and they focus more on organizations or the institutions of society as possible agents.

Criminal Agency—Individual versus Organizational Actor

The second controversy addresses the issues of criminal agency, that is, individual as actor versus organization as actor. Most study of crime focuses on the acts of individuals. In the study of conventional crime, exceptions to this pattern occur in the research on organized crime and juvenile gangs. However, criminologists who study crimes committed by the elite have recognized the importance of the organizational context for the action, although some hold that organizations cannot be considered criminal because of the issues of mens rea (criminal intent) and personal culpability. Only individuals working in organizations can be criminal, they say. Yet a number of criminologists studying corporate and state crimes are coming to focus on the organization as the unit of analysis or criminal agent.

The early studies of elite deviance emphasized the individual actor. For example, Edwin Sutherland, in his classic study of white-collar crime, stated that "persons of the upper socioeconomic class engage in much criminal behavior; that this criminal behavior differs from the criminal behavior of the lower socioeconomic class principally in the administrative procedures which are used in dealing with the offenders; and that variations in administrative procedures are not significant from the point of view of causation of crime" (1983, 8). He went on to define white-collar crime as crime committed by persons of respectability and high social status in the course of their occupations. Cressey more recently makes this same point in reaction to criminologists' increasing use of the organization as the unit of analysis. Cressey views the study of corporations as criminals as "self-defeating because it is based on the erroneous assumption that organizations think and act, thus saddling theoretical criminologists with the impossible task of finding the cause of crimes committed by fictitious persons" (1988, 32).

Nevertheless, researchers have accorded increasingly greater importance to social context as it relates to organizational forces (structures and processes) that lead to, or facilitate, the commission of criminal action. Some argue that we must look at corporate crime as a product of organizational actions, because the decisions to commit crime have a diffuse grounding; the criminal actions are products of the organizational structure of positions, roles, and culture—the context of human action (Fisse and Braithwaite 1983). Others, such as Ermann and Lundman (1992), similarly note that organizations are collections of positions occupied by people who are replaceable. In the case of organizational crime, the criminal behavior becomes institutionalized as part of the expectations of actors who occupy positions within the organized structure and culture. To ignore this organizational context, to define criminal behavior principally as the actions of individuals, denies its power.

Research on corporate crime increasingly focuses on such factors as the structure of the corporation, market structure and conditions, and corporate culture. For example, only in the context of the culture of William S. Merrill company and the role expectations of actors can we appreciate how product safety violations occurred in the case of MER 29. In another example, Ford Motor Company's safety engineers and corporate executives (such as Lee Iacoca) knew the inadvisability of locating the Pinto's gas tank just behind the rear bumper. Yet corporate decision makers applied a cost-benefit analysis to the issue: Which would cost more, changing the design to avoid injury and deaths or maintaining the product with the hazardous design?

In all cases of corporate crime, the profit motive has led companies to promote the commission of criminal acts by corporate elites. This is especially the case when the culture of the corporation supports illegal behavior to maximize profits. Furthermore, incentive systems are more often than not based on this profits-at-any-cost schema. Instances where the nature of the organization and its market are crucial to understanding the occurrence of crime include Union Carbide and the Bhopal disaster, Nestles and the marketing of infant formula in poor societies where most of the population has no access to clean drinking water, the Heavy electrical generator manufacturers and their price conspiracy, and the product-dumping cases uncovered by Dowie in the mid-1970s. The list of corporate crimes in which organizational forces were key is a long one (e.g., Mokhiber 1988).

It is useful here to distinguish between white-collar and corporate crime. White-collar crimes are noncoercive deviant acts committed by those in professional roles principally for their own interests and not necessarily in the interests of the organization. Corporate crimes are committed not principally in the personal interests of the actors but rather as corporate policy in the interests of the organization. Embezzlement is a classic example of white-collar crime; product safety violation and false advertising are examples of corporate crime.

In the study of elite crime, the focus has shifted from the individual as the agent of crime to the organization. Research on corporate crime today increasingly focuses on the nature of the organization (its culture and structure) and the interaction environment of the organization as defined in its national or international economic and political arenas.

Defining the Crime Problem—Masses versus Elites

The third controversy in the study of elite crime concerns the definition of the crime problem: crimes of the masses, or conventional crimes, versus crimes of elites. The vast majority of criminologists' writings deal with conventional crime, that is, with Part I offenses as listed in the FBI's Uniform Crime Report. Official government statistics generally do not include crimes committed by corporations or states. Likewise, crime control efforts concentrate almost entirely on conventional crimes or crimes of the working class. Crimes of elites, unless they are conventional offenses, are often not considered serious. In many cases of corporate crime the acts are not labeled crimes at all but violations of government regulations, for example, of environmental protection regulations or of worker health and safety regulations.

Michalowski (1985) notes that our cultural understandings of crime are produced by a crime control establishment that dedicates its resources to conventional crime. He calls the systematic generation and dissemination of crime statistics "culture work"—activity that serves to create or maintain widely accepted perceptions of the nature of reality. Insofar as the institutional mechanisms that gather and disseminate crime data shape our cultural understanding of crime, they shape our perceptions of what constitutes "real" crime. Often excluded from "real" crime in this scenario are harms committed by the elite in the United States in pursuit of profit and power.

Critical criminologists have struggled to help people see the significant contribution of elite crime to the crime problem. They view crimes of the elite as far more costly than conventional crimes in terms of lives and materials lost (Reiman 1994). They contend that those who have more power in stratified societies have greater power to commit crimes and to evade having their criminal acts defined as crimes.

Exploitation and Deviance by Elite Religious

Criminology as a specialization has generally ignored crime by religious elites. In any social scientific sense, it is a recent area of investigation. Anson Shupe, who has examined issues of religious deviance (1985, 1991), attempts in *In the Name of All That's Holy: A Theory of Clergy Malfeasance* (1995) to develop a sociological theory of clergy malfeasance, the first major effort to develop a theory of deviance to focus specifically on religious elites.

A fruitful avenue for predicting the direction of the study of religious crime and deviance is to examine how Shupe addresses the three controversies criminologists have wrestled with, as outlined here.

Defining Clergy Malfeasance

Shupe begins by defining religious deviance—what he more narrowly refers to as "clergy malfeasance"—in terms of violation of clergy fiduciary responsibility to lay persons. It is the "exploitation and abuse of a religious group's believers by elites and leaders of that religion in whom the former trusts" (Shupe 1995, 15). Although the inclusive terms *exploitation* and *abuse* lend themselves to conceptualization in a more critical criminological approach, Shupe leaves them relatively undefined, thereby narrowing the range of deviant behavior to violations of law (or normative violations as defined by the religious institutions themselves). The examples he gives are acts of sexual abuse and theft by religious elites or outright physical abuse of parishioners. Left out are other religious crimes that transcend the normative boundaries of our social system—those that would fall within the conceptualization of crime or deviance as violations of human rights but not typically thought of as clergy malfeasance.

For example, Shupe (1995) correctly cites cases of clear economic fraud, such as the defrauding by Jim and Tammy Faye Bakker of the now-defunct PTL television ministry and by televangelist Robert Tilton of the Dallas "Success N' Life" ministry, as well as fraud by lesser-known con artists and schemers. He also catalogues a number of cases of ministerial authoritarian abuse, sometimes referred to as shepherding or discipling, in conservative churches, where religious elites exercise enormous influence over their followers and exact strict obedience from them. An extreme example was the Christian Alliance Holiness Church, wherein Rev. Wilbert Thomas has a follower of the church whipped by male members for allegedly "wasting" Thomas's time with a query about the parishioner's career goals. Thomas and two men in his church were arrested and charged with aggravated assault and criminal coercion. (Shupe also refers to studies debunking the fears that underground satanic-ritual abuse, either of children or adults, is rampant in this country [i.e., Victor 1993; Richardson, Best, and Bromley 1991]).

Shupe also examines the problem of interpersonal sexual violence. For example, in Chicago in the early 1990s a commission appointed by the archbishop, Joseph Bernardin, determined that sexual abuse complaints against thirty-nine priests were "well-founded," as Peter Steinfels of the *Fort Wayne [Indiana] Journal-Gazette* reported in "Abuse by Priests under Study by Chicago Diocese" on February 24, 1992. The case of Fr. James Porter, who admitted sexually abusing (by conservative estimates) at least 125 male and female students and who was convicted in 1992 of forty-six counts of sexual assault is perhaps the most sensational example. The Roman Catholic Church even established a now defunct retreat in New Mexico that for a time catered to sexually deviant priests. Shupe (1995) notes that the retreat hosted more than six hundred clerical deviants after it opened in 1975.

But the Roman Catholic Church is not the only one with such problems. Bonavoglia (1992) cites cases of rabbis who have resigned in the face of charges of sexual harassment, seduction, and infidelity. Several other studies have found similar problems among churches in Protestant denominations. For example, in a book targeted at evangelical Christians, Conway and Conway (1993) claim that 37 percent of ministers surveyed admitted to engaging in "inappropriate sexual behavior." Shupe (1995, 6, 106–107) cites the particularly extreme case of the Word of Life Church, whose pastor,

Donald Miller of Defiance, Ohio, was convicted in 1993 of seventeen counts of rape, sexual battery, child endangerment, and theft.

However, two areas of religious crime Shupe does not consider in his legalistic definition of clergy malfeasance occur when religious organizations are involved in violent acts either in support of the state or in rebellion against it (e.g., Tinker 1993; Gage 1991; Chomsky and Herman 1979; Fried et al. 1983; Wilson and Kvale 1994; Fisher 1989; Iadicola and Shupe, 1996). Here I refer to religions' complicity in the cultural and physical genocide of indigenous populations, with capitalists and missionaries often working in tandem. The history of religion wedded to violence is the history of conquest and imperialism. For example, the history of the Catholic Church from the fourth century to the seventeenth is replete with examples of torture and military violence against those the Church deemed pagans or heretics. The Spanish Inquisition, the Crusades, and the conquest of the Americas all used violence and theft to possess the property and energies of dominated peoples. Religious elites played a central role in furthering the violent conquest of peoples considered inferior to their Christian subjugators.

In more recent times, in many Latin American countries there are examples of the established church working with the military to terrorize dissident populations. In Paraguay, Bolivia, and Brazil, Protestant missionaries have succeeded the Catholic missionaries of an earlier era in representing the dominant imperial interests of Western capitalist countries. The German anthropologist Munzel, in discussing the missionary work in Paraguay, found that in one mission run by U.S. fundamentalist Christian missionaries the minister himself engaged in "Indian hunts" whose young child captives were sold into slavery (Chomsky and Herman 1979). According to Chomsky and Herman (1979, 122), North American missionaries from such groups as the Summer Institute of Linguistics and the Wycliffe Bible Translators have become the servants of right-wing military dictatorships in Bolivia and their supporters to the north. Fundamentalist missionaries in Guatemala played in important role in supporting General Rios Monte, himself a born-again Christian and member of the Church of the Word in California, who conducted a campaign of terror against the Guatemalan poor that continued throughout the 1980s (Fried et al. 1983).

Neither does Shupe include in his definition of clergy malfeasance the religious impetus behind government protesters in the United states, from the Ku Klux Klan to the Freemen, the Christian Identity Movement, the White Aryans, and similar possibly revolutionary and illegal groups. The list reaches beyond North America. Reiter (1983) documents how radical Catholic clergy and nuns in some dioceses helped supply arms and combatants and organize clandestine street committees in the overthrow of the Somoza regime in Nicaragua.

These significant categories of religious crime have been least studied, in large part because of the narrow definition of religious crime employed by Shupe and others.

Criminal Agency

Shupe's work is largely in the tradition of studies of white-collar crime: He has studied the organizational context for conventional crime by religious elites. Shupe observes that religious groups and institutions must be understood as hierarchies of unequal power. He maintains that the sources of this power are elites' and leaders' special access to spiritual wisdom, experience, or charisma, whether obtained through ordination, training, calling, or special enlightenment. He also notes that those in elite positions, whether priests, nuns, bishops, ministers, presbyters, deacons, superintendents, counselors, rabbis, gurus, or swamis, possess greater power of moral persuasion and in some cases even the theological authority to deny lay persons access to privileges of membership (including salvation).

Religious Organizations as Trusted Hierarchies. In one axiomatic statement Shupe defines churches as a unique type of group because (unlike most of their secular counterparts) they are "trusted hierarchies." That is, those persons of lower status in religious organizations trust or believe in the good intentions, unselfish motives, benevolence, and spiritual insights and wisdom of the upper echelons. According to Shupe, the nature of trusted hierarchies allows them to systematically provide opportunities and rationales for elite deviance, and indeed at times make such deviance likely to occur.

Certainly Shupe is correct that religious organizations are fundamentally based on trust and faith and that this trust-faith mix gives elites power over members' lives. However, one could argue the same for many other economic, professional, or political organizations. The corporation and the state are first of all hierarchies of unequal power. Those who dominate these organizations are believed, in part as a result of their position, to be superior in some regard. The dominant ideology and the historical myths of the society rationalize their superior position and the hierarchy of which it is a part.

Do not those in elite positions, whether we are speaking about kings, military rulers, presidents, entrepreneurs, or CEOs, generally possess greater powers of moral persuasion (at a minimum) and authority to deny civilians and workers access to privileges of membership, including ultimately the ability to live within the system? Furthermore, are not all organizations that make up the institutions of society trusted hierarchies to some extent in the eyes of their members? I would maintain that churches are less unique on the trust dimension than Shupe conceptualizes them.

Furthermore, all institutions are trusted hierarchies to the extent they provide special structures or avenues of potential exploitation, abuse, and manipulation of organizational resources (finances and members) by leaders. This is certainly the case with corporate and state crime. The refrain of offenders that they were only following orders is in part rooted in the trust that members have for the institution and the elites that are in control. We may need to recognize that trust is not an absolute factor. Some institutions are based on more or less trust of their members. The more the institutional organization relies on the trust of members, the more these members may be at risk.

External and Internal Power Hierarchies. Shupe looks at the nature of the hierarchical structure (hierarchical vs. congregational) as it relates to the occurrence of clergy malfeasance, neutralization, and normalization. He notes that in hierarchical groups local pastoral authority is an extension of a larger ecclesiastical authority that supervises it, not vice-versa. In congregational groups the local church leadership does not have to account to any other sacred or ecclesiastical authority. The point is not that there is an absence of hierarchy in a congregational group but that the local group is not part of any larger ecclesiastical structure, thus its leaders are only accountable to followers and to no other religious authorities (Shupe 1995, 17).

According to Shupe, hierarchical groups, as opposed to congregational groups, do better at helping keep secondary abusive deviance invisible, both because leaders are often not under the direct inspection of lay persons and because they typically create a greater mystique about the elites' authority that produces stronger assumptions of trust, obedience, and presumed virtue. However, according to Shupe, hierarchical groups ultimately do better in discouraging normalization of clergy malfeasance than do congregational groups. What normalization in this context means is that members come to accept or consider normal a form of elite deviance that abuses them. No outside controls on the local elites prevent this. Thus, the external relationship of the church with an outside religious organizational structure may increase the occurrence of clergy malfeasance by keeping the deviance invisible. However at the same time it may depress the level of clergy malfeasance by inhibiting the ability of the offender to normalize the deviance.

Focusing on the hierarchy of structures of the religious organization outside the local church is one power context. However, another important dimension of the power context as it relates to deviance is the distribution of power within the church where the deviance occurs. This local power distribution may actually have more influence over the occurrence and normalization of the deviant act. Because potentially greater power is dispersed to members of a church with a congregational structure, one could argue that church leaders would have less ability to normalize their deviance. Thus, I think we need to address both the internal and external religious power structures, although they may overlap, especially in episcopalian groups. On the other hand, a congregational group may provide the most variation in the two power structures.

Shupe also focuses on the nature of the organizational structure in terms of its ability to neutralize fallout. Neutralization in this context means how elites contain or even squelch the publicity and damage to an organization's reputation once the secondary deviance is revealed. Hierarchical groups generally provide greater opportunities for elites to neutralize the fallout from clergy malfeasance than do congregational groups. They may even have publicists who act for them. More importantly, their greater normative weights of tradition, respectability, and authority, compared to more precarious congregational groups, can be called on to defuse scandal. However, in the long run hierarchical groups are more likely to address the malfeasance, where congregational groups may dissolve or deteriorate.

In terms of external power hierarchies, one can see how an independent congregational church may not have the support of structures outside the organization, which may weaken it. On the other hand, congregational churches with power more dispersed internally might be better able to respond to deviance. With power vested in the members of the church and not the church hierarchy, there would be greater freedom of action to resolve deviance problems. In the church with a strict internal hierarchy, such a problem could cause a chain reaction of one church leader covering up for another.

Shupe mentions the precarious position of congregational groups confronting scandals. Are years of existence or number of members relevant to the impact of clergy malfeasance? Certainly, a church with a large membership, long history, and large bureaucratic structure would be better able to handle cases of clergy malfeasance. A new church with a small membership is likely to experience a more serious, potentially fatal impact.

Regarding victims' responses, Shupe contends that "victims in hierarchical groups, as opposed to those in congregational groups, initially experience more ambivalence, guilt, and reluctance to expose the secondary deviance. . . . However, ultimately victims in hierarchical groups are more likely to become empowered to focus their grievances on group-specific reforms while still remaining within the tradition" (1995, 119). Congregationalists, he notes, are more likely to quit or move on. Whether victim response is a result of external or internal hierarchical structures remains unclear.

In regard to internal hierarchy, one could argue that, with power more dispersed in some congregational groups, members experience more ambivalence, guilt, or reluctance to address the problem. In these cases the membership may feel more responsible for the deviance, since they are more involved in the church governance. On the other hand, given the sense of empowerment that may go with participation in the governance structure, they may be more likely to respond to the clergy malfeasance. This is also likely in the case of congregational churches with less internal hierarchic structure, because the structures for membership participation and response to problems of church governance are present.

In terms of external hierarchical structures, what would seem important is less the nature of the distribution of power than the nature of the network present in an externally hierarchical church organization. Members have other organizational structures in the hierarchy outside of their local church to respond to, thus increasing the likelihood of victim response. On the other hand, members of a church organization isolated from other church organizations or an equal affiliate with other organizations—that is, with a low level of external power hierarchy—may feel more powerless to respond. Further research needs to focus on the patterns of victim response as they relate to external and internal power hierarchy dimensions.

Confounding the definition of power with style of leadership presents a greater problem. To argue that clerical authority in congregational groups finds its basis more in the nonrational and consciously antibureaucratic criterion of a calling confounds the power variable with the type or style of leadership variable. Not all congregational churches have charismatic leaders. What about those that hire a preacher to work for the congregation? Most of the examples of congregational churches Shupe cites are Bible/charismatic/fundamentalist congregations or parachurches run by televangelists, all ef-

External Power Hierarchy

		Low	High
		Low	Lowest Rate of Clergy Malfeasance	Moderate Rate of Clergy Malfeasance
Internal Power Hierarchy	High	Moderate Rate of Clergy Malfeasance	Highest Rate of Clergy Malfeasance

External and Internal Power Hierarchy and Clergy Malfeasance

fectively independent of denominational supervision or control. Again, the church founded and run by charismatic leaders with little or no governance structure other than the dictates of the prophet or enlightened one is logically the most centralized and therefore the most internally hierarchical. Nevertheless, this is a separate variable that needs to be measured in its effect on malfeasance, normalization, and neutralization.

The tables reflect hypothetical situations of external and internal power hierarchy and their relationship to clergy malfeasance, normalization, and neutralization. Where the external power hierarchy is low, power is decentralized or no organizational structure exists outside the immediate organization where the deviance takes place. Where the internal power hierarchy is low, dispersed among the members of the congregation, clergy malfeasance is at its lowest. The independent congregational charismatic church may be of this type.

In the opposite case, where the external power hierarchy is high, with power centralized in an organizational structure outside the immediate organization in which the deviance takes place, and internal power is highly centralized in the hands of a minister or prophet, clergy malfeasance is at its highest. A Roman Catholic church may fit this type.

In regard to an institution's neutralization of deviant acts, the power hierarchy variables work in the same manner. High levels of power hierarchy,

External Power Hierarchy

	Low	High
Low	Moderate Rate of Normalization	Lowest Rate of Normalization
High	Highest Rate of Normalization	Moderate Rate of Normalization

(left axis label: Internal Power Hierarchy)

External and Internal Power Distribution and Normalization of Clergy Malfeasance

both internally and externally, increase the likelihood of neutralization. Where the internal and external power hierarchy is low, so is the level of neutralization.

In the case of the normalization variable, the hypothesized pattern changes. Normalization is highest where external power hierarchy is low and internal power hierarchy high, centralized in the church leader or prophet. Where the external power hierarchy is high and the internal power hierarchy low, normalization is lowest.

A variable not addressed here may influence the nature of the relationship of hierarchical structure and deviance—the stability of dogma and rituals. Some religious organizations, either hierarchical (internally or externally) or congregational, are very stable, with an elaborate process required to make or modify dogma and rituals—think of this as the stability of the normative system. Others, where church leaders or offenders have the power to change dogma or rituals at will, are very unstable. Churches with highly stable normative structures experience more reaction to violation by elites. In this case, the normative structure has more power than the individual leaders and thus serves as a significant control on their behavior. On the other hand, with a highly unstable normative structure, elites have more power of action. Thus,

External Power Hierarchy

		Low	High
Internal Power Hierarchy	Low	Lowest Rate of Neutralization	Moderate Rate of Neutralization
	High	Moderate Rate of Neutralization	Highest Rate of Neutralization

External and Internal Power Distribution and Neutralization of Clergy Malfeasance

high levels of normative or doctrine instability lead to higher levels of clergy malfeasance; low levels have the opposite effect.

Furthermore, normalization is more likely to occur in groups with unstable normative structures, for here elites can more easily redefine or reinterpret norms to excuse or legitimate their actions. Similarly, we would expect higher levels of neutralization in organizational environments characterized by high levels of normative or doctrine stability. In these situations, it is easier to separate the offending elites from the doctrine that forms the foundation of the organization. On the other hand, where the doctrine or normative environment is unstable, subject to the frequent revision and interpretation of elites, neutralization becomes more difficult because of the close connection between the offending elites and the doctrinal foundation of the organization.

As we add additional variables, contingency tables become cumbersome in theory building. Figure 1 is a hypothetical path diagram that presents a modification of Shupe's model that incorporates the additional variables discussed here. Beginning with the internal power dimension, the more that power is centralized internally (hierarchical), the higher the incidence of clergy malfeasance, the higher the likelihood of normalization, and the greater the organization's ability to neutralize negative fallout. The more power is

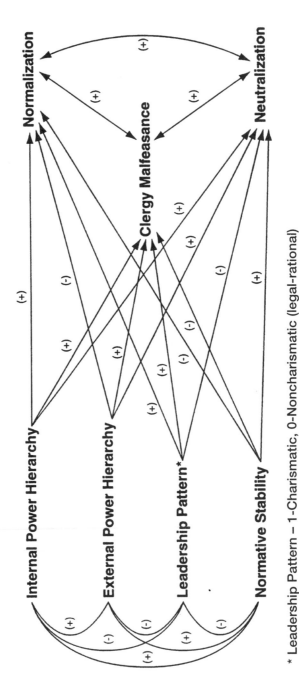

FIGURE 1. Modified Model of Clergy Malfeasance, Normalization, and Neutralization.

dispersed internally (congregational), the lower the incidence of clergy mal-feasance, the lower the likelihood of normalization, and less ability the organization has to neutralize the negative response of the community. Consistent with Shupe's thesis, the more hierarchical the external power structure, the higher the incidence of clergy malfeasance, the greater the organization's ability to neutralize the negative response of the community, however, the lower the likelihood of normalization.

In regard to leadership patterns, as leadership tends more toward the charismatic, the greater the likelihood of malfeasance, the greater the group's ability to normalize the deviant behavior, and less its ability to neutralize the negative response of the community. As stated earlier, because a charismatic leader involved in deviance is often identified as the church, once the offense becomes public it is difficult to separate the offender from the organization, thus making neutralization difficult. Conversely, the more leadership patterns follow a more legal/rational model, the less the likelihood of malfeasance, the less the group's ability to normalize the deviant behavior, and the more likely to neutralize the negative response of the community—because of the presence of a bureaucratic process within such organizations that allows for controlling behavior, defining doctrine, and separating the offender from the organization when deviance occurs.

In regard to the normative stability dimension, the more stable the normative structure or religious doctrine, the lower the incidence of clergy malfeasance, the lower the group's ability to normalize the deviance, and the greater its ability to neutralize the negative response of the community. Conversely, the more unstable the doctrine or the more subject to interpretation by church leadership, the greater the likelihood of malfeasance, the greater the likelihood of normalization of the deviance, and the lower the group's ability to neutralize the negative response of the community. Normative stability defends against the occurrence of clergy malfeasance, in that rules or doctrine are clearly defined and more rigidly defended. Furthermore, as a result of the stability of the doctrine, normalization is less likely to occur. Lastly, where the doctrine is very stable it is defined as the basis or foundation of the religious organization. Thus, individual offenders are easily separated from the doctrine, thereby helping to neutralize negative community response.

Taking into account these four factors, a religious organization most likely to experience clergy malfeasance would have hierarchical internal and external power structures, charismatic leadership, and highly unstable normative doctrine. Clergy malfeasance is least likely to occur in an organization with more egalitarian internal and external power structures, a legal/rational leadership, and highly stable doctrine.

Defining the Religious Crime Problem

Although Shupe's theory focuses on the crimes of elites, limiting clergy malfeasance to crimes as defined by the law of the state narrows that focus to conventional crime by elites. The larger areas of crimes committed by religious organizations in the process of conversion and conquest fall outside his scope. Nevertheless, as the study of white-collar crime expanded to larger areas of organization crime, we can construct the bridge to this second area of religious crime by looking at the connections between religious organizations, the economy, and the state, and at the position of religious elites in the entire system of social stratification.

Clergy malfeasance—A Prolegomenon

The study of religious crime and deviance is in its infancy. Shupe's work provides an excellent starting point for developing a theory to account for conventional crime by religious elites. Like Sutherland's early work on white-collar crime, Shupe's calls attention to a long-neglected area of research and theorizing. Like the study of corporate and state crime, the study of religious crime eventually will focus on organizational religious crime, not just on the organizational context for conventional crime by religious elites. Researchers in the field will broaden the definition of religious crime to cover larger, more devastating cases, such as the perpetuation of systems of domination, nationally and internationally. With this leap, theoretical models will move beyond the organizational context of the behavior to political-economic contexts in the larger social system.

References

Aho, James A. 1990. *The Politics of Righteousness: Idaho Christian Patriotism*. Seattle: University of Washington Press.
Bonavoglia, Angela. 1992. "The Sacred Secret." *Ms* (March–April): 4–5.
Chomsky, Noam, and Edward S. Herman. 1979. *The Washington Connection and Third World Fascism*. Boston: South End.
Conway, Jim, and Sally Conway. 1993. *Sexual Harassment No More*. Downers Grove, Ill.: InterVarsity.
Cressey, Donald R. 1988. "The Poverty of Theory in Corporate Crime Research." In *Advances in Criminological Theory*, edited by W. S. Laufer and F. Adler. Vol. 1. New Brunswick, N.J.: Transaction.

Ermann, M. David, and Richard J. Lundman. 1992. *Corporate and Governmental Deviance.* New York: Oxford University Press.

Fisher, Jo. 1989. *Mothers of the Disappeared.* Boston: South End.

Fisse, Brent, and John Braithwaite. 1983. *The Impact of Publicity on Corporate Offenders.* Albany: State University of New York.

Fried, Jonathan L., Marvin E. Gettleman, Deborah T. Levenson, and Nancy Peckenham. 1983. *Guatemala in Rebellion: Unfinished History.* New York: Grove.

Gage, Susan. 1991. *Colonialism in the Americas.* Victoria, B.C.: Victoria International Development Education Association.

Gurr, Ted Robert. 1986. "The Political Origins of State Violence and Terror: A Theoretical Analysis." In *Government Violence and Repression: An Agenda for Research*, edited by M. Stohl, and G. A. Lopez. New York: Greenwood.

Iadicola, Peter, and Anson Shupe. 1996. *Violence, Inequality, and Human Freedom.* New Jersey: General Hall.

Lemert, Edwin. 1958. "The Behavior of the Systematic Check Forger." *Social Problems* 6 (Fall): 141–149.

Michalowski, Raymond. 1985. *Order, Law, and Crime: An Introduction to Criminology.* New York: Random House.

Mokhiber, Russell. 1988. *Corporate Crime and Violence.* San Francisco: Sierra Club.

Reiman, Jeffery. 1994. *The Rich Get Richer, the Poor Get Prison.* New York: Macmillan.

Reiter, Jackie. 1983. "A Church Divided." In *The Nicaragua Reader*, edited by Peter Rosset and John Vandermeer. New York: Grove.

Richardson, James T., Joel Best, and David G. Bromley. 1991. *The Satanism Scare.* New York: Aldine de Gruyter.

Rossetti, Stephen J. 1990. *Slayer of the Soul: Child Sexual Abuse and the Catholic Church.* Mystic, Conn.: Twenty-Third Publications.

Schwendinger, Herman, and Julia Schwendinger. 1975. "Defenders of Order or Guardians of Human Rights?" In *Critical Criminology*, edited by Ian Taylor, Paul Walton, and Jock Young. London: Routledge and Kegan Paul.

Shupe, Anson. 1995. *In the Name of All That's Holy: A Theory of Clergy Malfeasance..* Westport, Conn.: Praeger.

Simon, David, and Stanley D. Eitzen. 1990. *Elite Deviance.* 3d ed. Boston: Allyn and Bacon.

Sivard, Ruth Leger. 1986. *World Military and Social Expenditures.* 1986. Washington, D.C.: World Priorities.

Sutherland, Edwin. 1983. *White Collar Crime.* New Haven: Yale University Press.

Tinker, George E. 1993. *Missionary Conquest.* Minneapolis: Fortress.

Victor, Jeffrey S. 1993. *Satanic Panic.* Chicago: Open Court.

Wilson, Margaret, and Ingrid Kvale. 1994. "They Do Not Know Us Yet." *New Internationalist* (June 17).

CHAPTER 13

Future Study of Clergy Malfeasance

‑‑ ‑‑‑‑ ‑‑

ANSON SHUPE

*A*ll of the essays in this volume deal with clergy malfeasance scandals occurring between the mid-1980s and the early 1990s. Examining cases across time, one develops strong suspicions that such malfeasance is in no way unique to our modern generation or even to our century. Indeed, some of the most recent revelations of malfeasance in North America involve incidents of abuse that took place decades ago. And unlike the largely baseless hysteria of well-meaning "child savers" and those fearful of underground satanic networks allegedly abducting and ritually abusing children (see, e.g., Victor 1993; Richardson et al. 1991; Hicks 1991; Shupe 1991, 106–123; Best 1990), the malfeasance discussed here is undeniably real. We know this not just through victims' testimonies but also from law enforcement investigations, court adjudications, and perpetrators' confessions.

And the malfeasance apparently goes on. For example, despite Philip Jenkins's (1996, 167) constructionist conclusion that the "contemporary abuse crisis" in the Roman Catholic Church "directly affects perhaps a few hundred priests on one continent," the abuse controversy is not limited to North America nor is some narrow nationalist contingent of clergy responsible for it. Nancy Nason-Clark, Theresa Krebs, and A. W. Richard Sipe provided evidence of the international scope of the sexual abuse problem just within Catholicism. Moreover, E. Burke Rochford, Robert Kisala, and myself (among others) have demonstrated that clergy malfeasance is "ecumenical"—it transcends denominations and faith traditions in the same way that domestic violence recognizes no social class, racial-ethnic, or gender lines. The Linkup, the nation's largest victims' advocate organization that addresses Catholic as well as Protestant concerns, constructed a "wall of shame" for its fourth annual conference in September 1996. As keynote speaker, I observed that wall-length banner which contained 666 names of abusive Catholic clergymen. I commented on it to the conference coordinator, who told me: "We have many more names, but the number's theologically significant. And we ran out of room to include more."

Six Examples of the Ongoing Discovery of Clergy Malfeasance

To illustrate the continuing process of uncovering and revealing clergy malfeasance across groups, I offer the following six brief examples that came into my files in just several weeks' time as this volume was going to press.

First, in February 1997 a major scandal broke in West Lafayette, Indiana (Lafayette diocese), when it became public knowledge that twelve identified priests (perhaps as many as sixteen) may have sexually abused as many as forty victims over a twenty-five year period. The bishop, William L. Higi, only revealed these numbers to parishioners when it was learned that two Indianapolis newspapers were to carry investigative series on the malfeasance. Bishop Higi promptly hired a public relations firm to manage "damage control" for the diocese.

There were calls for Higi's resignation when it came out that he had assigned abusive priests to counseling and soon afterward reassigned them to pastoring in unsuspecting parishes. Furthermore, Higi downplayed the ephebophilia problem by suggesting that some adolescents and young teenagers might be partly responsible for their own victimization (i.e., "consented" to and even invited sex by priests), some as young as thirteen. Such young persons were technically not minors, he maintained. Higi claimed his dealings with the allegations of sexual abuse were "successful" Mark Rahner reported in "Higi: Success, Not Men" in the *West Lafayette [Ind.] Journal and Courier* on February 20. That claim rang hollow, particularly to victims, who termed Higi's approach "unchecked arrogance," according to Julie McClure in "Catholic Clergy to Confer Today on Sexual Allegations" in the *Journal and Courier* of February 27. At a special session called for diocesan priests to discuss the matter, one priest who did not wish to be identified told Rahner: "The bishop has yet to admit he has made any mistake. And I find that outrageous" ("Grieving, Denial Mark Priests' Session," *Journal and Courier*, February 27).

Second, in Huntington, Indiana, a youth pastor and director of the

Huntington County Youth Services Bureau was arrested and charged with two counts of felony child molesting, one count of felony sexual misconduct with a minor, and two misdemeanor counts of battery. These alleged actions occurred during the summers of 1994 and 1995 with boys between thirteen and seventeen years old. The alleged perpetrator was a youth pastor in the United Brethren Church, as Mark Harper reported in "Youth Pastor Faces Sex Count" in the *Fort Wayne (Ind.) Journal Gazette* on March 6.

Third, in 1996 the first volume of the *Case Reports of the Mormon Alliance* (Anderson and Allred 1996) was published. The alliance was organized in July 1992 "to counter spiritual and ecclesiastical abuse in the [LDS] Church," with several of its original trustees ultimately excommunicated by Mormon leaders. The group sponsors quarterly meetings and publishes a quarterly newsletter and annual case reports volumes. The tone of the writers and editors has been low key, and the articles are well documented. Interestingly, the editors' definition of authoritative abuse resembles my own: "Ecclesiastical abuse occurs when a Church officer, acting in his official capacity and using the weight of his office, coerces compliance, imposes his personal opinions as church doctrine or policy, or resorts to such power plays as threats, intimidation, and punishment to insure that his views prevail in a conflict of opinion" (Anderson and Allred 1996, 3). The editors of volume 1 go on to enumerate seven factors that characterize most spiritually abusive encounters between laypersons and clergy, which resemble remarkably emerging statements in other denominations (e.g., Yeakley 1988). The Mormon Church hierarchy has been under much criticism in the 1990s for excessive intellectual control of its members (i.e., authoritative ecclesiastical abuse), in particular of its own academics and intellectuals (e.g., Knowlton 1996; Shupe 1995, 43–46).

Fourth, the senior pastor of the First United Methodist Church in Fort Worth, Texas, Rev. Barry Bailey, was being sued for more than $14 million in damages shortly before the Christmas season, 1996, by eight women accusing him of sexual exploitation. He was specifically accused of "misusing his high-ranking position by making unwanted sexual advances and lewd phone calls, sexually harassing several female church employees and seducing two women who sought counseling in his private office and elsewhere," reported Linda Campbell in "8 Women Seek $14 Million from Ex-Pastor" in the *Fort Worth Star Telegram* on December 3. All the women contended that Bailey's activities caused them an array of physical and emotional problems. Several stated that he had telephone them and discussed masturbation in detail, according to Campbell in "Bailey Denies Seducing Women" in the

Telegram on December 5. One woman alleged that Bailey had given her a job in order to facilitate a sexual relationship. One husband also filed a lawsuit for $100,000, claiming that Bailey had caused him to lose "consortium" with his wife. Bailey denied these accusations, but shortly before they were filed he retired from the church pastorate and surrendered his ministerial credentials to the denomination.

Fifth, a Naples, Florida, Catholic priest was one of nine men accused in late January 1997 of molesting twelve- and thirteen-year-old boys as long as fifty years ago. Rev. Marcial Maciel Degollado, seventy-six years old, founder of an order called the Legionaries of Christ, was accused of sexually abusing boys in Spain and Italy between the 1940s and the 1960s, according to Gerald Renner and Jason Berry in "Catholic Official Accused of Abuse" in the *Sarasota Herald Tribune* on February 24. One of his accusers was a sixty-year-old priest. Another, who claims he was inducted into the order at ten years of age and taken to a seminary in Spain, said he underwent a sexual relationship with Maciel into his twenties.

Sixth, a Sarasota, Florida, Catholic priest was charged in early 1997 with attempting a lewd and lascivious act with a minor. Rev. Jeremiah Michael Spillance of the Church of the Incarnation had tried to arrange a sexual encounter with a thirteen-year-old male via computer. He was arrested at a Clearwater gas station by a police detective posing as the young teenager, Juli Cragg Hilliard reported in "Parish Reacts to Priest's Arrest" in the *Herald Tribune* on February 13. Spillance made a full confession of soliciting sex and was carrying condoms, lubricants, and homoerotic magazines, according to Hilliard in "Diocese Places Priest on Leave" in the *Herald Tribune* on February 24.

Future Directions in Conceptualization

So the clergy malfeasance problem even across only Christian groups, as my brief sampler here and this book demonstrate, will likely linger for the indeterminate future, just as it has existed in the indeterminate past. In an earlier work (Shupe 1995, 59) I argued that "[c]lergy malfeasance, or something we moderns could recognize as such, is probably as old as practiced religion itself." Certainly one can find evidence in the history of Christendom. It is endemic to religious organizations because of power differentials between leaders and followers, in turn ubiquitous in human organizations.

But we need to move research on malfeasance into more faith traditions.

To be sure, there have been some reliable journalistic and scholarly studies of clergy malfeasance in neo-Christian, Jewish, quasi-Islamic, and non-Christian groups, but not nearly enough. For example, when the suicidal UFO cult group now better known as Heaven's Gate stunned the nation in 1997 (Evan et al. 1997), Robert W. Balch (whose work appears in this volume) had studied leadership issues in Heaven's Gate's earlier incarnation, the Bo and Peep UFO cult during the mid-1970s (Balch 1982). Balch (1995) went on to research a Seattle-based cult loosely grounded in Jewish teaching and operated by a corrupt, self-centered, charismatic leader named Love Israel. Angela Bonavoglia (1992) has written of the "zipper factor" among California rabbis who seduce female congregants.

A self-defined neo-Jewish group of so-called Black Hebrews, following the commands of a ruthless, self-aggrandizing prophet calling himself Yahweh ben Yahweh (literally, God the son of God), engaged in extortion and violence against both followers and nonfollowers. Yahweh ben Yahweh is now in jail, as the *Miami Herald* reported on January 6, 1996 (Sydney P. Freedberg, "Yahweh's Conviction Confirmed"). And the Nation of Islam has come in for investigative criticism among allegations that leader Louis Farrakhan has enriched both himself and his family at the expense of the movement and that the movement's chief doctor was dispensing in Washington, D.C., a bogus drug called Alim that purported to cure AIDS, a disease movement leaders allege was introduced by whites intent on the genocide of blacks (David Jackson and William Gaines, "Nation of Islam: Power of Money" and "AIDS Hope or Hoax in a Bottle," *Chicago Tribune*, March 12, 1995).

I suggest a conceptual agenda for the future of clergy malfeasance studies, not as a mere sop to readers in closing out an edited volume but because of an urgent theoretical need to push our understandings of recently collected data further.

First, as Peter Iadicola argues in the final essay of this volume, sociologists of religion and deviance/criminology need to take model building beyond the closed system approach I developed in *In the Name of All That's Holy* (1995). Much as Sipe and Jenkins also contended in their essays, the sociocultural contexts of a congregation, the local community, the denomination's oversight, and understandings built from media exposure provide a complicated yet not inscrutable feedback loop that conditions how perpetrators, religious elites, and victims experience the recidivism of victimization. In Shupe 1995 I found differences in these reactions by denominational polity: episcopalian (extremely hierarchical), presbyterian (representative or republican), and congregational (democratic). Donald C. Houts (1995, 371–

372), a former parish pastor, hospital chaplain, seminary professor, and career support specialist for Illinois pastors, offers the same prescription for understanding sexual abuse: "My clear impression is that church structure largely predicts a style of response to the crisis of integrity in the area of clergy sexual ethics."

Sociologists are not psychologists, thus their agenda must focus on the multiple audiences who react to revelations of religious elite deviance rather than on deviant motives, personalities, and so forth. This is no small charge. One has only to consider the final diagram in the Iadicola chapter to appreciate the measurement challenge. But how else could we fully consider the West Lafayette, Indiana, Roman Catholic scandal (along with others) in its cultural and international systemic implications? As I have come to see, no congregation or even denomination stands alone in societal reaction to clergy malfeasance.

Second, clergy malfeasance needs to be connected conceptually beyond religion and criminology/deviance to other forms of violence, among them sexual, familial, and economic. Why reinvent the wheel? Violations of fiduciary responsibilities have been much analyzed in health care, legal, and therapeutic/educational professions (e.g., Gonsiorek 1995; Rutter 1989); these analyses should serve as models for bridging understandings of clergy malfeasance to similar deviance in other areas of power inequity between clients and service providers. Nancy Nason-Clark, whose chapter in this volume dealt with victims and victims' families in the Newfoundland priest-abuse scandal, offers an example of such an ongoing effort.

Finally, many of our data on clergy malfeasance are anecdotal, qualitative, and "cluster based," that is, we have solid knowledge of multiple-victim cases caused by individual perpetrators such as Father James Porter or Father David Holley. Writes Walter H. Bera, an educational psychologist who has worked in the field of sexual abuse for two decades: "Over the last five years, I have treated nearly sixty male victims of clergy sexual abuse. The denominations involved were various. Most were members of a 'cluster' of victims by a single offender. The largest cluster was a group of about 30 men who ranged in age from nineteen through forty-eight who all had been abused by the same pastor during his thirty-year perpetration career. Similar numbers were seen in other clusters, but with similar dynamics" (Bera, 1995: 91).

We needed victimization surveys that tap general public awareness of the clergy malfeasance problem as well as self-reports of its extent. In addition, data comparing the extent of self-reported alleged clergy-initiated abuse to self-reported alleged accountant/attorney/school teacher/sports coach/police abuse would provide the broader picture we badly need. What differences exist among denominations in monitoring initial offences and repeat offences? How efficacious is counseling of clergy, by denominational background and sexual orientation? How do victim responses differ across denominations? No one even has a hypothesis. A host of questions awaits a new wave of social science research. Clergy malfeasance has the potential to become a "growth industry" for research even if the media spotlight cools after initial sensational revelations of scandal. After all, with power differentials inherent in religious organizations, the opportunity structures for exploiting that power by leaders are never going to disappear in any religion of which we can conceive.

References

Anderson, Lavina Fielding, and Janice Merrill Allred (eds.). 1996. *Case Reports of the Mormon Alliance: Volume 1, 1995*. Salt Lake City, Utah: Mormon Alliance.

Balch, Robert W. 1995. "Charisma and Corruption in the Love Family: Toward a Theory of Corruption in Charismatic Cults." In *Sex, Lies, and Sanctity: Religion and Deviance in Contemporary North America*. Edited by Mary J. Neitz and Marion S. Goldman. Greenwich, Conn.: JAI Press.

———. 1982. "Bo and Peep: A Case Study of the Origins of Messianic Leadership." In *Charisma and Millennialism*. Edited by Roy Wallis. Belfast, Northern Ire.: Queen's University of Belfast.

Best, Joel. 1990. *Threatened Children: Rhetoric and Concern about Child-Victims*. Chicago: University of Chicago Press.

Bonavoglia, Angela. 1992. "The Sacred Secret." *Ms.* (March–April): 2–5.

Evan, Thomas, et al. 1997. "The Next Level." *Newsweek*, April 17.

Gonsiorek, John C., ed. 1995. *Breach of Trust: Sexual Exploitation by Health Care Professionals and Clergy*. Thousand Oaks, Calif.: Sage.

Hicks, Robert D. 1991. *In Pursuit of Satan*. Buffalo: Prometheus.

Houts, Donald C. 1995. "Training for Prevention of Sexual Misconduct by Clergy." In *Breach of Trust: Sexual Exploitation by Health Care Professionals and Clergy*, edited by John C. Gonsiorek. Thousand Oaks, Calif.: Sage.

Jenkins, Philip. 1996. *Pedophiles and Priests: Anatomy of a Contemporary Crisis*. New York: Oxford University Press.

Knowlton, David C. 1996. "Authority and Authenticity in the Mormon Church." in *The Issue of Authenticity in the Study of Religion*, edited by Lewis Carter. Greenwich, Conn.: JAI Press.

Richardson, James T., Joel Best, and David G. Gromley, eds. 1991. *The Satanism Scare*. New York: Aldine de Gruyter.

Rutter, Peter. 1989. *Sex in the Forbidden Zone*. Los Angeles: Tarcher.

Shupe, Anson. 1995. *In the Name of All That's Holy: A Theory of Clergy Malfeasance*. Westport, Conn.: Praeger.

————. 1991. *The Darker Side of Virtue: Corruption, Scandal, and the Mormon Empire.* Buffalo: Prometheus.

Victor, Jeffrey S. 1993. *Satanic Panic: The Creation of a Contemporary Legend.* Chicago: Open Court.

Yeakley, Flavil R., Jr. 1988. *The Discipling Dilemma.* Nashville: Gospel Advocate College.

INDEX

ABOUT THE CONTRIBUTORS

ROBERT BALCH is professor of sociology at the University of Montana in Missoula. He has been conducting participant observation studies of unconventional religions since 1975. His published professional articles and monographs deal with conversion, commitment, defection, failed prophecy, the corruption of power among religious elites, and critiques of methodologies for studies of such phenomena as rumors about satanism in the Mountain West.

DAVID G. BROMLEY is professor of sociology at Virginia Commonwealth University. He has written extensively about the sociology of law and the new religious movements/anticult movements controversy. He has been editor of the *Journal for the Scientific Study of Religion* and is coeditor (with Jeffrey K. Hadden) of *The Handbook of Cults and Sects in America* (1994).

PETER IADICOLA is associate professor of sociology at the joint campus of Indiana University-Purdue University Fort Wayne. He is coauthor (with Anson Shupe) of *Violence, Inequality, and Human Freedom* (1997).

PHILIP JENKINS is chair of the Department of Religious Studies at the Pennsylvania State University. His most recent book is *Pedophiles and Priests: Anatomy of a Crisis* (1995).

ROBERT KISALA is assistant professor of religious studies at Nanzan University in Nagoya, Japan. As a member of the Nanzan Institute for Religion and Culture, his research has focused on the social ethics of Japanese new religious movements.

THERESA KREBS is a graduate student in the Department of Sociology at the University of Edmonton. She is researching sexual abuse by Roman Catholic clergy in North America (particularly Canada) and worldwide.

STEPHAN LANGDON is an undergraduate student at the University of Montana. He has done field research of several unconventional religious groups, among them the Church Universal and Triumphant, the Aryan Nation, and the Ordo Templi Orientis.

JOSEPH MAROLLA is chair and professor of the Department of Sociology and Anthropology at Virginia Commonwealth University. He has published extensively on the problem of rape.

JEANNE M. MILLER is founder and past president of The Linkup, the first national advocacy organization for (interdenominational) victims of clergy sexual abuse. She is the author of *Assault on Innocence: For the First Time the Untold Story of Pedophilia* and is a graduate of the Loyola University of Chicago School of Law.

NANCY NASON-CLARK is professor of sociology at the University of New Brunswick. She has published extensively in North American social science journals and is engaged in a long-term project exploring family violence issues in contemporary Christianity.

ELIZABETH PULLEN is a graduate student in the sociology of religion in the Religion and Society Program at Drew University. Her specialties are the use of power in religious institutions and social movements, the nature of religious authority, and the status of children in Christian churches.

E. BURKE ROCHFORD JR. is professor of sociology and anthropology at Middlebury College. For the past twenty years he has published numerous analyses of the Hare Krishna movement, both in North America and worldwide. He is currently writing a book on families and the second generation of cultural development among the Krishnas.

ANSON SHUPE is professor of sociology at the joint campus of Indiana University-Purdue University, Fort Wayne, and the author and editor of many books, professional articles, and book chapters, as well as popular writings.

Among his most recent works is *In the Name of All That's Holy: A Theory of Clergy Malfeasance* (1995).

A. W. RICHARD SIPE is an ordained Roman Catholic priest (now retired from active ministry), a psychotherapist in private practice, and a lecturer in family therapy in the Department of Psychiatry at the Johns Hopkins School of Medicine in Baltimore. He is the author of *A Secret World: Sexuality and the Search for Celibacy* (1990) and *Sex, Priest and Power: Anatomy of a Crisis* (1995).

JAMES G. THOMSON is a graduate student in the Department of Sociology and Anthropology at Virginia Commonwealth University and specializes in rhetorical aspects of clergy malfeasance scandals.